BEST of the BEST
from

UTAH

COOKBOOK

Selected Recipes from Utah's
FAVORITE COOKBOOKS

A 45-minute hike brings visitors to Delicate Arch, one of more than 2,000 sandstone arches found in Arches National Park.

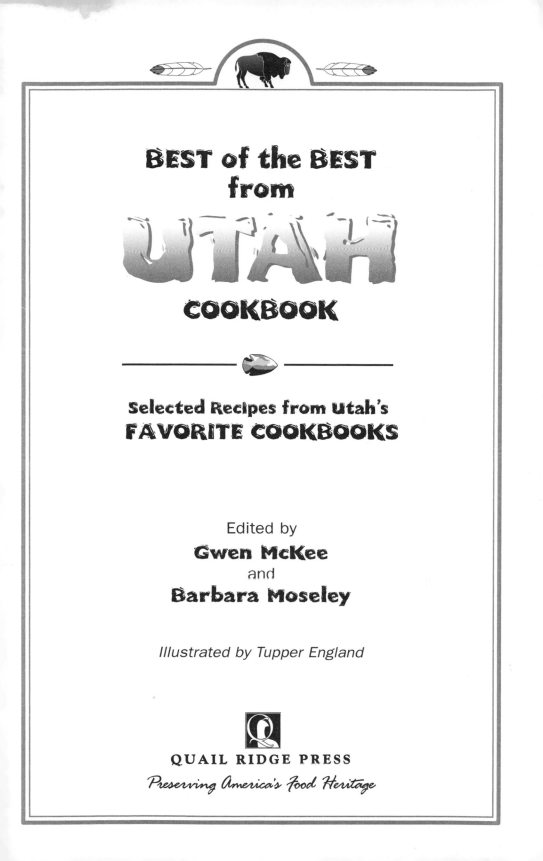

BEST of the BEST
from

UTAH

COOKBOOK

Selected Recipes from Utah's
FAVORITE COOKBOOKS

Edited by
Gwen McKee
and
Barbara Moseley

Illustrated by Tupper England

QUAIL RIDGE PRESS
Preserving America's Food Heritage

Recipe Collection ©2004 Quail Ridge Press, Inc.

Reprinted with permission and all rights reserved under the name
of the cookbooks, organizations or individuals listed below.

All That Jam: 101 Recipes to Make with a Jar of Jam ©2003 by Hollee Eckman and Heather Higgins; *Always in Season* ©1999 Junior League of Salt Lake City, Inc.; *Aromatherapy in the Kitchen* ©2002 by Melissa Dale and Emmanuelle Lipsky; *Back to the House of Health* ©1999 Hikari, LLC.; *Backyard Dutch Oven* ©2000 by Bill LeVerre; *The Beginner's Guide to Dutch Oven Cooking* ©2000 Horizon Publishers & Distributors, Inc.; *A Century of Mormon Cookery, Volume 1* ©2002 Horizon Publishers & Distributors, Inc.; *A Century of Mormon Cookery, Volume 2* ©2002 Horizon Publishers & Distributors, Inc.; *Championship Dutch Oven Cookbook* ©1988 Val and Marie Cowley; *Chocolate Snowball* ©1999 Letty Holloran Flatt; *The Cowboy Chuck Wagon Cookbook* ©2003 by E. W. Allred; *Doin' Dutch Oven: Inside and Out* ©1990 Horizon Publishers & Distributors, Inc.; *Dutch Oven AND Outdoor Cookbook, Book Two: Homespun Edition* ©1999 Larry A. and Jeanie S. Walker; *Dutch Oven AND Outdoor Cooking, Y2K Edition* ©2001 Larry A. and Jeanie S. Walker; *Dutch Oven Delites* ©1995 Val and Marie Cowley; *Dutch Oven Gold* ©1990 Val and Marie Cowley; *The Dutch Oven Resource* ©2000 by Camp Chef and Gerry and Chauna Duffin; *Dutch Oven Secrets* ©1995, 1998 Horizon Publishers & Distributors, Inc.; *Enjoy! Again and Again* ©1997 by Fred Wix; *The Essential Mormon Cookbook* ©2004 by Julie Badger Jensen, 2003 Deseret Book Company; *Favorite Utah Pioneer Recipes* ©2000 Horizon Publishers & Distributors, Inc.; *Five-Star Recipes from Well-Known Latter Day Saints* ©2002 Deseret Book Company; *Friends of Old Deseret Dutch Oven Cookbook* ©1996 Duffin's Dutch Ovens; *Heritage Cookbook* ©1975 Junior League of Salt Lake City, Inc.; *How to Enjoy Zucchini* ©1983 Josie's Kitchen; *How to Win a Cowboy's Heart* ©1995 by Kathy Lynn Wills; *JLO Art of Cooking* ©2003 Junior League of Ogden, Inc.; *Let's Cook Dutch: A Complete Guide for the Dutch Oven Chef* ©1979 Horizon Publishers & Distributors, Inc.; *Lion House Desserts* ©2000 Hotel Temple Square Corporations, Deseret Book Company; *Lion House Entertaining* ©2003 Hotel Temple Square Corporations, Deseret Book Company; *Lion House Recipes* ©1980 Hotel Temple Square Corporations, Deseret Book Company; *Lion House Weddings* ©2003 Hotel Temple Square Corporations, Deseret Book Company; *Log Cabin Campfire Cookn'* ©2001 Log Cabin Cookbooks; *Log Cabin Dutch Oven* ©1993 Log Cabin Grub Cookbook* ©1990 by Colleen Sloan; *Log Cabin Holidays and Traditions* ©1999 by Colleen Sloan; *Log Cabin Presents Lewis and Clark* ©2003 LCG Cookbooks; *Making Magic* ©2003 Virginia Tanner Creative Dance Programs and Children's Dance Theatre; *A Mormon Cookbook* ©2002 by Erin A. Delfoe; *101 Things to Do with a Cake Mix* ©2002 by Stephanie Ashcraft; *101 Things To Do With a Slow Cooker* ©2003 by Stephanie Ashcraft and Janet Eyring; *A Pinch of Salt Lake Cookbook* ©1986 Junior League of Salt Lake City, Inc.; *The Practical Camp Cook* ©1988 Horizon Publishers & Distributors, Inc.; *Quick & Easy Cooking* ©1989 Horizon Publishers & Distributors, Inc.; *Recipes for Roughing it Easy* ©2001 by Dian Thomas; *Roughing It Easy at Girl's Camp* ©2003 by Dian Thomas, Deseret Book Company; *Savor the Memories* ©2002 by Marguerite Marceau Henderson; *30 Days to a Healthier Family* ©2003 by Peggy J. Hughes, Deseret Book Company; *Ultimate Dutch Oven Cookbook: Sharing Recipes with You* ©2003 by Camp Chef; *Utah Cook Book* ©1999 Golden West Publishers; *Vacation Cooking: Good Food! Good Fun!* ©1989 Horizon Publishers & Distributors, Inc.; *World Championship Dutch Oven Cookbook* ©1989 by Dick Michaud

Library of Congress Cataloging-in-Publication Data

Best of the best from Utah cookbook : selected recipes from Utah's favorite cookbooks /
    edited by Gwen McKee and Barbara Moseley ; illustrations by Tupper England.
    p. cm.
    Includes index.
    ISBN 1-893062-63-5
    1. Cookery, American 2. Cookery—Utah. I. McKee, Gwen. II. Moseley, Barbara.

    TX715.B485617 2004
    641.59792—dc22   2004005800

Front cover: "Thor's Hammer," is one of Bryce Canyon's most impressive
multi-hued sandstone pinnacles. Photo by Frank Jensen, courtesy of State of Utah
Division of Travel Development. • Back cover photo by Greg Campbell
Design by Cynthia Clark • Printed in Canada

First printing, June 2004 • Second, January 2006

QUAIL RIDGE PRESS
P. O. Box 123 • Brandon, MS 39043 • 1-800-343-1583
email: info@quailridge.com • www.quailridge.com

Contents

In 1997, the Utah State Legislature designated the Dutch oven as the state cooking pot. The World Championship Dutch Oven Cookoff is held annually in Sandy.

Preface

Utah is a land like no other. Gazing across the panorama of contrasting sky, desert, and rock formations, I can't begin to comprehend how long it took the forces of prehistoric times to sculpt this dramatic landscape. The Great Salt Lake and the Bonneville Salt Flats are both amazing remnants of those times. Every turn reveals Utah's diverse countryside—the canyons, mountains, deserts, lakes, rivers, valleys, forests, salt flats, old mining towns, and bright city lights. There is never a shortage of places to explore and activities to pursue, from hiking and boating in the summer, to snow skiing and snow boarding in the winter. So famous for its slopes is Utah that the 2002 Olympic Winter Games were held here, literally transforming Salt Lake City into a winter Olympic wonderland! Five national parks, seven national monuments, two national recreation areas, a national historic site, and forty-one state parks preserve the land and cultural heritage. Utahns are certainly proud of the fact that 50,000 square miles of their state are reserved for recreational activities.

And they are proud of their cooking, too! Along with preserving the land and historic places, preserving Utah's food heritage is equally important. After researching, testing, and tasting recipes from the Beehive State's most popular cookbooks, we've come up with a collection of more than 300 recipes that define Utah's cooking. Within these pages you'll find the culinary traditions of Utah's strong Mormon background, its Native American heritage, its Wild West days, and also the more urban, modern Utah. Included are numerous recipes for outdoor Dutch-oven cooking that Utahns have so beautifully and deliciously perfected. They work just as well for modern-day pioneers, but inside ovens can also be used to make delicious recipes like Cowboy Cheese Bread, Son-of-a-Gun Stew, Honey Peach Crisp. . . .

Utah's livestock and livestock products (cattle, sheep, wool, milk, hogs, etc.) account for three-fourths of the state's agriculture cash receipts. Utahns grow lots of barley, wheat, beans, potatoes, onions, and corn, and are especially proud of their homegrown sweet corn and tomatoes, which are sold at local farmers' markets. In addition, Utah ranks second in the United States in tart cherries, third in apricots,

fifth in sweet cherries, ninth in pears, and seventeenth in both peach and apple production. Recipes like Best in the West Beans, Blackberry-Glazed Pepper Steaks, and Utah Valley Applesauce Bread reflect the state's wonderful bounty.

Choosing the recipes from all the wonderful cookbooks submitted was no easy task. We appreciate each of the outstanding cooks who so graciously shared their favorite dishes with us. (You can learn more about each contributing cookbook on page 259.) Every person we called upon for help was courteous and friendly and most definitely helpful. It is always such a joy getting to know the people who live in each state, and Utahns were no exception.

Nestled among the recipes is interesting information about the state, including a listing of state parks, a bit of history from the Church of Jesus Christ of Latter-day Saints, and a sprinkling of state facts. For example, did you know Rainbow Bridge is the world's largest natural bridge at 290 feet high with a 275-foot span? And that legend says if you take even one piece of petrified wood from the Escalante State Park, you will face nothing but bad luck—not to mention, it's against the law!

In addition to these facts, you'll also enjoy photographs of famous places such as the Salt Lake Temple and Arches National Park and charming illustrations that make you feel like you are there. Thank you to all who provided interesting information about the state, and to those who supplied such beautiful photographs. And to our BEST OF THE BEST artist, Tupper England, thank you for showing us Utah as you see it.

Utah is a feast for your eyes as well as your palate! Welcome to colorful, flavorful Utah!

Gwen McKee and Barbara Moseley

Contributing Cookbooks

All That Jam
Always in Season
Aromatherapy in the Kitchen
Back to the House of Health
Backyard Dutch Oven
The Beginner's Guide to Dutch Oven Cooking
A Century of Mormon Cookery, Volume 1
A Century of Mormon Cookery, Volume 2
Championship Dutch Oven Cookbook
Chocolate Snowball
Cherished Recipes
A Complete Guide to Dutch Oven Cooking
The Cowboy Chuck Wagon Cookbook
Doin' Dutch Oven: Inside and Out
Dude Food
Dutch Oven and Outdoor Cooking, Book Two: Homespun Edition
Dutch Oven and Outdoor Cooking, Y2K Edition
Dutch Oven Delites
Dutch Oven Gold
The Dutch Oven Resource
Dutch Oven Secrets
Enjoy! Again and Again
The Essential Mormon Cookbook
Family Favorites from the Heart
Favorite Recipes from Utah Farm Bureau Women
Favorite Utah Pioneer Recipes
Five-Star Recipes from Well-Known Latter Day Saints
Friends of Old Deseret Dutch Oven Cookbook
Heritage Cookbook
How to Enjoy Zucchini
How to Win a Cowboy's Heart
JLO Art of Cooking
Ladies' Literary Club Cookbook
Let's Cook Dutch
Lion House Desserts
Lion House Entertaining
Lion House Recipes

Contributing Cookbooks

Lion House Weddings
Log Cabin Campfire Cookn'
Log Cabin Dutch Oven
Log Cabin Grub Cookbook
Log Cabin Holidays and Traditions
Log Cabin Presents Lewis and Clark
Making Magic
A Mormon Cookbook
No Green Gelatin Here!
101 Things To Do With a Cake Mix
101 Things To Do With a Slow Cooker
Only the Best
Patty's Cakes and Things
A Pinch of Salt Lake Cookbook
Pleasures from the Good Earth
The Practical Camp Cook
Quick & Easy Cooking
Recipes & Remembrances
Recipes for Roughing It Easy
Recipes Thru Time
Roughing It Easy at Girl's Camp
Savor the Memories
Smoothies & Ice Treats
Tasteful Treasures Cookbook
30 Days to a Healthier Family
Ultimate Dutch Oven Cookbook
Utah Cook Book
Vacation Cooking: Good Food! Good Fun!
World Championship Dutch Oven Cookbook

Beverages and Appetizers

PHOTO COURTESY OF UTAH STATE PARKS.

Sailing is very popular on the Great Salt Lake. On overcast days, the horizon on the lake blends into the sky, making sailboats and the lake's islands appear to float in midair.

Cowboy Cider

1 cup sugar	½ teaspoon ground ginger
3 cups water	3 cups orange juice
12 whole cloves	8 cups apple cider
4 allspice berries	2 cups lemon juice
2 or 3 sticks cinnamon	

Boil sugar and water for 10 minutes. Add cloves, allspice berries, cinnamon, and ginger. Cover and let stand for 1 hour. Strain, then add orange juice, apple cider, and lemon juice. Bring to a light boil and serve.

The Cowboy Chuck Wagon Cookbook

Caramel Apple Cider

CINNAMON SYRUP:

1 cup sugar	5 or 6 (6-inch) cinnamon sticks
1 cup water	

In a saucepan, stir together sugar and water. Heat and stir until sugar dissolves. Reduce heat, add cinnamon sticks, and allow to simmer and reduce for 30–40 minutes. (You don't want sugar crystals forming on the sides of the pan, which happens if you simmer too long.) Allow to cool slightly, strain into a jar, and use as needed.

CIDER:

1 (64-ounce) bottle apple juice	Caramel sauce (ice cream
¼–½ cup Cinnamon Syrup	topping)
Spray can whipped cream	

Heat apple juice either on the stove top or in a crockpot. Stir in Cinnamon Syrup and heat to desired serving temperature. To serve, pour juice in mug, squirt whipped cream on top, and drizzle with caramel sauce.

Only the Best

Slush Punch

1 large can grapefruit sections
1 large can crushed pineapple
  with juice
1 cup sugar
2 cups water

Juice of 3 lemons
1 drop peppermint extract
1 tablespoon grenadine (cherry
  juice)
1 (2-liter) bottle 7-UP

Blend grapefruit sections and crushed pineapple with juice in blender. In saucepan, combine sugar and water, and bring to a boil until sugar is dissolved. Add cooled sugar-water to fruit mixture. Add lemon juice, peppermint extract, and grenadine. Freeze in clean one gallon milk container. Remove from freezer about 45 minutes to an hour before serving to begin to melt. Cut off top of milk container to remove. In punch bowl, break frozen mixture into a slush and add 7-UP just before serving. Don't make up the mixture until you need it, as it will melt and not be slushy.

Patty's Cakes and Things

Lime Slush

2 cups sugar
8 cups water
1 (12-ounce) can frozen limeade

5 fresh limes, juiced
2 (12-ounce) cans lemon-lime soda

Combine sugar and water in a large saucepan and heat slightly until sugar is dissolved. Add frozen limeade and juice of 5 limes. Mix and pour into shallow pan. Freeze. Remove from freezer about an hour before serving and break up into slush. Pour into punch bowl and add lemon-lime soda. Makes 18 (4-ounce) servings.

Lion House Weddings

Sixty-five percent of Utah's land is owned by the federal government.

13

Berry Frappe

1 gallon strawberry ice cream
1 pint vanilla ice cream
2 cups whole milk

4 cups lemon-lime soda
20 fresh strawberries or
   20 sprigs fresh mint

Let ice cream soften on counter top for 15 minutes. Place softened ice cream in a large container and blend with the milk, using a steel spoon or hand mixer.

When ice cream is well blended, pour in the soda and mix only enough to incorporate it. (Mixing too much will make the soda go flat and destroy the bubbly texture.) Pour the frappe into chilled glasses and serve garnished with a fresh berry or mint sprig. Makes 24 (8-ounce) servings.

Note: Raspberry ice cream can be substituted. Garnish with mint sprig or fresh raspberries instead of strawberries.

Lion House Weddings

Piña Colada

2 cups pineapple juice
½ cup cream of coconut or
   coconut milk

1 cup plain nonfat yogurt
1 cup ice
Whipped cream for garnish

Pour pineapple juice, cream of coconut, and yogurt into smoothie container. Add ice and press mix button; let run for 30 seconds. Rotate stir stick counterclockwise while mixing. Press the smooth button and let run for 45 seconds. Continue to rotate stir stick. Press mix button; place glass under spout and pour. Top with whipped cream.

Smoothies & Ice Treats

Strawberry Cheesecake Smoothie

You can never go wrong with cheesecake. Now you can have it anytime with only half the guilt. This smoothie version of the classic dessert is lower in calories and fat, but high in taste!

1 (14-ounce) can sweetened
   condensed milk
2 tablespoons lemon juice
   concentrate
1 (8-ounce) can crushed
   pineapple, undrained
1 (3-ounce) package cream
   cheese, softened

1 banana, sliced
1 cup strawberries (fresh or
   frozen)
1 cup ice
Fresh strawberries for garnish

Pour condensed milk, lemon juice, and crushed pineapple with juice into smoothie container. Add cream cheese, banana, strawberries, and ice. Insert stir stick in top and press mix button. Mix for 30 seconds while rotating stir stick counterclockwise. Press smooth button and let run for 45 seconds, continuing to rotate stir stick. Press mix button and pour into glass from spout. Garnish with strawberries, if desired.

Smoothies & Ice Treats

Banana Split Smoothie

Your kids will love this smooth and creamy beverage that tastes just like a banana split. They'll never know it's good for them, too!

1½ cups milk
2 tablespoons honey
2 bananas, sliced
1 (8-ounce) can crushed
  pineapple, drained

½ cup sliced strawberries (fresh
  or frozen)
1 cup ice

Add milk, honey, and fruits to liquids line on smoothie container. Add ice. If using stir stick, place in hole in top; press mix button and let run for 30 seconds, rotating stick counterclockwise. Press the smooth button and let run for 45 seconds, continuing to rotate stir stick. Pour and enjoy.

Smoothies & Ice Treats

Thirty Second Dynamite Dinner

You can add different fruits to this basic smoothie to fit your mood. It's great for a snack before or after dinner, and it's packed with protein.

1 cup milk
1 cup sliced peaches
2 tablespoons wheat germ

Dash nutmeg
Dash cinnamon
1½ cups ice

Pour milk into smoothie container. Add peaches, wheat germ, and spices, then ice. If using stir stick, place in hole in top. Press the mix button and let run for 30 seconds, rotating stir stick counter-clockwise while mixing. Press down the smooth button and let run for 45 seconds, continuing to rotate stir stick. Press mix button and press thumb tab on spout to pour.

Smoothies & Ice Treats

Sweet & Spicy Meatballs

MEATBALLS:

2 eggs, slightly beaten	½ teaspoon salt
1 onion, diced fine	½ teaspoon pepper
¾ cup bread crumbs	2 pounds hamburger

Mix eggs, onion, bread crumbs, and seasonings together, then add the hamburger and mix well with your hands. Form small Meatballs, about golf-ball size, out of the mixture. In a Dutch oven, cook over bottom heat only using 16–20 coals (400°), until well browned. Cook several Meatballs at a time, removing them when done. When all the Meatballs are browned, drain any leftover grease from the Dutch oven. Return the Meatballs to the Dutch oven and cover them with Sauce.

SAUCE:

1 (12-ounce) jar grape jelly	Juice of 1 lemon
1 (12-ounce) jar chili sauce	½–1 teaspoon hot sauce

Mix the Sauce ingredients together, then pour over the Meatballs. Cover and simmer with medium bottom heat (13–19 coals) for about 20–25 minutes. Stir occasionally while cooking. Serve as an appetizer, or make the Meatballs larger and serve them over rice as a main dish. Serves 8–12.

The Beginner's Guide to Dutch Oven Cooking

Perhaps the greatest influence on Utah's topography is ancient Lake Bonneville. Fossilized shoreline evidence of the great lake that once covered most of Utah and portions of Idaho and Nevada can still be found, including the remains of mammoth, musk ox, ancestral camel, horse, deer and mountain sheep that once roamed the area. Geologists believe the lake originated during the last ice age. At its crest, Lake Bonneville was over 5,200 feet in elevation and 1,050 feet deep, 145 miles wide and 346 miles long. Today's Great Salt Lake is a large remnant of Lake Bonneville, and occupies the lowest depression in the Great Basin.

Parks in Utah

With some of the most popular public parks in America, Utah is a dream come true for people who love the outdoors. Biking, hiking, boating, fishing, horseback riding, golfing, camping, skiing, snowboarding . . . you name it and one of Utah's parks has it. From desert landscapes to pristine lakes, from mountains to salt flats, you can find it all in Utah.

UTAH'S 41 STATE PARKS

- Anasazi State Park Museum
- Antelope Island State Park
- Bear Lake State Park
- Camp Floyd/Stagecoach Inn State Park and Museum
- Coral Pink Sand Dunes State Park
- Dead Horse Point State Park
- Deer Creek State Park
- East Canyon State Park
- Edge of the Cedars State Park Museum
- Escalante State Park
- Fremont Indian State Park and Museum
- Goblin Valley State Park
- Goosenecks State Park
- Great Salt Lake State Marina
- Green River State Park
- Gunlock State Park
- Historic Union Pacific Rail Trail State Park
- Huntington State Park
- Hyrum State Park
- Iron Mission State Park Museum
- Jordanelle State Park
- Kodachrome Basin State Park
- Millsite State Park
- Otter Creek State Park
- Palisade State Park
- Piute State Park
- Quail Creek State Park
- Red Fleet State Park
- Rockport State Park
- Sand Hollow State Park
- Scofield State Park
- Snow Canyon State Park
- Starvation State Park
- Steinaker State Park
- Territorial Statehouse State Park Museum
- This Is The Place Heritage Park
- Utah Field House of Natural History State Park Museum
- Utah Lake State Park
- Wasatch Mountain State Park
- Willard Bay State Park
- Yuba State Park

Horseback riders enjoy the magnificent views of Courthouse Wash, a short, pretty canyon near the entrance to Arches National Park.

NATIONAL PARKS

- Arches National Park
- Bryce Canyon National Park
- Canyonlands National Park
- Capitol Reef National Park
- Zion National Park

NATIONAL RECREATION AREAS

- Flaming Gorge National Recreation Area
- Glen Canyon/Lake Powell National Recreation Area

HISTORIC SITE

- Golden Spike National Historic Site

NATIONAL MONUMENTS

- Cedar Breaks National Monument
- Dinosaur National Monument
- Grand Staircase-Escalante National Monument
- Hovenweep National Monument
- Natural Bridges National Monument
- Rainbow Bridge National Monument
- Timpanogos Cave National Monument

Cranberry Meatballs

These are very good for a Christmas buffet; may be frozen and later served with pasta.

2 eggs, beaten
1 cup dry bread crumbs
⅓ cup minced fresh parsley
⅓ cup ketchup
2 tablespoons finely chopped onion

2 tablespoons soy sauce
¼ teaspoon minced garlic
½ teaspoon salt
½ teaspoon pepper
2 pounds lean ground beef

In a bowl, combine all ingredients except beef. Add beef and mix well. Shape into 1-inch balls. Place in an ungreased 10x15-inch pan and bake, covered, at 450° for 8–10 minutes, until no longer pink. Transfer to crockpot.

SAUCE:

1 (16-ounce) can whole cranberry sauce
1 (12-ounce) bottle chili sauce
1 tablespoon brown sugar

1 tablespoon prepared mustard
1 tablespoon lemon juice
¼ teaspoon minced garlic

Combine Sauce ingredients and simmer for 10 minutes. Pour over meatballs and cook on LOW for an hour or more, or until ready to serve. Makes about 50 meatballs.

No Green Gelatin Here!

Deviled Egg Boats

These are worth "stowing away" for your gourmet picnic.

12 hard-cooked eggs
3 tablespoons Miracle Whip
  salad dressing
Salt and pepper to taste

Dill or sweet pickle, chopped
3 slices Cheddar cheese (1 ounce
  each, individually wrapped)

Peel eggs and slice in half lengthwise. Remove yolks and mash with a fork. Blend in other ingredients, except cheese. Fill egg whites with mixture. Line egg carton with plastic wrap. Put egg halves back together and place in egg carton for easy transport.

When you arrive at destination, set eggs on serving plate. Cut each cheese slice into 8 triangles. Push toothpick through cheese "sails" and place one in each egg half to make your boats. Makes 24 egg boats.

The Essential Mormon Cookbook

Cowboy Caviar

2 tablespoons red wine vinegar
1½ teaspoons oil
1½–2 teaspoons hot sauce
1 clove garlic, minced
⅛ teaspoon pepper
1 firm ripe avocado
1 (15-ounce) can black-eyed
  peas
1 (11-ounce) can corn, or kernels
  from 2 ears of fresh corn,
  blanched

⅔ cup chopped cilantro
⅔ cup thinly sliced green
  onions
8 ounces Roma tomatoes, coarsely
  chopped
Salt to taste

Mix vinegar, oil, hot sauce, garlic, and pepper in a bowl. Cut avocado into ½-inch cubes and add to the vinegar mixture, mixing gently. Drain and rinse the peas and corn. Add to the vinegar mixture with cilantro, green onions, and tomatoes; mix gently. Add salt to taste. Serve with tortilla chips. Serves 10–12.

Always in Season

Gabby's Fresh Watermelon and Peach Salsa

This is a tasty condiment for roasted lamb or grilled white fish. Really wonderful and just as great on a tortilla chip. Try!

2 cups fresh, sweet watermelon, seeded and finely diced

1½ cups fresh sweet peaches, skinned, pitted, and finely chopped

1 cup finely chopped fresh tomato

1 small red Bermuda onion, finely chopped

1–2 red jalapeño peppers, very finely chopped

1 clove garlic, finely minced

3 tablespoons finely chopped fresh cilantro

1½ teaspoons finely chopped fresh mint

1 tablespoon dried oregano leaves

½ teaspoon dried ground cumin

3 tablespoons seasoned rice vinegar*

1 tablespoon extra virgin olive oil

1 teaspoon salt, or to taste

Prepare all of the fresh ingredients as indicated. It is best if these ingredients are all hand minced or chopped instead of processing in a food processor.

In a large mixing bowl, combine all the ingredients, and mix well. Taste for proper seasoning and adjust as desired. Cover with plastic wrap and place in the refrigerator to chill until serving. Makes just over a quart.

*If you prefer less sweetness, use regular rice vinegar in place of seasoned vinegar.

Enjoy! Again and Again

"Oh, give me a home where the buffalo roam. . . ." These lyrics to an 1873 cowboy ballad still hold true if you are adventurous enough to go to the remote Henry Mountains. This isolated pocket of wilderness is home to a herd of some 300 buffalo—the largest free-roaming, hunted buffalo herd in the nation. The region is very rugged and dry, and carries warnings of danger from washouts, rockslides, snow, and dangerous animals and reptiles—"badder than the badlands," some say. But the deer and the antelope play there . . . and the buffalo . . . and they like calling it home.

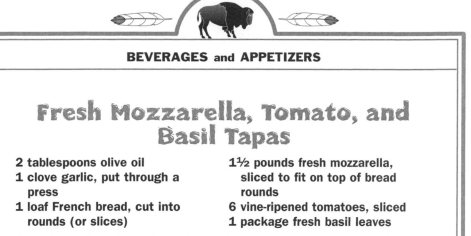

Fresh Mozzarella, Tomato, and Basil Tapas

2 tablespoons olive oil
1 clove garlic, put through a press
1 loaf French bread, cut into rounds (or slices)

1½ pounds fresh mozzarella, sliced to fit on top of bread rounds
6 vine-ripened tomatoes, sliced
1 package fresh basil leaves

Combine olive oil and garlic, and brush mixture on top of bread rounds. Place fresh mozzarella slices on top of bread. Place tomato slices on top of cheese, and one basil leaf on top of tomato. Place under broiler until brown. Serve hot.

Making Magic

Wild Rice in Cherry Tomatoes

1 (6-ounce) package wild rice
8 ounces hot sausage, cooked, drained and crumbled
½ cup finely diced celery
¼ cup chopped green onions
1 tablespoon chopped fresh parsley

⅓ cup mayonnaise
1 tablespoon lemon juice
2 pounds cherry tomatoes
Parsley for garnish

Prepare wild rice as directed on package. Cook and drain sausage. Add to rice. Add celery, green onions, parsley, mayonnaise, and lemon juice. Mix well and chill.

Wash and dry cherry tomatoes. Cut around the stem, remove, and hollow out tomato. Stuff tomatoes with rice mixture and place a tiny parsley sprig on top. Yields 40 tomatoes.

A Pinch of Salt Lake Cookbook

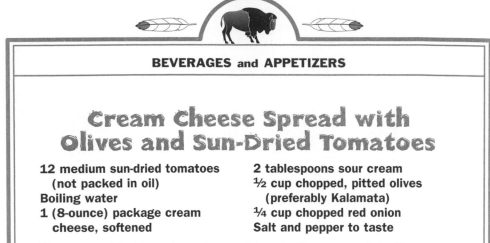

Cream Cheese Spread with Olives and Sun-Dried Tomatoes

12 medium sun-dried tomatoes (not packed in oil)	2 tablespoons sour cream
Boiling water	½ cup chopped, pitted olives (preferably Kalamata)
1 (8-ounce) package cream cheese, softened	¼ cup chopped red onion
	Salt and pepper to taste

Place sun-dried tomatoes in small bowl. Pour enough boiling water over tomatoes to cover. Let tomatoes stand until soft—about 10 minutes. Pat tomatoes dry and chop finely. Mix cream cheese and sour cream in medium bowl until smooth. Mix in olives, onion, and sun-dried tomatoes. Season to taste with salt and pepper. Cover and refrigerate. Let stand at room temperature for one hour before serving.

Note: Prepare this one or two days ahead to allow the flavors to blend.

Recipes & Remembrances

Ham Spread

1 (8-ounce) tub soft-style cream cheese with chives and onion	⅓ cup finely chopped, fully cooked ham
½ teaspoon Dijon mustard	¼ cup shredded Cheddar cheese
1 tablespoon mayonnaise	Crackers, bread, or celery sticks

In a small mixing bowl, stir together cream cheese, mustard, and mayonnaise. Stir in ham and Cheddar cheese. Cover and chill. Spread on crackers, bread, or celery sticks. Cover and store leftover spread in the refrigerator for up to 5 days. Makes enough spread for 6 slices of bread.

Variations: To make roast beef spread, substitute cooked roast beef for the ham, and Swiss cheese for the Cheddar. To make turkey spread, substitute cooked turkey for the ham, and mozzarella cheese for the Cheddar.

Lion House Entertaining

Lemon Garlic Shrimp

2 pounds large shrimp (21-26 per
  pound) peeled, deveined,
  and cooked, tails on
¼ cup olive oil
2 lemons, zest and juice
¼ cup chopped fresh parsley

1 tablespoon minced garlic
1 tablespoon chopped fresh
  dill, or 1 teaspoon dried dill
½ teaspoon salt
Pinch of red pepper flakes

In a bowl, combine all ingredients. Stir well. Taste for seasoning. Cover; refrigerate until ready to use. Serve with lemon slices and parsley sprigs. Can be made hours ahead. Serves 8–10, allowing 5–6 shrimp per person.

Savor the Memories

Shrimp with Ginger Butter

This very simple preparation pairs the ever-sultry shrimp with the sensuously spicy ginger to make a great start to a fabulous evening of romantic dining. Go ahead and get your hands a little messy with this fun and tantalizing dish! A loaf of crusty French bread makes a great accompaniment to soak up all of the delicious sauce.

1 pound raw shrimp, shells on
1 stick (½ cup) butter
1 tablespoon minced gingerroot
1 garlic clove, finely chopped

2 tablespoons chopped fresh
  parsley
Salt and pepper

Preheat oven to 400°. Place shrimp in baking dish. Melt butter in a small saucepan. Add ginger, herbs, salt and pepper, and cook over medium heat for about 2 minutes. Pour over shrimp and bake in oven for 5 minutes. The shrimp should be pink and opaque. Remove the shrimp to a serving bowl, and drain the sauce into another bowl for dipping.

    Have ready a bowl for the shells, and a couple of small bowls with some water and lemon for cleansing your hands as you dive into this peel-and-eat appetizer. Serves 2–4 as a first course.

Aromatherapy in the Kitchen

Miniature Crab Cakes

1 pound crabmeat
¼ cup finely diced onion
¼ cup finely diced red bell
  pepper
3 cups fresh bread crumbs,
  divided
½ cup mayonnaise
¼ cup cream cheese, softened

1 tablespoon Dijon mustard
1 egg
Pinch of cayenne pepper
⅛ teaspoon paprika
¼ teaspoon salt
1 tablespoon finely chopped
  parsley

In a medium bowl, mix crabmeat, onion, bell pepper, 1 cup bread crumbs, mayonnaise, cream cheese, mustard, egg, cayenne, paprika, salt, and parsley. Refrigerate for 1 hour. Place remaining bread crumbs in a shallow bowl. Using a tablespoon, form a crab cake about 1 inch in diameter. Coat both sides with bread crumbs and place on baking sheet which has been sprayed with vegetable or olive oil spray. Continue until all crabmeat mixture is used. This can be done a day ahead, covered with plastic wrap, then refrigerated until ready to use.

Bake at 375° for 10–12 minutes or until golden brown. Serve warm with a dollop of Chipotle Mayonnaise on top. Makes about 24 mini crab cakes or 12 large crab cakes.

CHIPOTLE MAYONNAISE:

2 whole chipotle chiles (canned
  smoked jalapeño peppers)
1 cup mayonnaise

1 tablespoon minced garlic
½ cup chopped fresh parsley
¼ teaspoon salt

Place all ingredients in blender or processor and blend until smooth. This can be made a day ahead. Makes about 1 cup.

Savor the Memories

Beginning on July 24, 1847, construction of Salt Lake Temple took 40 years to complete. Granite used at the site was quarried in Little Cottonwood Canyon, 20 miles southeast of Temple Square, and transported to the site by teams of oxen. Four days of travel was required for each wagonload to reach the temple site.

Crab Napoleon

1 (16-ounce) package wonton
  wrappers
1 (8-ounce) package cream
  cheese, softened
2 tablespoons Old Bay Seafood
  Seasoning

1 pound crabmeat, defrosted
  if frozen
1 cup alfalfa sprouts

Heat a deep saucepan or fryer with shortening to 350° according to manufacturer's directions. Carefully place individual wonton wrappers into the fry oil and fry until golden brown. The wontons will continue to brown when removed from the oil, so care must be taken with this step. Drain on paper towels.

In a medium bowl, mix the cream cheese and Old Bay Seasoning with a metal spoon. (For a stronger flavor, add more Old Bay.) Add the crabmeat and incorporate into the cream cheese. Organize a work area with the crab mixture, fried wontons, and the sprouts within easy reach. Take a wonton skin and spread a small amount of the sprouts onto the skin. Spoon a tablespoon of the crab mixture onto the sprouts. Place on a serving platter and serve immediately or hold for up to 2 hours. Makes 20 servings.

Lion House Weddings

Warm Crab Dip

1 (8-ounce) package cream
  cheese, softened
1 tablespoon milk
1 (6½-ounce) can crabmeat,
  flaked
2 tablespoons finely chopped
  onion

½ teaspoon cream-style
  horseradish
¼ teaspoon salt
Dash of pepper
Sliced almonds

Combine cream cheese and milk. Add remaining ingredients and blend well. Spoon into oven-proof dish. Sprinkle with sliced almonds. Bake at 375° for 15 minutes. Serve immediately.

A Century of Mormon Cookery, Volume 1

Glen Canyon Dip

3 ripe avocados
2 teaspoons lemon juice
1 cup sour cream
1 cup mayonnaise
1 package taco seasoning
2 (9-ounce) cans bean dip

1 bunch green onions, chopped
3 medium tomatoes, chopped
1 (6-ounce) can pitted olives, sliced
8 ounces Cheddar cheese, grated

Peel and mash avocados in a bowl, add lemon juice and set aside. Combine sour cream, mayonnaise, and taco seasoning in another bowl and set aside. Spread bean dip on a serving plate, spread avocado mixture over bean dip and then layer with sour cream mixture. Top with onions, tomatoes, and olives, and sprinkle all with cheese. Serve with your favorite chips or crackers.

Utah Cook Book

Defiance House, three miles up the middle fork of Forgotten Canyon, is one of the best-preserved Ancestral Puebloan dwellings in Glen Canyon National Recreation Area. In 1959, while exploring the area where Lake Powell was to be created, University of Utah archeologists found a site where as they described it, "most of the roofs were still in place, and . . . two perfect red bowls still had scraps of food in them." They named the site Defiance House because of the large pictograph (rock painting) of three warriors brandishing clubs and shields.

Warm Blue Cheese, Bacon, and Garlic Dip

7 slices bacon, chopped
2 cloves garlic, minced
1 (8-ounce) package cream
  cheese, softened
¼ cup half-and-half
1 (4-ounce) package blue cheese,
  crumbled

2 tablespoons chopped fresh
  chives
3 tablespoons chopped smoked
  almonds

Cook bacon in a large skillet over medium-high heat until almost crisp, about 7 minutes. Drain excess fat from skillet. Add garlic and cook until bacon is crisp, about 3 minutes. Beat cream cheese until smooth. Add half-and-half and mix until combined. Stir in bacon mixture, blue cheese, and chives. Transfer to a 2-cup, oven-proof serving dish and cover with foil. Bake until thoroughly heated, about 30 minutes. Sprinkle with chopped almonds. Makes 2 cups.

Making Magic

Creamy Spinach Dip

Healthy as well as delicious.

1 (10-ounce) package frozen
  chopped spinach, thawed
  and well drained
1 cup salad dressing (Miracle
  Whip)

1 cup sour cream
½ cup chopped parsley
½ cup chopped green onions
1 teaspoon dill weed
½ teaspoon lemon or lime juice

Combine ingredients in a 1-quart bowl. Mix well with a wooden spoon. This dip will store for one week in the refrigerator in a plastic container. Serve with assorted vegetables and crackers. Makes 2½ cups.

Vacation Cooking: Good Food! Good Fun!

Chili Bean Cheese Dip

This dip is also great on baked potatoes or buns.

1 pound hamburger meat	**1 (16-ounce) can chili**
½ pound bulk sausage	**⅓ cup BBQ sauce**
1 large onion, chopped	**2 cups shredded cheese**
1 cup chopped red bell peppers	**Chips or crackers**
1 (15-ounce) can kidney beans	

Brown hamburger meat and sausage. Add onion and peppers; cook until tender. Add beans, chili, and BBQ sauce. Add cheese; stir well and serve on chips or crackers.

Log Cabin Dutch Oven

Pizza Fondue

1 (26- to 28-ounce) jar spaghetti sauce with meat	**½ cup sliced pepperoni**
2 teaspoons Italian seasoning	**1 cup grated mozzarella cheese**
1 tablespoon cornstarch or instant tapioca	

Combine all ingredients except mozzarella cheese in greased 2- to 3½-quart slow cooker. Cover and cook on LOW heat for 2–3 hours. Add cheese the last hour of cooking. Serve with bread sticks, pita bread, or chunks of crusty Italian bread for dippers. Makes 8–10 servings.

101 Things To Do With a Slow Cooker

Bread and Breakfast

The Watchman Peak stands guard over the south entrance to Zion National Park. The hiking trail to Watchman Peak offers scenic views of the park as well as the nearby town of Springdale.

Corn Bread

1⅓ cups cornmeal
⅔ cup self-rising flour
2 tablespoons sugar
2 tablespoons baking powder

2 teaspoons salt
2 eggs
Milk
2 tablespoons oil

Mix together all the dry ingredients. Add eggs and enough milk to make the consistency of cake batter. Pour into a 12-inch preheated Dutch oven that has a little hot oil in the bottom. Cook until the corn bread is golden brown (about 30 minutes). Make sure to keep enough heat on the bottom to cook it evenly.

Dutch Oven and Outdoor Cooking, Y2K Edition

Patty's Version of Corn Bread

2 small boxes Jiffy Corn Bread
  Mix
2 eggs
¼ cup oil
4 tablespoons sugar

½ (15-ounce) can of creamed
  corn
Milk
2 tablespoons margarine

Mix corn bread mix, eggs, oil, sugar, and corn; do not overmix. Add enough milk to make a thick mixture. Melt margarine in a 10- to 12-inch iron frying pan, and heat in 375° oven until the pan is really hot. Take the pan out of the oven and pour in the corn bread mixture, then return to the oven. Bake approximately 20–25 minutes until done, but don't overcook. Serve from the frying pan.

Patty's Cakes and Things

Natural Bridges National Monument was established in 1908, making it the oldest National Park Service site in Utah. The monument protects three of the ten natural stone bridges in the world. They are named: Kachina, Owachomo and Sipapu.

Cowboy Cheese Bread

2½ cups flour
2 teaspoons baking powder
¾ teaspoon salt
¼ teaspoon garlic powder
2 tablespoons dried parsley
1½ teaspoons dried onion
1 tablespoon sugar

¼ cup butter-flavored
  shortening
½ cup butter, divided
2 eggs
½ cup milk
1 cup grated Cheddar cheese
¼ cup Parmesan cheese

Mix all dry ingredients and seasonings together. (Do not mix in either cheese at this time.) Cut shortening and ¼ cup butter into dry ingredients; mix until it resembles coarse meal. Mix eggs and milk together, then add to flour mixture, and mix again. Add both cheeses, and knead until the cheese is worked through. Roll dough out into a 12-inch circle, then cut with a pizza cutter into pie-shaped wedges. Place wedges the way they were cut into an oiled Dutch oven, then melt remaining butter and drizzle over wedges. Cover and cook with 16–22 coals (400°), with a ratio of 1 (bottom)/3 (top), for 20–30 minutes or until no longer doughy inside. Serves 8–10.

The Beginner's Guide to Dutch Oven Cooking

Cheesy French Bread

1 tablespoon sugar
1½ teaspoons salt
1 tablespoon cooking oil
1 tablespoon yeast dissolved in
  1½ cups warm water

4 cups flour
½ teaspoon garlic powder
½ teaspoon onion salt
2 cups grated Cheddar cheese
Poppy seeds

Mix sugar, salt, oil, and yeast mixture in large bowl. Add flour and mix well. Punch dough down 5 times at 10 minute intervals. Turn onto floured board and divide in half. Shape each into rectangle. Sprinkle each with garlic powder, onion salt, and cheese. Roll each firmly into a roll lengthwise. Slash tops. Place into Dutch ovens and let rise until double. Brush tops with egg white and sprinkle with poppy seeds. Bake at 400° for 30–35 minutes or until bread sounds hollow when tapped. Makes 2 loaves.

Championship Dutch Oven Cookbook

Bread on a Stick

1 dowel or roasting stick for
   each person
1 box Bisquick mix
About 1 cup water, divided

½ cup (1 stick) butter or
   margarine
1 cup honey or jam

Using the end of the stick, make a little well in the open box of Bisquick. Pour 1 tablespoon of water into the well. Place stick in well and begin stirring until a small ball of dough forms around stick. Lift stick out of box and press dough firmly around end of stick. Pass the box and water to the next person to repeat.

Grill dough stick over a bed of hot coals and turn often. When your bread is golden brown and cooked throughout, slide it off the stick and slather it with butter, honey, or jam. Sit back and enjoy until the box makes its way again to you. A large box of Bisquick makes more than 20 servings.

Roughing It Easy at Girls Camp

Sky-High Biscuits

2 cups all-purpose flour plus
  1 cup whole-wheat flour
  (or 3 cups all-purpose flour)
4½ teaspoons baking powder
2 tablespoons sugar

½ teaspoon salt
¾ teaspoon cream of tartar
¾ cup butter or margarine
1 egg, beaten
1 cup milk

In a bowl, combine flour, baking powder, sugar, salt, and cream of tartar. Cut in butter or margarine until mixture resembles coarse cornmeal. Add egg and milk, stirring quickly and briefly. Knead lightly on floured surface. Roll or pat gently to 1-inch thickness. Cut into 1- to 2-inch biscuits. Place in a 12- to 14-inch Dutch oven. Bake over a 450° fire for 10–12 minutes. Makes about 12 biscuits.

Dutch Oven Secrets

Yam Biscuits

1 egg
⅓ cup lard, butter, or
  shortening
1 cup cooked, mashed yams

2 tablespoons sugar
1 cup flour
2 teaspoons baking powder
½ teaspoon salt

Mix egg, shortening, and yams in a bowl until fluffy. Gradually stir in sugar. Now add flour, baking powder, and salt. Blend well and drop by tablespoons onto lightly greased pan. Bake at 375° until done, 10–20 minutes. Check after 10 minutes for doneness.

Log Cabin Grub Cookbook

The Bonneville Salt Flats are one of the only places in the United States where you can see the curvature of the earth over dry land. The flats are a salt (potash) floor from one to six inches thick, and are actually the bed of what was ancient Lake Bonneville.

Easy Onion Rolls

2 cups flour
½ teaspoon salt
1 tablespoon baking powder
½ cup butter or butter-flavored
   vegetable shortening
½ cup sour cream

½ cup milk
2 tablespoons butter
1 small red onion, chopped
1 small white onion, chopped
½ teaspoon ground thyme
1 teaspoon rosemary leaves

Preheat oven to 425°. Lightly grease or spray cookie sheet. In a large mixing bowl, blend dry ingredients. Cut in butter until mixture resembles coarse meal. Add sour cream and stir until barely mixed. Add milk, and mix or knead until a rich elastic dough forms. Set aside.

In a heavy skillet over medium heat, melt butter and sauté chopped onions with spices until soft and transparent. Cool slightly. Roll out dough in a large rectangle, approximately ¼ inch thick. Spread onion mixture over dough, and roll into a tight log. Cut into 1-inch slices and place approximately ½ inch apart on cookie sheet. Bake for 15 minutes.

How to Win a Cowboy's Heart

As Utah's largest national park, Canyonlands has been naturally divided by the Colorado and Green Rivers into four districts: the Island in the Sky, the Needles, the Maze and the Rivers themselves. To the north between the rivers, and serving as an observation tower, The Island in the Sky offers a view of hundreds of miles across Utah. Arches, rock spires, gardens, canyons, potholes, prehistoric Native American ruins, and pictographs surround the Needles. Lying to the west, in the most remote region of the park (and only accessible via off-road vehicles), is the Maze with its maze-like canyon of tall standing rocks and fins of colorful sandstones. There are two major entrances to Canyonlands National Park—one found 35 miles northwest of Moab, the other lies 22 miles north of Monticello.

Parmesan Dinner Rolls

2 tablespoons dry yeast
2 cups warm water
⅓ cup sugar
⅓ cup oil
1½ teaspoons salt

1 egg
⅔ cup nonfat dry milk
5–6 cups flour
½ cup butter, melted
1 cup Parmesan cheese

Combine yeast, water, and sugar. Let sit until foamy (about 5 minutes). Add oil, salt, and egg. Mix dry milk with 2 cups flour; add to the liquid. Beat until smooth. Add flour mixture 1 cup at a time. Mix until smooth. Dough should be very soft but workable.

Knead dough until smooth and satiny. Oil bowl and return dough to rise until triple. Pinch off ball of dough; roll in melted butter, then in Parmesan cheese. Place balls in lightly greased 12-inch Dutch oven and let rise. Bake 15–20 minutes with coals placed around perimeter of bottom and checkerboard-style on lid. Loosen edges with a knife and tip rolls out of pan to cool.

Friends of Old Deseret Dutch Oven Cookbook

Potato Rolls

1 tablespoon yeast
¾ cup warm water
⅛ cup sugar
¾ teaspoon salt
⅓ cup shortening

1 egg
½ cup lukewarm mashed
 potatoes
3½–4 cups flour, divided

Dissolve yeast in warm water. Stir in sugar, salt, shortening, egg, potatoes, and 2 cups flour. Beat until smooth. Mix in enough remaining flour to make dough easy to handle. Turn dough onto floured board; knead until smooth, about 5 minutes. Place in greased bowl; cover tightly. Refrigerate at least 8 hours (dough can be kept for 5 days).

Form rolls and place in a 12-inch Dutch oven and let rise 1 hour before baking. Bake with 6 coals on bottom and 16 on lid for 15–25 minutes until brown.

Friends of Old Deseret Dutch Oven Cookbook

Dutch Oven Rolls

To watch Juanita Kohler generate these at a workshop is to watch an artist at work.

1 tablespoon yeast	**1 cup warm milk**
¼ cup warm water	**1 tablespoon butter**
⅛ teaspoon plus 1 tablespoon	**1 teaspoon salt**
sugar	**3 cups flour, divided**

Mix dry yeast in water; sprinkle ⅛ teaspoon sugar over the yeast mixture to activate. Mix milk, butter, salt, and remaining sugar; stir well. Add ½ amount of flour; mix thoroughly. Add yeast mixture, stir well, then add all but ½ cup of the remaining flour. Dust a flat surface with the ½ cup. Knead until dough is smooth. Place dough in greased bowl; cover and let rise until double in bulk (approximately one hour). Shape dough into about 12 smooth rolls and place in greased 12-inch Dutch oven. Cover and let rise until double in bulk. Place Dutch oven on 1 or 2 shovels of hot coals and also put a shovel of coals on the top of the lid. Bake approximately 10–15 minutes. Remove Dutch oven from coals and continue baking with coals on top for approximately 10–15 minutes or until rolls are golden brown. Makes about a dozen rolls.

Variations:

Orange Rolls: ½ stick butter, rind from 1 orange, ½ cup sugar.

Cinnamon Rolls: brown sugar, cinnamon, raisins or nuts as desired. Roll dough in a flat rectangle shape (approximately ¼ inch thick). Spread or sprinkle filling on the rolled dough. Roll up and pinch edges together. Cut in 1-inch slices and place in greased Dutch oven, edges touching. Let rise until double in bulk. Bake in the same manner as the Dutch Oven Rolls.

World Championship Dutch Oven Cookbook

All-In-One Cinnamon Rolls

2 packages dry yeast
2½ cups milk, scalded
½ cup packed brown sugar
1 tablespoon salt
5 tablespoons margarine,
  softened
6–7 cups flour, divided

½ cup dried chopped currants
½ cup chopped nuts
1 teaspoon cinnamon
Oil
1 pound powdered sugar
Milk

Dissolve yeast in warm milk. In a bowl, mix well the sugar, salt, and margarine. Add 3 cups flour and yeast mixture; beat well. Mix in currants and nuts. Continue adding flour a little at a time until a soft dough forms. Add cinnamon and knead well. Place in lightly oiled bowl and let double in size.

Form dough into balls and place into a lightly oiled 12-inch Dutch oven; let rise double again. Bake at 400° for 30–35 minutes (8–10 coals on bottom, 18–20 coals on top). When done, remove from oven. Mix powdered sugar and just enough milk to make a thin glaze. Drizzle over rolls. Makes 1 dozen large rolls. Enjoy.

Dutch Oven Gold

Simply Superb Cinnamon Rolls

I looked and looked for the perfect cinnamon roll—one that was moist, but not overly gooey, and that could be done in the bread machine. Since creating this, I haven't had a finer cinnamon roll—and they are easy, too!

½ cup milk
½ cup water
2 tablespoons butter
1 egg
¼ cup white sugar
3 cups flour
¾ teaspoon salt

2¼ teaspoons bread machine yeast
2 tablespoons softened butter
½ cup softly packed brown sugar
¾–1 teaspoon ground cinnamon

Combine and cook for 1 minute on HIGH in the microwave the milk, water, and butter. Place in bread machine pan in order suggested by the manufacturer: the milk mixture, egg, sugar, flour, salt, and yeast. Select dough cycle and press start.

When dough is ready, roll into a large rectangle and spread with the softened butter. Sprinkle with brown sugar and cinnamon. Starting from long side, roll up and pinch to seal. Cut into 12 slices (using dental floss is easiest).

Place on greased jellyroll pan, cover, and let rise in a warm place for 30 minutes. Bake at 375° for 15 minutes. Let cool for a few minutes, then spread with frosting and enjoy! These can be refrigerated and then reheated in the microwave for 10–20 seconds on LOW, if absolutely necessary, but they are truly best when fresh.

CREAM CHEESE FROSTING:
4 ounces cream cheese, softened
2–3 tablespoons butter, melted

2–2½ cups powdered sugar
½ teaspoon vanilla

Beat cream cheese and butter until smooth. Add sugar and vanilla, and beat until creamy.

ORANGE ROLL VARIATION:
3 round tablespoons butter, softened

⅓–½ cup white sugar
Grated rind of 1 orange

Onto rolled-out dough rectangle, spread butter, white sugar, and orange rind. Finish as for cinnamon rolls, or cut dough in half, fold over each half and cut into strips. Twist each strip and place on

(continued)

(Simply Superb Cinnamon Rolls continued)

cookie sheet. Bake. Add fresh orange zest to Cream Cheese Frosting and a bit of fresh orange juice, if desired. Frost twists.

CARAMEL APPLE VARIATION:

¾ cup brown sugar
¼ cup flour
2 teaspoons cinnamon

⅓ cup butter, softened
2 apples, peeled and chopped

Double dough recipe to make 24 rolls. Combine sugar, flour, cinnamon, and butter. Sprinkle onto dough. Evenly sprinkle on apples. Finish as for cinnamon rolls, but frost with Caramel Frosting.

CARAMEL FROSTING:

½ cup butter
1 cup brown sugar
½ cup milk or half-and-half

2–4 cups powdered sugar
1 teaspoon vanilla

Melt butter in saucepan, then add brown sugar. Bring to a low boil and stir for 2 minutes. Add milk and bring back to a boil. Remove from heat and beat in powdered sugar and vanilla to desired consistency. Frost rolls.

Only the Best

Facts about The Great Salt Lake:
• The largest salt lake in the western hemisphere.
• The largest U.S. lake west of the Mississippi River.
• The 4th largest terminal lake (no outlet) in the world.
• It is a remnant of Lake Bonneville, a prehistoric freshwater lake that was 10 times larger than the Great Salt Lake.
• It is about 75 miles long, and 28 miles wide, and covers 1,700 square miles.
• It has a maximum depth of about 35 feet.
• It is typically 3 to 5 times saltier than the ocean.
• It has no fish, the largest aquatic critters are brine shrimp.
• It is one of the largest migratory bird magnets in Western North America.
• The salt industries extract about 2.5 million tons of sodium chloride and other salts and elements from the lake annually.
• No streams empty from the lake, and its high salinity is caused by the accumulation of minerals with no removal and the accompanying water evaporation.

Balloon Buns

2 tablespoons yeast
⅔ cup warm water
½ cup shortening
4 cups hot water
6+ cups flour
½+ cup sugar

2 teaspoons salt
2 eggs
Large marshmallows
Melted butter
Cinnamon sugar

Dissolve yeast in warm water. Add shortening to the hot water and let it sit until melted and cooled to lukewarm. Add flour, sugar, and salt to yeast mixture. Add eggs (and a little more sugar, if you like your bread sweeter). Add more flour until dough is thick but moist. Turn dough out onto a floured surface and knead until smooth and bubbly. Let rise until double; punch down and let rise again.

Break pieces off one at a time. Flatten dough. Roll a large marshmallow in melted butter, then cinnamon sugar mixture, and put in the center of the dough piece. Fold dough around it and seal together. Put sealed-side-down in a greased 16-inch Dutch oven after dipping top in melted butter. Let rise about one hour. Bake at 350° for 15–20 minutes or until golden brown. Makes about 24 Balloon Buns.

Dutch Oven Secrets

Cinnamon Breakfast Squares

1 cup peeled, seeded, and
   shredded zucchini
¼ cup oil
1 teaspoon vanilla
1 egg
¼ cup brown sugar
¼ cup white sugar

1 cup flour
1 teaspoon baking soda
½ teaspoon salt
½ teaspoon cinnamon
1 tablespoon grated orange rind
   (optional)

Combine zucchini with oil and vanilla. Stir in unbeaten egg. Add sugars and blend. Sift dry ingredients together and add to mixture. Stir until well mixed (do not beat). Blend in orange peel. Spread into a greased 8x8-inch pan. Bake at 350° for 30 minutes. Cool 10 minutes. Cut into squares and break open like muffins; spread with honey butter.

How to Enjoy Zucchini

Sloans S-Nut Rolls

2 loaves frozen bread dough,
   thawed
1 cup creamy small-curd cottage
   cheese
1 egg

½ cup butter, melted
1 cup brown sugar
1 cup chopped nuts (optional)
1 teaspoon vanilla or maple
   syrup

Roll both loaves of dough out in a rectangle. Combine remaining ingredients and divide in half; spread on top of each rectangle. Roll the side up and cut into ½-inch thick rolls. Warm and grease a 12-inch Dutch oven, or 2 (10-inch) Dutch ovens. Take each roll and twist once into an S shape. Place in ovens and let rise till double in size (about 30 minutes in the Dutch oven with the lid on; will take 1–1½ hours on a cookie sheet). Bake on 12 briquettes in your Volcano, or 10 on bottom and 15 on top in open air. In your oven at home, bake at 350° for 25–30 minutes or until you get the smell. Should make about 2 dozen rolls.

Log Cabin Campfire Cookn'

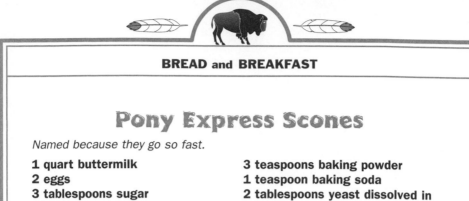

Pony Express Scones

Named because they go so fast.

1 quart buttermilk
2 eggs
3 tablespoons sugar
1½ teaspoons salt
2 tablespoons oil

3 teaspoons baking powder
1 teaspoon baking soda
2 tablespoons yeast dissolved in
  ½ cup warm water
7–8 cups flour

Heat buttermilk until it curdles. Add eggs, sugar, salt, oil, baking powder, and baking soda. Add yeast mixture. Mix in flour and knead well. Let rise, then punch down and place in fridge. The dough can be kept in the refrigerator for 2 weeks.

To make the scones, roll dough out to ½-inch thickness. Cut into square pieces with a pizza cutter. Let rest for a few minutes and deep-fry in oil until golden brown.

Recipes Thru Time

Quick Scones

A convenient way to use leftover pancake batter. This is one of the best scones you will ever eat; the center is never doughy.

1 cup vegetable oil for frying
4–6 English muffins, cut in half
2–3 cups prepared pancake
  batter

Toppings of your choice

In a large, deep skillet, heat oil until a drop of pancake batter dropped into the skillet sizzles. With a fork, dip muffins into the pancake batter and carefully add to the hot oil. Cook on both sides until golden brown. Remove and drain on paper towels. Serve hot, plain, or with Toppings, as desired. Serves 4.

TOPPINGS:

Sugar, powdered sugar, brown
  sugar, or cinnamon sugar
Honey, jam, jelly, or syrup
  (flavored, if desired)

Powdered sugar and fresh lemon
  juice

Recipes for Roughing It Easy

Six Weeks on the Trail Muffins

2 cups boiling water
5 cups bran, divided
5 cups whole-wheat flour
5 teaspoons baking soda
1½ teaspoons salt
2 teaspoons cinnamon
1 cup wheat germ

1 cup oil
1 cup honey or molasses
4 eggs, beaten
4 cups buttermilk or yogurt
1 cup dates, raisins, chopped
  apple, or nuts

Pour boiling water over 2 cups bran. In another bowl, sift flour, soda, salt, and cinnamon. Add wheat germ and remaining bran. Combine with wet bran. Stir until moist. Add oil, honey, eggs, buttermilk, and fruit or nuts. Pour into desired number of well-greased muffin tins. Bake at 400° for 15–20 minutes. Keep dough in refrigerator to use as needed.

The Cowboy Chuck Wagon Cookbook

Blueberry-Pumpkin Muffins

1⅔ cups plus 1 tablespoon
  flour, divided
1 teaspoon baking soda
½ teaspoon salt
1 teaspoon cinnamon
½ teaspoon allspice
1 cup cooked pumpkin

¼ cup evaporated milk
⅓ cup butter, softened
1 cup firmly packed light brown
  sugar
1 egg
1 cup blueberries

Combine 1⅔ cups flour, soda, salt, cinnamon, and allspice together in a mixing bowl; stir and set aside. Mix pumpkin and evaporated milk until blended and set aside. Cream butter and sugar together in large mixing bowl. Add egg to sugar mixture and blend until mixture is fluffy. Add flour mixture to butter mixture, alternating with pumpkin mixture, until all ingredients are well blended. Combine blueberries with 1 tablespoon flour, and gently fold into batter. Fill 18 paper-lined muffin cups ¾ full. Bake in preheated 350° oven for 40 minutes.

Utah Cook Book

Grandma Kygar's Banana Bread

1 cup sugar	1 teaspoon baking soda
½ cup vegetable oil	½ teaspoon baking powder
2 eggs, beaten	½ teaspoon salt
3 bananas, mashed to a pulp	½ cup chopped nuts
2 cups flour	1 teaspoon vanilla

Combine sugar and oil, and mix well. Add beaten eggs and mashed bananas; beat well. Sift together flour, baking soda, baking powder, and salt; add to mixture and beat well. Stir in nuts and vanilla. Lightly flour and oil a 12-inch Dutch oven. Pour batter into Dutch oven and bake at 350° for one hour (6–10 coals on bottom, 12–16 coals on top). Invert and frost, or eat as is.

Dutch Oven Gold

Pumpkin Bread

2 eggs	¾ teaspoon salt
1½ cups sugar	½ teaspoon cloves
1 cup pumpkin	½ teaspoon cinnamon
½ cup oil	½ teaspoon nutmeg
1½ cups flour	1 cup chopped nuts
1 teaspoon baking soda	1 cup raisins
¼ teaspoon baking powder	

Beat eggs and sugar until light. Add pumpkin and oil. Mix flour, soda, baking powder, salt, cloves, cinnamon, and nutmeg, and add to pumpkin mixture. Fold in nuts and raisins. Pour into a well-greased, floured loaf pan and bake for 1 hour at 325°.

Note: May substitute 1 cup applesauce or 4 cups grated zucchini for pumpkin.

Quick & Easy Cooking

Utah Valley Applesauce Bread

Applesauce bread can be made a month in advance and frozen for holiday giving. It stays very moist because of the applesauce and slices easily.

4 cups flour	½ teaspoon nutmeg
2 tablespoons cornstarch	½ teaspoon salt
2 cups sugar	1 cup vegetable oil
4 teaspoons baking soda	3 cups applesauce
1 teaspoon cinnamon	1 cup raisins
½ teaspoon cloves	½ cup chopped pecans
½ teaspoon allspice	

Mix the first 9 (dry) ingredients in a bowl. In another bowl, combine the remaining ingredients. Combine both mixtures and mix well. Spoon batter into 2 greased 5x9-inch loaf pans. Bake at 350° for one hour. Cool in pans for several minutes; remove to wire racks to cool completely.

Utah Cook Book

Applesauce

Apples were a staple here in the West. As pioneers traveled, they often planted apple seeds along the way to help feed the thousands that were to follow in the years to come. Apples were stored all winter long in root cellars covered with sawdust or straw, or dried and used in baking.

4 cups peeled, cored and sliced apples	Sugar to taste
	Cinnamon to taste

Place apples in medium-size saucepan. Cover with water and cook until tender. Drain most of the liquid and mash apples with potato masher or food processor. Season to taste with sugar and cinnamon. Serve hot, or allow to cool in refrigerator.

Favorite Utah Pioneer Recipes

Coconut Bread

4 eggs
2 cups sugar
1 cup oil
2 teaspoons coconut flavoring
1 cup buttermilk
1 cup flaked coconut

1 cup chopped walnuts
3 cups flour
½ teaspoon baking soda
½ teaspoon baking powder
½ teaspoon salt
Coconut Syrup

Beat eggs; add sugar, oil, coconut flavoring, buttermilk, flaked coconut, and walnuts. Mix together flour, baking soda, baking powder, and salt. Add dry ingredients to moist mixture. Grease 4 small loaf pans; pour in batter. Bake at 325° for 40–45 minutes. While hot, spoon Coconut Syrup over loaves. Cool in the pans for a few minutes; then put loaves on a cake rack until cold.

COCONUT SYRUP:

½ cup sugar
¼ cup water

1 tablespoon butter
½ teaspoon coconut flavoring

Put sugar, water, butter, and coconut flavoring in saucepan; bring to a boil. Then simmer for 5–10 minutes; spoon over hot loaves.

Ladies' Literary Club Cookbook

Spudnuts

2 cups milk
1 package yeast
½ cup warm water
½ cup white sugar, divided
7 cups white flour, divided
3 eggs

1 cup mashed potatoes (instant works fine)
½ cup shortening, melted
1 tablespoon salt
2 teaspoons cinnamon

Scald milk. Dissolve yeast in warm water. Add 1 tablespoon white sugar to water and yeast and let stand for 15 minutes. When milk has cooled to lukewarm, add 2 cups of the flour. Beat to a smooth batter and add the yeast. Let this rise for 20 minutes. Add eggs to mashed potatoes; add melted shortening and whip until very smooth. Potato mixture must be warm. Add to the batter and mix well.

Add remaining flour to which salt and cinnamon have been added. Mix and knead to a smooth dough. Let rise once and knead down. The second time it rises, roll out to ½ inch thickness and cut as for doughnuts. Let rise and drop into hot grease (350°) and cook for 3–4 minutes or until light golden brown. Drain on paper towels. Coat with remaining sugar, or when cool, dip one side in a thin icing of confectioners' sugar and milk.

A Century of Mormon Cookery, Volume 2

Utah has five major Indian tribes: Ute, Navajo, Paiute, Goshute and Shoshoni.

Raised Pancakes

These are similar to sourdough pancakes.

1 package dry yeast	1⅔ cups milk
¼ cup warm water	2 cups Bisquick
1 egg	½ teaspoon salt

In a medium bowl, dissolve yeast in warm water. With a wooden spoon or wire whip, stir in the egg, milk, Bisquick, and salt. Beat until smooth. Cover and allow to stand at room temperature for 1 hour, then refrigerate overnight.

Pour 2 tablespoons batter for each pancake onto a lightly greased hot griddle. Flip pancakes when bubbles appear all over them. Serve with butter and syrup. Makes 20 cakes.

Vacation Cooking: Good Food! Good Fun!

Sweet Potato Pancakes

2 large sweet potatoes, peeled and grated	½ teaspoon salt
1 pear or apple, grated	¾ teaspoon nutmeg
4 eggs, beaten	¾ teaspoon cinnamon
9 crackers (Ritz or other butter crackers, or saltines), crumbled to fine meal	Dash of black pepper
	Light oil for frying

Mix all ingredients, except the oil, in a large bowl until well blended. Pour oil to ¼ inch deep in heavy skillet and place over medium-high heat until very hot (but not smoking). Oil should sizzle when a drop of water hits the pan. Drop sweet potato batter into hot oil by rounded tablespoonfuls. Fry on each side until golden brown. Repeat with remaining batter, adding more oil to pan if necessary. Serve with applesauce.

How to Win a Cowboy's Heart

Johnny Cakes

6 eggs
1 (8.5-ounce) package corn
  muffin mix
1 (8-ounce) can whole-kernel
  corn, drained

1 cup Filling
1 teaspoon cooking oil
1 cup sour cream
1 cup salsa

In a small mixing bowl, beat eggs until foamy, then add unprepared muffin mix until thoroughly blended. Add corn and desired Fillings, blending well. In a large frying pan on medium, heat oil. Spoon about ¼ cup of batter for each cake into hot pan. When bubbles appear at edges, turn over and cook until lightly browned. Serve with sour cream and salsa. Serves 4.

FILLING SUGGESTIONS:

Chopped ham
Diced cooked bacon
Thinly sliced green onions

Mushrooms
Red or green pepper, chopped
Or a combination of several

Recipes for Roughing It Easy

Stuffed French Toast with Strawberries

8 slices white or wheat bread,
   cut 1 inch thick
1 (8-ounce) package cream
   cheese, softened
6 tablespoons strawberry
   preserves
1⅓ cups milk

4 eggs
2 teaspoons granulated sugar
2 teaspoons vanilla
1 teaspoon cinnamon
4 cups sliced strawberries
4 tablespoons powdered sugar

Cut each bread slice in half crosswise. With a sharp knife, cut a horizontal slit in each half slice to make a pocket. In a medium bowl, combine cream cheese and preserves. Spread ¹⁄₁₆ of the mixture inside each bread pocket. Pinch edges of bread together to hold filling. In a shallow bowl, whisk together milk, eggs, sugar, vanilla, and cinnamon. Dip filled bread slices in egg mixture to coat. Cook about 6 minutes or until golden brown, turning once. Top with strawberries and sprinkle with powdered sugar.

Pleasures from the Good Earth

Banana Pecan Waffles

2 cups flour
2 tablespoons sugar
1 tablespoon baking powder
1 teaspoon salt
1½ cups milk

6 tablespoons vegetable oil
2 eggs, separated
2 bananas, mashed
¾ cup chopped pecans

Sift flour, sugar, baking powder, and salt into a bowl. Whisk milk, oil, and egg yolks in another bowl until blended and add to flour mixture. Stir until moistened. Beat egg whites until stiff (but moist) peaks form. Fold into batter. Fold in mashed bananas and pecans. Bake in hot waffle iron.

Note: Leftover waffles can be frozen between sheets of wax paper and stored in freezer bags.

Favorite Recipes from Utah Farm Bureau Women

Utah Strawberry Days Waffles

A sourdough variety for people who love crisp, light waffles.

SOURDOUGH STARTER:

½ package dry yeast
1½ tablespoons water (110°)

2 cups buttermilk or sour milk
1 cup flour

Dissolve yeast in water. Add buttermilk and flour. Let stand at room temperature overnight. Next day, refrigerate (up to 3 weeks).

¾ cup Sourdough Starter
2 cups flour
1½ cups warm water
4 tablespoons sugar, divided
¾ teaspoon baking soda
¾ teaspoon salt

2 egg whites
2 egg yolks, beaten
¼ cup vegetable oil
1 cup heavy cream
2 cups fresh strawberries,
    sliced

Put Sourdough Starter in a large bowl. Gradually mix in flour. Thoroughly blend in warm water. Cover. Put in warm place overnight (90°).

Next day, combine 2 tablespoons sugar, baking soda, and salt. Set aside. Beat egg whites just until stiff peaks form. Set aside. Mix egg yolks and vegetable oil into Sourdough Starter. Stir in sugar mixture. Gently fold in egg whites. Bake in hot waffle iron 4–5 minutes (until golden brown). While baking, whip heavy cream and remaining 2 tablespoons sugar. To serve, put a scoop of whipped cream on each waffle. Top with fresh strawberries. Yields 4 waffles.

Heritage Cookbook

Utah is the rooftop of the United States. The average elevation of the tallest peaks in each of Utah's counties is 11,222 feet above sea level—higher than any other state.

Frittatas

The Frittata is like an omelet but easier to make—you don't have to try and fold it over with all the goodies in the middle. Everything is cooked inside the Frittata.

2 eggs	**Salt and pepper to taste**
¼ cup diced ham	**Parmesan cheese**
2 tablespoons chopped onion	**1–2 tablespoons olive oil**
Oregano to taste	

Whisk eggs in a medium-size bowl. Add diced ham and onion. Add seasonings to taste. Sprinkle with Parmesan cheese to taste. Heat olive oil in bottom of sauté pan. Pour in frittata mixture and cook until one side is done. Flip and cook the other side until golden brown. Drain on paper towels. Serve for breakfast.

Note: Substitute other veggies and cooked meats, if desired.

Cherished Recipes

Jalapeño Jam

1 pound sweet red bell peppers, seeded and ribs removed	**Fresh lime juice, as needed**
	3 pounds sugar
¼ pound jalapeño peppers, seeds and pits removed	**1 (1¾-ounce) package powdered pectin**
1½ cups cider vinegar, divided	**Hot pepper sauce, as desired**
1 teaspoon salt	

In food processor, finely chop the red peppers and jalapeños with a little of the vinegar. Place in a stainless steel pan and add the rest of the vinegar and salt. Bring to a boil, then simmer over medium heat for about 5 minutes. Remove from heat and measure, adding lime juice, if necessary, to make 3 cups. Place back in pan and stir in the sugar and pectin. Mix well; stir while bringing to a rolling boil. Cook for 4–5 minutes. Remove from heat and skim foam. If desired, add hot pepper sauce. Ladle into 4 hot, sterilized half-pint jars or 2 pint jars, leaving ¼-inch headspace. Adjust two-piece lids and process in boiling-water canner 5 minutes.

All That Jam

Shorty's Scramble

6 eggs
½ cup cooked sausage, ham,
  or bacon pieces
½ bell pepper, chopped

½ onion, chopped
1 tomato, chopped
½ cup grated cheese
Salsa

Scramble eggs in mixing bowl and pour into greased frying pan. Cook over medium heat for 1½ minutes, until eggs start to thicken. Add meat, pepper, onion, tomato, and cheese. Mix and cook until eggs are cooked all the way. Top with salsa to taste.

Tho Cowboy Chuck Wagon Cookbook

Crustless Quiche

6 eggs, beaten
2 tablespoons heavy cream
1 (10¾-ounce) can cream of
  celery soup

1 cup Cheddar cheese
1 cup provolone cheese
1 teaspoon seasoned salt
2 cups Filling

Prepare quiche by combining eggs, cream, cream of celery soup, cheeses, and salt. Add Filling ingredients of your choice. Be creative with herbs and spices.

    Spray 10-inch pie plate with nonstick cooking spray and bake one hour at 350° or until set. Cool 10 minutes before cutting.

FILLING SUGGESTIONS:

Garden vegetables with spinach
Feta and colorful peppers
Shrimp
Fresh dill and asparagus or
  artichokes

Ham
Mushrooms and asparagus
Fresh corn and bacon

Variation: Quiche can also be baked in mini muffin tins, sprayed with nonstick cooking spray, for 15–20 minutes. Serve these for afternoon tea or appetizers.

JLO Art of Cooking

Scrambled Egg Cupcakes with Cheddar Cheese Frosting

BREAD BASKETS:

8 slices white bread,
  crusts removed

2 tablespoons butter or
  margarine, softened

Flatten bread slices with rolling pin. Spread butter on one side of each slice. Press bread, buttered-side-down, into 8 muffin cups. Bake at 350° for 12–15 minutes or until lightly toasted.

EGGS:

2 tablespoons butter or
  margarine, softened

7 eggs, beaten

3 tablespoons chopped fresh
  chives, or 1½ teaspoons
  dried chives

Salt (optional)

8 (2x2-inch) squares sharp
  Cheddar cheese

Melt butter in large skillet. Add beaten eggs and chives and cook over medium-low heat until softly scrambled. Season with salt, if desired. When Bread Baskets are done, increase oven temperature to 475°. Fill baskets with scrambled eggs; top each with a square of Cheddar cheese. Return to oven for about 2 minutes or until cheese is melted.

Pleasures from the Good Earth

Chile Relleno Eggs with Stewed-Tomato Sauce

2 (4-ounce) cans whole green
  chiles, or 8 fresh roasted
2 cups grated Monterey Jack
  cheese, divided
6 eggs

1 tablespoon flour
2 cups milk
½ teaspoon nutmeg
1½ tablespoons butter

Preheat oven to 325°. Slit each chile down one side and fill loosely with grated cheese, using one cup of cheese for all the chiles. Lay filled chiles in lightly buttered, oven-proof casserole dish or shallow bowl.

In separate bowl, beat eggs and flour, then mix in milk and nutmeg. When blended well, fold in remaining grated cheese. Pour egg mixture over filled chiles, dot with butter, and bake for 45 minutes to 1 hour, until top is bubbly and knife inserted near center comes out clean. To serve, spoon Stewed-Tomato Sauce over eggs.

STEWED-TOMATO SAUCE:

2 (16-ounce) cans stewed
  tomatoes
1 teaspoon garlic powder
1 teaspoon basil flakes
1 tablespoon parsley flakes

½ teaspoon onion powder
½ teaspoon salt
¼ teaspoon black pepper
¼ teaspoon allspice
2 tablespoons butter

Combine all ingredients in a medium saucepan. Simmer over medium heat for 15–20 minutes, until heated through.

How to Win a Cowboy's Heart

Cowtown All Day Breakfast

Oft times in the West, a breakfast had to last you all day long. So, the camp cook would feed the wranglers a hearty meal to last them till supper. The following is one of those breakfasts.

¼ cup bacon grease or shortening

1 large onion, sliced

6 medium potatoes, washed and sliced

2 tablespoons seasoned salt, or salt and pepper to taste

8 eggs

1 cup diced ham, fried bacon, or sausage

Melt grease in a large fry pan or in the bottom of a 12-inch Dutch oven. Add onion, potatoes, and seasonings. Cook till tender. Break eggs over the potatoes and pour meat on top. Cover and cook 7–10 minutes. Spoon onto plates or cut in pie-like wedges.

Variations: Add grated cheese over top just before serving; salsa and sour cream for a zesty flavor; green and yellow or red peppers; mushroom soup mixed with eggs; ground beef for a hearty beef meal; or kidney or pinto beans mixed with the potatoes.

Log Cabin Campfire Cookn'

A One-Pot Breakfast

1–1½ pounds ground sausage
1 medium to large onion,
  chopped
1 (4-ounce) can sliced mushrooms
  (or fresh)
1 green pepper, chopped

1 (28-ounce) package cubed hash
  brown potatoes
¼ cup milk
8–10 eggs, beaten
½ pound Cheddar cheese,
  grated

In a large (12-inch) Dutch oven, heating just from below for now, brown the sausage, keeping it broken up in small pieces. Just before it is thoroughly browned, add onion, mushrooms, and green pepper. Once the vegetables are semicooked, add hash browns, mix, and cook for about 10 minutes.

Mix milk with eggs and pour over hash brown mixture. Stir, cover, and cook (adding coals to the top of the oven) at 325°–350° for about 20 minutes or until eggs are firm. Be careful not to burn the bottom at this stage. In the last 5 minutes of cooking, sprinkle cheese over top of egg mixture, cover once again, and cook until cheese has melted. Serve with your favorite salsa for a delicious one-pot breakfast.

Backyard Dutch Oven

The Jardine Juniper tree, in Logan Canyon, is said to be the oldest living tree in the Rocky Mountains. It was once thought to be over 3,000 years old, but a core sample taken in the 1950s found it to be 1,500 years old.

Mexican Breakfast Burritos

1½ pounds ground sausage
1 onion, diced
½ green pepper, diced
1 (4-ounce) can diced green
   chiles
10 potatoes, diced

Seasoning to taste
10 eggs, beaten
3 cups shredded Cheddar cheese,
   divided
Flour tortillas
Salsa

Fry sausage in a Dutch oven until color changes; add onion, green pepper, and chiles. Sauté until tender. Add potatoes and cook until tender (may need to add a little water). Season to taste. Pour eggs and 2 cups cheese on top, and stir until done to taste. Fill warm tortillas with the mixture; top with more cheese and salsa. Enjoy.

Dutch Oven and Outdoor Cooking, Book Two: Homespun Edition

Sausage Casserole

4 slices bread
1 pound sausage, browned
1 cup shredded Cheddar
2 cups milk
5 eggs, beaten

1 teaspoon salt
½ teaspoon pepper
1 (4-ounce) can mushrooms,
   drained
1 tablespoon butter

Tear bread into pieces and put into a Dutch oven. Spread browned sausage on top and sprinkle with cheese. In separate bowl, beat milk into eggs, then add salt and pepper. Add mushrooms, and pour over sausage and bread. Dot with butter. Cover and cook on coals for 35–40 minutes.

Dutch Oven and Outdoor Cooking, Y2K Edition

Sundance Chicken Hash

Foods served in the Foundry Grill at Sundance Resort represent the best of fresh American home-style cooking, often created over a wood-fire grill with fresh ingredients from Sundance's own gardens and local purveyors. This is Chef Trey Foshee's version of comfort food.

2 tablespoons clarified butter or vegetable oil
3 cups peeled, cubed (½ inch) potatoes
¾ cup red onion pieces (½ inch)
¾ cup peeled, roasted red bell pepper pieces (½ inch)

1 cup shredded roasted chicken
¼ cup minced scallions
1 tablespoon chopped parsley
Salt and pepper to taste
6 large eggs, cooked as you like

Heat a large nonstick sauté pan over high heat. Add clarified butter and potatoes. Cook until well browned, tossing occasionally. Reduce heat to medium and add onion. Sauté for 3–4 minutes or until tender. Add bell pepper and chicken and cook until heated through. Add scallions, parsley, salt and pepper. Mound onto 6 serving plates. Top each serving with an egg. Serves 6.

Always in Season

Breakfast Potato Boats

8 left-over or freshly baked potatoes	2 teaspoons seasoned salt, divided
¼ cup chopped onion	1 teaspoon paprika
½ cup butter	2 cups grated cheese
½ teaspoon salt	2 cups cooked and crumbled bacon
¼ teaspoon pepper	

Make a cut in the top of the potatoes and scoop out all the insides, reserving shells. Or make 8 boats out of tin foil and use mashed potatoes. Mix potatoes, onion, butter, and seasonings (reserve 1 teaspoon seasoned salt). Spoon mixture back into potato shell and bake in a 12-inch Dutch oven that has been warmed and lightly oiled. Bake 30 minutes on 10–12 briquettes in your Volcano, or 10 briquettes on the bottom and 15 on top for outdoor cooking; on a propane fire, cook very low with 10 briquettes on top. Remove lid and put reserved seasoning, grated cheese, and bacon bits on top. Serve with bacon, hot rolls, or pancakes.

Log Cabin Campfire Cookn'

Records and firsts at the 2002 Salt Lake City Olympic Winter Games: Athletes from a record eighteen nations earned gold medals. Georg Hackl became the first person in Olympic history to earn a medal in the same individual event five times in a row. Yang Yang became the first Chinese athlete to win a gold medal at the Winter Games. Vonetta Flowers became the first black athlete to earn winter gold, while Jarome Iginla followed as the first black male winner. Participation included: seventy-seven National Olympic Committees (Nations), 2,399 athletes (886 women, 1,513 men), 22,000 volunteers, and 8,730 media (2,661 written press, 6,069 broadcasters).

Soups, Chilies, and Stews

Snow sport enthusiasts love the skiing at Park City Mountain, Deer Valley, and the Canyons, all world-class resorts in the Park City area. Long before it became a world-class mountain resort and venue for the 2002 Olympic Winter Games, Park City was famous as a silver mining town, and boasts a lively and colorful past.

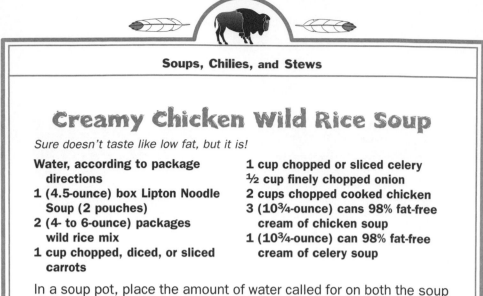

Creamy Chicken Wild Rice Soup

Sure doesn't taste like low fat, but it is!

Water, according to package directions
1 (4.5-ounce) box Lipton Noodle Soup (2 pouches)
2 (4- to 6-ounce) packages wild rice mix
1 cup chopped, diced, or sliced carrots
1 cup chopped or sliced celery
½ cup finely chopped onion
2 cups chopped cooked chicken
3 (10¾-ounce) cans 98% fat-free cream of chicken soup
1 (10¾-ounce) can 98% fat-free cream of celery soup

In a soup pot, place the amount of water called for on both the soup mix and rice mix packages. Bring to a boil and add soup broth (noodles also, if you like) and all the wild rice mix, including seasonings. Boil 15 minutes, then add celery, carrots, onion, and chicken. Boil 10 minutes or until veggies are tender. Stir in cream soups. At this point, depending on desired thickness, add 1 cup of water if needed. Simmer for 5 minutes and serve. Yields 12–14 servings (recipe fills a 5-quart crockpot).

Note: The soup will thicken more upon cooling. When reheating, add whatever water you want. This soup freezes very well.

Only the Best

Homemade Chicken Noodle Soup over Mashed Potatoes

When I ask the men in my family what they want for their birthday dinner, this is their request.

1 large chicken
1 onion, quartered
2 carrots, chopped
2 stalks celery
2 cloves garlic, minced
1 tablespoon chicken bouillon
  granules

2 carrots, grated
¼ cup minced fresh parsley
1 package fresh linguine noodles,
  cut into 2-inch pieces
1½ cups frozen petite peas
Mashed potatoes

Place chicken in large pot and cover with water. Add onion, chopped carrots, and celery stalks. Bring to a boil; simmer gently about 2 hours or until tender.

Remove chicken from stock, and let cool; remove meat from bones. Cut up chicken and store in the refrigerator until ready for use. Strain broth and chill. Remove fat from top of cooled broth.

About 30 minutes before serving, place broth in pot, adding garlic, bouillon, grated carrots, and minced parsley. Add more water as needed to make enough broth. Bring to a boil, then add chicken pieces, linguine noodle pieces, and peas. Cook until noodles are done. Serve in bowls over mashed potatoes. Serves 8–10.

Recipe by Bruce and Christine Olsen
Five-Star Recipes from Well-Known Latter Day Saints

CURSE OF THE PETRIFIED WOOD
Some say if even one piece of petrified wood is removed from the Escalante State Park, the taker will face nothing but bad luck. A recent visitor to the park secretly removed a piece, and upon returning home faced nothing but terrible luck. The petrified wood was quickly sent back to the park with a letter of apology. Is the wood really haunted or is it just a silly myth? Escalante State Park is located approximately four hours south of Salt Lake City near the town of Escalante. (Reprinted by permission from Utah State Parks.)

Gayle's Chicken Tortilla Soup

2 (14-ounce) cans chicken broth
2 cups diced, cooked chicken
1 (4-ounce) can mild diced green
  chiles
1 (15-ounce) can corn, drained
1 (10¾-ounce) can 98% fat-free
  cream of chicken soup
½ teaspoon ground cumin

Fresh chopped cilantro to taste
Fresh lime juice (optional)
Condiments: shredded cheese,
  crushed tortilla chips, diced
  tomatoes, diced avocado, sliced
  green onions, sliced black olives,
  sour cream

Bring broth to a boil and add remaining ingredients, except condiments. Simmer for a few minutes to blend flavors, then ladle into bowls. Top immediately with desired condiments and serve.

Note: You can place condiments in bowl first and pour soup on top.

Only the Best

White Bean Soup

½ pound dry navy beans, rinsed,
  or canned white beans, rinsed
2 celery stalks, cut up
1 carrot, sliced
1 onion, chopped
1 clove garlic, minced
1 tablespoon olive oil

1 large can low-sodium chicken
  broth
1 (10-ounce) package frozen
  chopped spinach
½ cup elbow macaroni or other
  small pasta, cooked

Bring dry beans to boil in pan of water; boil 5 minutes. Remove from heat. Cover and let stand 1 hour. Drain. Stir-fry celery, carrot, onion, and garlic in oil about 5 minutes. Add beans and chicken broth and bring to a boil; cover and simmer until beans are tender—about 1 hour. Add spinach; boil, then simmer until spinach is heated. Add cooked pasta.

30 Days to a Healthier Family

Potato Soup with Riffles

3–4 potatoes
3 cups water
Salt and pepper to taste
1 cup milk

1 tablespoon butter
1 cup flour
1 egg

Peel and dice potatoes. Cook in 3 cups water with salt and pepper to taste. When tender, add milk and butter and bring to a simmer. In a mixing bowl, add flour and break an egg in the center; stir quickly leaving small chunks. Pour into simmering potato liquid, then cover, cooking until riffles are cooked thoroughly (about 20 minutes). Be careful not to let the pot run over.

Variation: Add diced onion to potatoes. Shredded cheese may be added, if desired.

Cherished Recipes

Potato Bisque

2 medium onions, diced
1½ cups diced celery
2–3 tablespoons margarine
8–10 potatoes, diced ½ inch
2 cups water

4 chicken bouillon cubes
3 cups milk, divided
4–6 tablespoons cornstarch
2 tablespoons salt, or to taste
Sprinkle of chopped parsley

Fry onions and celery in margarine. Add potatoes, water, and bouillon cubes; cover and cook 15–20 minutes until potatoes are tender. Add 2½ cups milk and bring to a boil. Mix ½ cup milk with cornstarch. Pour into pot, add salt, and stir well. Cook 3–5 minutes more to thicken. Sprinkle with parsley.

Championship Dutch Oven Cookbook

Split Pea Soup with Ham

2 pounds cooked ham
1 (16-ounce) package (2 cups)
   dried split peas
1 teaspoon salt
½ teaspoon basil leaves

1 large onion, chopped
¼ teaspoon pepper
8 cups water
4–5 celery stalks, sliced
5–6 carrots, peeled and sliced

Cut ham into ½- to 1-inch cubes. In a 12-inch Dutch oven, combine all ingredients except celery and carrots. Simmer, covered, at about 325°–350°, for one hour. (Heat from bottom only). Stir in celery and carrots. Continue simmering, covered, for ½–1 hour, or until peas are tender and soup thickens.

Backyard Dutch Oven

Santa Fe Cheese Soup

1 pound Velveeta cheese, cubed
1 pound ground beef, browned
   and drained
1 (15¼-ounce) can whole-kernel
   corn, with liquid
1 (15-ounce) can kidney beans,
   with liquid

1 (14½-ounce) can diced
   tomatoes with green chiles,
   with liquid
1 (14½-ounce) can stewed
   tomatoes, diced with liquid
1 envelope taco seasoning mix
Corn chips

Combine all ingredients in greased 4½- to 6-quart slow cooker. Cover and cook on HIGH heat 3 hours or on LOW heat 4–5 hours. Serve with corn chips. Makes 6–8 servings.

101 Things To Do With a Slow Cooker

Quick Crab Soup

2 cans bean-bacon soup
2 cans split pea soup
2 cans tomato soup

1 cup imitation crab
2 teaspoons butter

Heat soups according to can directions. Heat crab in butter. Just before serving soup, sprinkle crab on top. Serves 6–8.

Family Favorites from the Heart

Hotel Utah Borscht

4 cups beet juice
4 cups chicken or beef stock,
　divided
Juice of 1 lemon
Sugar to taste
Salt to taste
¼ cup cornstarch

1 cup sour cream
1 or 2 egg yolks
Additional sour cream for
　garnish
Chopped parsley for garnish
Hard-cooked eggs, diced for
　garnish

Bring beet juice and 3½ cups stock to a boil. Stir in lemon juice, sugar, and salt. Combine remaining ½ cup stock and cornstarch until smooth. Stir into soup. Cook and stir until thickened. Combine sour cream and egg yolks. Gradually stir 1 cup of hot liquid into egg mixture. Then, stirring constantly, slowly add warmed egg mixture to hot liquid. Heat to boiling. Strain. Serve hot or cold garnished with sour cream, parsley, and diced eggs. Serves 8.

A Century of Mormon Cookery, Volume 2

The 10-acre Temple Square is one of Salt Lake City's most visited places. Centerpiece of the Square are the Salt Lake Temple and the domed Tabernacle, home of the famous Mormon Tabernacle Choir and the great Tabernacle organ. Other places of interest within the Square are two visitors centers, an assembly hall, the Mormon Handcart Statue, the Seagull Monument, and other statuary and fountains.

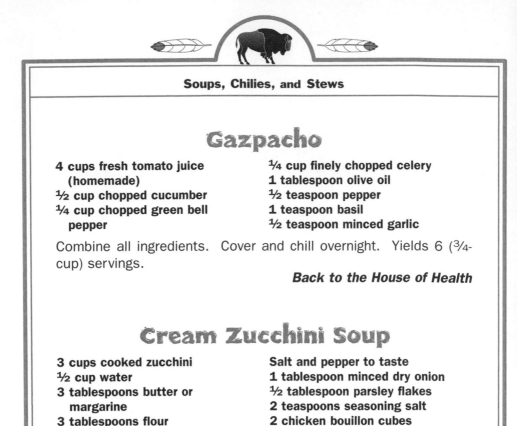

Gazpacho

4 cups fresh tomato juice
  (homemade)
½ cup chopped cucumber
¼ cup chopped green bell
  pepper

¼ cup finely chopped celery
1 tablespoon olive oil
½ teaspoon pepper
1 teaspoon basil
½ teaspoon minced garlic

Combine all ingredients. Cover and chill overnight. Yields 6 (¾-cup) servings.

Back to the House of Health

Cream Zucchini Soup

3 cups cooked zucchini
½ cup water
3 tablespoons butter or
  margarine
3 tablespoons flour
2 cups milk

Salt and pepper to taste
1 tablespoon minced dry onion
½ tablespoon parsley flakes
2 teaspoons seasoning salt
2 chicken bouillon cubes

Halve zucchini lengthwise and remove seeds, but do not peel. Cut in chunks and cook in water until soft. Set aside. Make white sauce with next 4 ingredients. Cook and stir until thickened. Add onion, parsley, seasoning salt, and bouillon. Put cooked zucchini in blender and purée. Add to white sauce. Add additional salt and pepper if desired. Serve hot.

How to Enjoy Zucchini

Creamy Vegetable Soup

This rich soup gets its creaminess from tofu. Be sure to blend it thoroughly (I think a blender is best) so you get a rich, even, smooth, creamy texture.

1 cup chopped onion
2 cloves garlic, minced
3 celery stalks, chopped
2 cups shredded green cabbage
½ pound asparagus, cut small
2 large leeks, chopped
4 cups vegetable broth

2 tablespoons chopped fresh
  parsley
2 teaspoons dried dill
2 teaspoons dried basil
1 teaspoon dried oregano
Salt and pepper to taste
1 package soft fresh tofu

In a skillet, steam-fry onion and garlic for a few minutes. Add celery, cabbage, and asparagus. Transfer to a large pot; add leeks and vegetable broth. Stir in parsley, dill, basil, oregano, salt and pepper. Simmer just to brighten veggies. Let cool a bit, then purée in a blender or food processor 2 cups at a time with some of the tofu, and return to another pot. Heat soup, not to exceed 118°, and serve. Serves 10.

Back to the House of Health

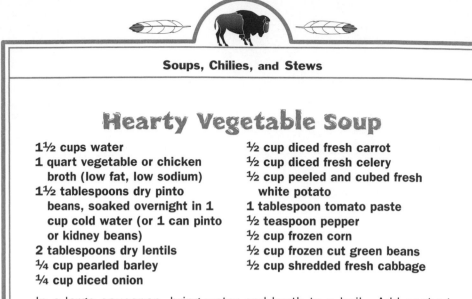

Hearty Vegetable Soup

1½ cups water
1 quart vegetable or chicken broth (low fat, low sodium)
1½ tablespoons dry pinto beans, soaked overnight in 1 cup cold water (or 1 can pinto or kidney beans)
2 tablespoons dry lentils
¼ cup pearled barley
¼ cup diced onion

½ cup diced fresh carrot
½ cup diced fresh celery
½ cup peeled and cubed fresh white potato
1 tablespoon tomato paste
½ teaspoon pepper
½ cup frozen corn
½ cup frozen cut green beans
½ cup shredded fresh cabbage

In a large saucepan, bring water and broth to a boil. Add soaked beans (discard water and rinse beans), lentils, barley, onion, carrot, celery, potato, tomato paste, and pepper. Cover and simmer for 20 minutes. Add corn, green beans, and cabbage. Simmer, covered, for 15 minutes. If using canned beans, add them at this stage.

Nutrients: Calories 122; Sodium 65mg (more if using canned beans); Protein 8g; Carbohydrate 21g; Fiber 5g; Total Fat 1g; Cholesterol 0mg.

30 Days to a Healthier Family

Spicy Southwestern Chowder

2 slices uncooked bacon, chopped
1 medium onion, chopped
1 cup shredded carrots (about 2
    medium)
1–2 jalapeño peppers, seeded
    and minced
2 cloves garlic, minced
1½ teaspoons chili powder
½ teaspoon ground cumin
3 cups low-fat milk

2 cups reduced-sodium chicken
    broth
3 cups cooked brown rice
1 (16-ounce) package frozen corn
    or 1 (17-ounce) can corn,
    drained
6 large sourdough round rolls,
    hollowed out, leaving ½-inch
    walls
Green onions for garnish

Cook bacon in Dutch oven over medium-high heat 5–7 minutes, stirring until bacon is crisp. Drain all but 1 tablespoon fat. Add onion, carrots, jalapeños, garlic, chili powder, and cumin. Cook 3–5 minutes, stirring constantly until onion is tender. Reduce heat to medium. Add milk, broth, rice, and corn. Cook, stirring, 10–12 minutes until mixture boils. Cook 1 minute more; remove from heat. Ladle into bread rounds. Garnish with green onions. Makes 6 servings.

Nutrients: 590 Calories; 7g Fat; 15mg Cholesterol; 780mg Sodium, 110g Carbohydrate; 5g Dietary Fiber; 10g Protein.

30 Days to a Healthier Family

"Hoodoos" color the landscape of Bryce Canyon National Park. These land formations stand in horseshoe-shaped amphitheaters along the eastern edge of the Paunsaugunt Plateau.

Broccoli Cheese Chowder

Your family will love this rich and smooth broccoli chowder. Try serving it in bread bowls.

**2 bunches (about 1 pound)
   fresh broccoli**
1 medium onion, chopped
¾ cup butter, divided
½ cup flour

4 cups milk
1 cup chicken broth
1½ teaspoons salt
2 cups grated Cheddar cheese

Cook broccoli just until tender. Do not overcook. Drain and cut into small pieces; set aside. Sauté chopped onion in ¼ cup butter until tender; set aside. In a large saucepan or soup pot, prepare a white sauce: melt remaining ½ cup butter over medium heat, then stir in flour until well blended. Gradually stir in milk, chicken broth, and salt. Stir constantly until mixture reaches a boil. Cook 1–2 minutes, until thickened. Add broccoli and onion. Stir in cheese. Cook briefly over medium heat. Avoid bringing to a boil. Serve immediately or keep warm over low heat. Makes 6–8 servings.

The Essential Mormon Cookbook

Mongolian Hot Pot

½ pound bacon, diced
1 pound lean ground beef, or
  2 cups diced cooked ham
1 (10½-ounce) can condensed
  beef broth, or 3 teaspoons beef
  soup base
1 quart water
1 onion, chopped
1 green pepper, chopped
1 carrot, sliced

1 tablespoon soy sauce
1 (16-ounce) can tomatoes
1 (10-ounce) package frozen
  mixed vegetables
1 zucchini, sliced
2 teaspoons salt
⅛ teaspoon pepper
1 tablespoon finely chopped
  parsley (optional)

Fry bacon in large, heavy saucepan until crisp; drain on absorbent paper. Pour off all but 2 tablespoons bacon fat. Sauté beef or ham in the 2 tablespoons bacon fat. Add next 7 ingredients and simmer gently for about one hour. Add mixed vegetables and zucchini, and simmer another 10 minutes. Add salt and pepper. Taste to correct seasoning. Add chopped parsley just before serving. Makes about 10 cups, or 10 (1-cup) servings.

Lion House Recipes

No Alarm Chili

5 pounds cubed beef
2–3 tablespoons margarine
4 large onions, chopped
2 green peppers, chopped
1 clove garlic, minced
8 bay leaves
2 tablespoons chili powder
1 tablespoon paprika
4 cups tomato sauce

2 tablespoons bouillon in ½ cup
  red wine vinegar
¾ teaspoon red pepper
1 tablespoon oregano
1 (7-ounce) can diced green
  chiles
1½ tablespoons cumin
Salt and pepper to taste

Brown meat in Dutch oven with margarine. Add onions and bell peppers. Cook 10–15 minutes. Add remaining ingredients; mix well. Cover and simmer 2–3 hours. Add more red pepper if you like it hot.

Championship Dutch Oven Cookbook

Baked Chili

CHILI:

1 pound ground beef
1 large onion, chopped
1 large green pepper, chopped
1 (16-ounce) can kidney beans, rinsed and drained
1 (15¼-ounce) can whole-kernel corn, drained
1 (15-ounce) can tomato sauce
1 (14½-ounce) can diced tomatoes
1 (4-ounce) can diced green chiles
2 teaspoons chili powder
½ teaspoon sugar
1 teaspoon salt
1 teaspoon ground cumin
½ teaspoon garlic powder

In a Dutch oven or large 4-quart pan, cook beef, onion, and green pepper over medium heat until meat is cooked through. Drain. Rinse and drain kidney beans; add to meat mixture. Add drained corn, tomato sauce, tomatoes, green chiles, chili powder, sugar, salt, cumin, and garlic powder. Bring to a boil, stirring occasionally. Reduce heat; cover and simmer for 10 minutes.

CORNBREAD BISCUITS:

1 cup all-purpose flour
1 cup cornmeal
2 teaspoons baking powder
⅛ teaspoon salt
1 egg
½ cup milk
½ cup sour cream

Combine flour, cornmeal, baking powder, and salt in a medium bowl. In a separate bowl, beat egg, milk, and sour cream until smooth; stir into dry ingredients just until moistened. Set aside.

Transfer Chili to an ungreased 9x13-inch baking dish. Drop biscuit batter by heaping teaspoonfuls onto hot Chili. Bake uncovered at 400° for 15–17 minutes or until biscuits are lightly browned. Makes 8 servings.

Lion House Entertaining

Son-of-a-Gun Stew

½ pound bacon
2 pounds cubed beef
3 medium onions, chopped
1 pound carrots, sliced
3 pounds potatoes, diced
2 green peppers, chopped

5 stalks celery, sliced
1 quart tomatoes
2 tablespoons Worcestershire
  sauce
¾ cup soy sauce
7–8 drops Tabasco

Fry bacon in Dutch oven. Add meat and onions. Brown well. Add remaining ingredients and stir well. Bring to a boil. Remove from heat and cover lid completely with coals. Stir occasionally and cook until vegetables are tender.

Championship Dutch Oven Cookbook

Mulligan Stew

The best Mulligan Stew to come out of my Dutch oven was a mixture of steak, pork, and roast, and some leftover vegetables and gravy. It was a meal fit for a king!

Leftover gravy from roast, or
  packaged gravy mix
Leftover cooked meat, fat and bones
  removed, chopped or shredded

Raw diced vegetables, if needed
Leftover cooked vegetables
  (potatoes, onions, carrots,
  celery, beans, corn, etc.)

In a 14-inch Dutch oven, pour all the leftover gravy, roast juice, etc. Level your oven on the fire and let it simmer. Add all the leftover meat. While this is simmering, prepare raw vegetables, diced smaller than for regular stew so they will be done when stew is ready. Add them to the meat, and add water if you need to. Cook for about 15–20 minutes, then add leftover vegetables. Cover again and cook until new vegetables are done. You can test them with a fork. This is a very tasty meal and helps with the food bill, too!

Let's Cook Dutch

Santa Fe Taco Stew

6 tablespoons vegetable oil, divided
2 pounds beef cube steak, cubed
Salt and pepper to taste
2 medium onions, diced
1 green pepper, diced
1 teaspoon garlic salt
1 teaspoon dried parsley flakes
1 package Lawry's Taco Spices and Seasonings
1 (28-ounce) can diced tomatoes
1 (14-ounce) can diced tomatoes
3 (15-ounce) cans pinto/red/kidney beans, drained
1 (16-ounce) package frozen corn, thawed
1 (8-ounce) can diced green chiles, drained
2 cups beef broth
1 tablespoon cornstarch
Tortilla chips

Place approximately 24 briquettes under a 12-inch Dutch oven and heat 2 tablespoons of oil. Add meat, salt and pepper, and brown until all the pink is gone. Remove meat and set aside. Heat remaining oil in the Dutch oven and sauté onions, green pepper, garlic salt, and parsley flakes until the onion is clear and tender. Add taco spices, tomatoes, beans, corn, and chiles. Blend well. Stir in the browned cube steak.

In a small bowl, gradually blend the beef broth into the cornstarch, using a wire whisk. Stir into stew. Bring to a boil, stirring frequently. Reduce heat (10 coals on bottom and 12 on top) and simmer for 30 minutes, stirring occasionally. If a thicker stew is desired, simmer for another 15 minutes, with the lid slightly ajar. Serve with chips.

Dutch Oven and Outdoor Cooking, Book Two: Homespun Edition

Notorious outlaw Butch Cassidy called Utah home. Robert LeRoy Parker (alias, Butch Cassidy) was born on April 13, 1866, in the small town of Beaver. Most of his outlaw activities happened outside the state, but Butch often sought protection and transportation in Utah. His original corral in Robbers' Roost remains in this once popular hideout located in southeastern Utah.

Beef Stew
with Potato Dumplings

This is a very hearty stew. In pioneer days, they probably would have used only a few of the vegetables listed below. They used vegetables that were in season or what they had stored for the winter.

STEW:

1 pound beef stew meat
Oil, lard, or bacon grease for
  frying
1 large onion, diced
2 tablespoons flour
3–4 cups beef broth or water
2 stalks celery, sliced

3 large carrots, sliced
Salt and pepper to taste
1 cup fresh or frozen peas
1 cup fresh, frozen, or canned
  corn
2 cups chopped cabbage

Brown meat in a small amount of oil in Dutch oven. Add onion and cook until tender. Sprinkle meat and onion with flour and let cook a few minutes more. Add beef broth or water, celery, carrots, and salt and pepper to taste. Cover and cook on stovetop at low heat until meat is very tender, about 45 minutes to 1 hour, stirring occasionally. Then add rest of ingredients and cook until all vegetables are tender. Add more broth if needed.

After vegetables are tender, drop Potato Dumplings by spoonful into the boiling stew. Cover, reduce heat, and cook for 20–30 minutes until dumplings are done. Add more broth if needed. You may also thicken stew (after dumplings are done) with a water-flour mixture, if a thicker broth is desired.

POTATO DUMPLINGS:

1 egg
¾ cup bread crumbs
1 tablespoon diced onion
1 tablespoon flour

½ teaspoon salt
Dash or 2 of pepper
2 cups shredded potatoes
Additional flour for coating

Combine egg and bread crumbs and mix well to soften bread crumbs. Add onion, flour, salt, and pepper; mix again. Stir in potatoes, then form into small balls (about golf-ball size) and roll in a small amount of flour. Cook in stew as directed above.

Favorite Utah Pioneer Recipes

Cowboy Stew

STEW:

1 cup dried beans	1 cup tomatoes or juice
2 ounces side pork (3 strips bacon)	1 onion, finely chopped
	½ cup celery
Flour	Salt and pepper to taste
1 pound stew meat	

Be sure to wash and soak beans overnight—this will help shorten cooking time. Cook pork until fat is fried out and pork is crisp. Remove pork from pan. Lightly flour chunks of meat (buffalo, elk, deer, beef, bear, etc.) and fry until brown. Add beans, tomatoes, onion, celery, and seasoning. Be sure to put pork back in stew. Cover and cook for 2–3 hours. If you add ½ cup water, dumplings can be put on top 20 minutes before serving.

NEVER FAIL DUMPLINGS:

2 cups sifted flour	1 egg
½ teaspoon salt	Enough milk to fill cup with beaten egg
4 level teaspoons baking powder	

Sift together dry ingredients. Break egg into measuring cup. Beat lightly with fork and fill cup to top with milk. Pour into mixing bowl, add dry ingredients, and mix enough to moisten dry ingredients. Let stand for 5 minutes to rise. Drop batter by spoonfuls onto stew. Cover and cook for 20 minutes. These are just as good warmed the next day.

Log Cabin Grub Cookbook

THE LEGEND OF DEAD HORSE POINT

From Dead Horse Point State Park, the desert landscape stretches as far as the eye can see. The labyrinths of Canyonlands National Park, carved by the Colorado River, appear a maze of seemingly uninhabitable land. As legend has it, cowboys gave Dead Horse Point its name. Using the Point as a natural corral, horses left high on the Point by these cowboys died of thirst in clear view of the Colorado River far below. The park has been the backdrop for several movies including *Mission Impossible 2* and *Thelma and Louise.* Dead Horse Point State Park is located four hours southeast of Salt Lake City, near Moab. (Reprinted by permission from Utah State Parks.)

Salads

PHOTO BY JAN MARIE ALBERT.

Named after the Mormon pioneer Ebenezer Bryce, Bryce Canyon became a national park in 1924. This area boasts some of the world's best air quality, offering panoramic views of Utah, Arizona, and New Mexico, and approaching 200 miles of visibility.

Tropical Green Salad with Apricot Vinaigrette

2 ripe, firm pears, cored and
   sliced
Lemon juice
8 cups bite-size pieces leafy
   greens (green and red leaf
   lettuce, spinach, romaine)

4 or 5 ripe kiwis, peeled and
   sliced
1 can Mandarin oranges, well
   drained
¼ cup chopped honey roasted
   almonds

Soak pears briefly in lemon juice to prevent browning. In a large salad bowl, combine and lightly toss the greens, kiwis, pears, oranges, and almonds. Set aside.

APRICOT VINAIGRETTE:

¼ cup white wine vinegar
½–¾ cup apricot all fruit jam

¼–½ cup canola oil
Sugar (optional)

In a blender, blend the vinegar and jam on low. With motor running, slowly add oil. Add some sugar if it is too tart for your taste. Pour into serving container and let individuals add dressing to their salad.

Only the Best

"Let Us Entertain You" Salad

*Such a versatile salad! The Relish may be used over greens for smaller sal-
ads. Ham and/or chicken and cheeses cut into julienne strips may be added
to make this a unique chef's salad. Looks great layered in a straight-sided
glass bowl.*

RELISH:

1 (6-ounce) can pitted ripe olives,
 drained and sliced
1 (16-ounce) can French-style
 green beans, drained
1 (17-ounce) can LeSueur peas,
 drained
1 (12-ounce) can shoe-peg corn
 (or tender young corn), drained
1 medium-size Bermuda onion,
 sliced into thin rings
1 medium-size red or golden
 pepper, sliced into thin rings
1 cup thinly sliced celery
½ cup vegetable oil
¼ cup tarragon vinegar
½ cup sugar
2 teaspoons water
½ teaspoon coarsely ground
 pepper

Toss the first 7 ingredients in a large mixing bowl suitable for marinating. Combine the next 5 ingredients in a jar and shake well.
Pour over Relish and allow to marinate, refrigerated, for 24 hours.

FETA DRESSING:

1 cup mayonnaise
1 (1.4-ounce) package Good
 Seasons Buttermilk Farm-Style
 Dressing
¼ cup sour cream
2 cups buttermilk
4 ounces crumbled feta cheese

Whisk mayonnaise, dressing mix, sour cream, and buttermilk
together in a wide-mouth quart jar. Add the feta cheese and refrigerate for 24 hours.

SALAD:

2 large heads iceberg lettuce,
 washed, drained, and torn into
 bite-size pieces
1 Relish recipe
3 large fresh tomatoes, peeled and
 cut into wedges (optional)
1 Feta Dressing recipe

Assemble the Salad in layers beginning with a layer of iceberg lettuce, then drained Relish, tomato if desired, and dollops of Feta
Dressing. Yields 12–16 servings.

A Pinch of Salt Lake Cookbook

Curried Spinach Salad

This salad is delicious served with pork.

CURRY DRESSING:

½ cup white wine vinegar
⅔ cup vegetable oil
1 tablespoon finely chopped
  chutney

1 teaspoon curry powder
1 teaspoon salt
1 teaspoon dry mustard
1–2 drops Tabasco sauce

Combine vinegar, oil, chutney, curry powder, salt, dry mustard, and Tabasco sauce in a jar and shake until blended well. For best flavor, allow dressing to stand for 2 hours at room temperature before serving.

SALAD:

2 pounds fresh spinach or
  romaine lettuce, cleaned
3 unpared apples, thinly sliced
½ cup golden raisins
¼ cup thinly sliced green
  onions

⅔ cup honey-roasted peanuts
1 orange, segmented with
  membrane removed
2 tablespoons sesame seeds

Combine spinach or romaine lettuce, apples, raisins, green onions, peanuts, orange, and sesame seeds. Toss with Curry Dressing. Yields 6–8 servings.

A Pinch of Salt Lake Cookbook

Rainbow Bridge is the world's largest natural bridge. From its base to the top of the arch, it is 290 feet and spans 275 feet across the river; the top of the arch is 42 feet thick and 33 feet wide. Rainbow Bridge is a sacred place and has tremendous religious significance to neighboring Indian tribes. As a result, visitors are asked not to walk under it or touch it. Although Rainbow Bridge is immediately adjacent to Glen Canyon National Recreation Area, it is a separate unit of the National Park System. On May 30, 1910, President William Howard Taft created Rainbow Bridge National Monument.

Rainbow Salad

Some people feel that eating a rainbow of colored foods supports the balance of the energy of the body. By choosing foods of many colors, you are ensuring a wide variety of electrical/magnetic frequencies that will increase the level of energy in the body.

Baby greens
Spinach
Lettuce
Grated red cabbage
Grated beets
Grated carrots
Grated squash (butternut, yellow,
**   zucchini)**
Grated jicama

Red, yellow, and orange bell
**   peppers**
Sprouts
Cucumbers
Fresh green peas from the pod
Lemon juice
Oil
Sesame seeds

Place fresh, dry greens in a big salad bowl. Arrange the colored vegetables on top, going from deepest dark colors to the lightest. Top with a dressing of lemon juice and desired oil, with a sprinkle of sesame seeds.

Back to the House of Health

Smoot Family's Famous Flavor-All Dressing

This dressing is great for tossed salads, or as a topping for baked potatoes, a light sauce over vegetables, steak sauce, or a great chip dip. This is a long-time family favorite.

1 (32-ounce) jar mayonnaise
1 (8-ounce) package cream
**   cheese, softened**
1 quart buttermilk

½ teaspoon onion salt
½ teaspoon black pepper
½ teaspoon garlic salt

Mix all ingredients thoroughly; pour into glass containers and store in refrigerator. Makes 1½ quarts.

Recipe by Mary Ellen Smoot
Five-Star Recipes from Well-Known Latter Day Saints

Sweet and Sour Pasta Salad

SALAD:

1 (16-ounce) package tricolor
spiral pasta
1 medium red onion, chopped
1 medium tomato, chopped

1 medium cucumber, peeled,
seeded, and chopped
2 tablespoons minced fresh
parsley

Cook pasta according to package directions; drain and rinse with cold water. Place in a large serving bowl. Add onion, tomato, cucumber, green pepper, and parsley; set aside.

DRESSING:

1½ cups sugar
½ cup vinegar
1 tablespoon ground mustard

1 teaspoon garlic powder
1 teaspoon salt (optional)

In a saucepan, combine sugar, vinegar, mustard, garlic powder, and salt. Cook over medium-low heat for 10 minutes or until sugar is dissolved. Pour over pasta salad and toss to coat. Cover and refrigerate for 2 hours. Makes 16 servings.

Lion House Entertaining

Pasta Salad
with Roasted Asparagus

1½ pounds asparagus,
   trimmed and cut diagonally
   into 1-inch pieces
1 red or yellow bell pepper, cored,
   seeded, and cut into 1-inch
   strips
3 tablespoons olive oil, divided
Coarse salt
½ pound pasta, spirals, or
   twists

1 tablespoon lemon juice
1–2 tablespoons chopped fresh
   herbs (basil, oregano, or thyme),
   chopped
Freshly ground black pepper to
   taste
¼ cup toasted pine nuts or sprigs
   of fresh herbs for garnish
   (optional)

Preheat oven to 500° and begin heating large pot of boiling salted water for pasta. Combine asparagus and peppers in large mixing bowl. Toss with 2 tablespoons olive oil. Spread on baking sheet and sprinkle with coarse salt. Roast for about 7 minutes, until asparagus is tender when pierced with fork. Return to bowl. Stir to cool.

Cook pasta until done. Drain and rinse thoroughly to cool. Toss with vegetables, remaining 1 tablespoon olive oil, lemon juice, and fresh herbs. Season to taste with pepper and additional salt or herbs, if needed. Garnish with pine nuts or fresh herbs, if desired. Serve at once. Serves 4–6.

JLO Art of Cooking

Bacon-Shrimp Potato Salad with Cayenne Pecans

As an artist, vibrant colors play a very important part in everything I do. Cooking is no exception.

CAYENNE PECANS:

½–1 cup pecan halves
¼ teaspoon salt
⅛ teaspoon ground cayenne
  pepper

⅛ teaspoon cumin
2 teaspoons butter, melted (more,
  if using more nuts)

Preheat oven to 350°. Prepare cayenne pecans by combining nuts, seasoning, and butter; spread on baking sheet; bake for 15 minutes. Set aside to cool. (Rather than baking the pecan mixture, it can also be sautéed in a nonstick pan until browned.)

HOT BACON DRESSING:

7 strips bacon
½ cup chopped green scallions
½ cup sherry vinegar
1 teaspoon mustard seeds,
  crushed
⅛ teaspoon salt
½ teaspoon pepper

2 tablespoons honey
2 tablespoons chopped fresh
  parsley
1 tablespoon chopped fresh dill,
  or 1 teaspoon dried dill
½ cup olive oil

To make dressing, sauté bacon in skillet until crispy. Drain on paper towels, crumble, and set aside for later use. Remove all but 1–2 tablespoons of drippings. Sauté scallions in drippings until soft. Remove pan from heat; whisk in sherry vinegar, crushed mustard seeds, salt, pepper, honey, parsley, and dill, until thoroughly mixed. Add oil in a slow stream, whisking until blended; set aside.

2 pounds potatoes (mixture of
  purple, red, or Yukon gold)
¼ cup chopped green scallions

½–1 pound cooked shrimp,
  medium or large, tails off

In a large pot, cover whole potatoes with skins in salted water. Bring to a boil and cook for 15–20 minutes, until tender (not mushy); drain. Pan-dry them (leave potatoes in pot over low heat for a minute or two). When cool enough to touch, slice the potatoes. If using purple potatoes, pull off skins.

(continued)

(Bacon-Shrimp Potato Salad with Cayenne Pecans continued)

Dress potatoes while still warm to allow them to absorb more flavor. Pour ⅔ of the dressing over potatoes; sprinkle with ½ of the crumbled bacon from the dressing recipe and ¼ cup scallions. Let stand at room temperature for 1 hour. Toss shrimp in remaining ⅓ of dressing; keep in refrigerator until ready to serve.

When ready to serve salad, toss dressed potatoes with shrimp, remaining bacon, and pecans, placing some attractively on top. Serves 6–8.

Recipe by Linda Mamone
Five-Star Recipes from Well-Known Latter Day Saints

Quilter's Potato Salad

Served frequently in women's homes when they came to quilt or sew carpet rags.

3 large potatoes	**¼ cup minced onion**
3 hard-cooked eggs	**Salt and pepper**

Cook potatoes in their jackets until tender, then cool, peel, and dice into ½-inch squares. Add chopped hard-cooked eggs, onion, salt and pepper to taste.

DRESSING:

1 teaspoon dry mustard	**3 tablespoons melted butter**
1 teaspoon salt	**½ cup hot vinegar**
3 tablespoons sugar	**1 cup heavy cream, whipped**
2 eggs	

Combine mustard, salt, and sugar. Add freshly beaten eggs with melted butter and hot vinegar. Cook in double boiler until thick. Chill. Combine with whipped cream and fold gently into remaining ingredients. Makes 6 servings.

Recipes Thru Time

Coleslaw Cardinal

3½ cups red seedless grapes,
   halved
3½ cups finely shredded
   cabbage
⅓ cup frozen orange juice
   concentrate, thawed
⅓ cup water

2 tablespoons cornstarch
Prepared mustard to taste
½ teaspoon salt
1 egg, beaten
Dash of hot pepper sauce
2 tablespoons lemon juice
½ cup sour cream

Toss grapes and cabbage together; cover and chill. Combine orange juice and water in a small saucepan; blend in cornstarch, mustard, and salt. Cook, stirring constantly, over medium heat until mixture boils. Stir a small amount of hot mixture quickly into egg; return egg mixture to pan. Add hot pepper sauce.

Cook over low heat, stirring constantly, until dressing thickens; remove from heat and blend in lemon juice. Allow to cool; cover and refrigerate until serving time. When ready to serve, blend sour cream into dressing; toss lightly with grapes and cabbage. Makes 8 servings.

Lion House Entertaining

 Protected within the Zion National Park's 229 square miles is Zion Narrows. Sculpted by the Virgin River, the Zion Narrows are 16 miles long, up to 2,000 feet deep, and at times only 20 to 30 feet wide. Zion is an ancient Hebrew word meaning a place of refuge or sanctuary.

River Trip Cabbage Salad

SALAD:

1 head cabbage
2 packages ramen noodles
(oriental or chicken flavor)
4 green onions, diced
2 tablespoons sesame seeds,
toasted
2 tablespoons slivered almonds,
toasted

Red seedless grapes
1 (11-ounce) can Mandarin
oranges, drained
1 (8-ounce) can sliced water
chestnuts, drained
4 tablespoons sunflower seeds
4 cups cooked chicken, fresh or
canned (optional)

Slice and chop cabbage into coarse bite-size pieces. Break uncooked ramen noodles over top of cabbage. Add diced green onions. Add toasted seeds and nuts to salad. Add washed grapes, Mandarin oranges, water chestnuts, and sunflower seeds. Add chicken, if desired. Pour Dressing over everything and toss all ingredients together. Serves 4–6 for a meal.

DRESSING:

¼ cup canola oil
8 tablespoons rice vinegar
2 tablespoons sugar
1 teaspoon salt

½ teaspoon pepper
1 flavor packet from ramen
noodles

Mix together and toss with Salad.

No Green Gelatin Here!

Fresh Mozzarella and Tomato Salad

2 pounds mozzarella balls, fresh
2 pounds Roma tomatoes
¼ cup fresh basil

¼ cup olive oil
1 teaspoon crushed red pepper

Cut the mozzarella balls into ¼-inch slices. Slice the tomatoes into ¼-inch-thick slices. Separate large basil leaves from the stems. Lay 5 leaves on top of one another and carefully cut the leaves into fine strips; repeat with remaining basil. Add the crushed red pepper to the olive oil and set aside to steep. Using a large serving platter, alternate slices of tomato with slices of mozzarella, working in concentric circles. When the platter is full, drizzle the olive oil and red pepper mixture over the tomatoes and mozzarella. Finally, sprinkle the shredded basil on top as a garnish. Hold for a maximum of 2 hours before serving. Makes 20 servings.

Lion House Weddings

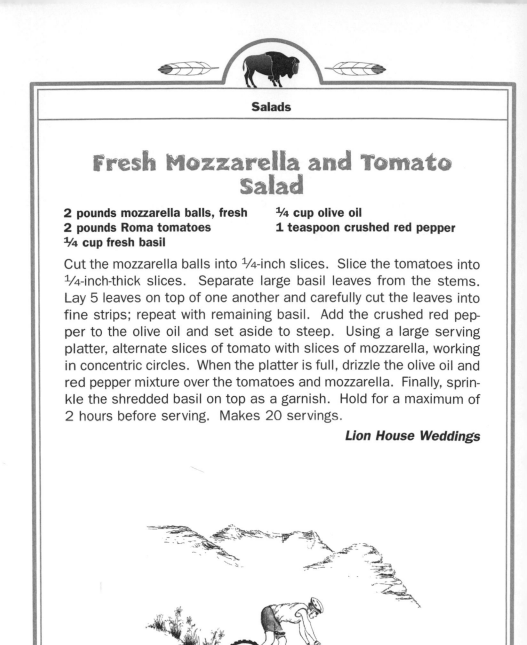

Craisin Salad

DRESSING:

½ cup chopped onion
1 cup sugar
1½ teaspoons salt

2 teaspoons dry mustard
½ cup red wine vinegar
1 cup oil

Mix ingredients in blender; set aside.

SALAD:

1 head red leaf lettuce
1 head green leaf lettuce
1 head iceberg lettuce
1 (8-ounce) package shredded
  mozzarella cheese
1 package shredded Parmesan
  cheese

1 pound bacon, cooked and
  crumbled
1 bag craisins
1 package sliced almonds,
  browned in oven or toaster oven
4–8 cooked and cut-up chicken
  breasts (optional)

Combine all Salad ingredients and toss with Dressing right before you serve. For a main meal salad, add cut-up chicken breasts. Serves 12.

Making Magic

Apple Walking Salad

This is one of my favorite snacks to take on a hike.

2 tablespoons chunky or plain
  peanut butter
2 tablespoons raisins

1 apple, cored
1 tablespoon lemon juice

In a small bowl, mix peanut butter and raisins. Slice the top off of an apple and brush lemon juice onto all cut areas. Spoon the mixture into the center and place the apple back together. Serves 1.

Roughing It Easy at Girl's Camp

Citrus Salad Toss

SUGARED PECANS:

¼ cup sugar   ⅔ cup pecan halves

Mix sugar with pecans in a small skillet. Cook over low heat until sugar melts, stirring to coat pecans well. Spread on foil and cool; break pecans apart.

CITRUS DRESSING:

⅔ cup vegetable oil   2 tablespoons sugar
¼ cup lime juice   1 teaspoon grated lime zest
2 tablespoons orange juice   1 teaspoon grated orange zest

Combine oil, lime juice, orange juice, sugar, lime zest, and orange zest in an airtight jar and shake well. Chill until serving time.

SALAD:

8 cups torn leaf lettuce   1 pint strawberries, cut into
8 cups torn romaine lettuce   halves
1 red onion, thinly sliced   2 avocados, thinly sliced
1 large orange, peeled, sliced

Combine lettuces, onion, orange slices, and strawberries in a large salad bowl and toss gently. Chill until serving time. Add avocados to the salad just before serving. Drizzle with Citrus Dressing and toss gently. Top with Sugared Pecans. Serves 4–6.

Note: Mandarin oranges may be substituted for the fresh orange.

Always in Season

Lagoon Park is the sixth oldest theme park still operating in the United States. The roller coaster is the eighth oldest coaster still operating in the United States. The oldest ride currently operating at Lagoon is the carousel, built in 1893 and moved to the park in 1906. Lagoon Park is located seventeen miles north of Salt Lake City.

The Relief Society's 5-Cup Salad

1 cup mini marshmallows
1 cup Mandarin oranges,
   drained

1 cup pineapple tidbits, drained
1 cup sour cream
1 cup coconut

Mix all together and refrigerate for several hours before serving.

A Mormon Cookbook

Indian Paintbrush Fruit Salad

1 (5-ounce) package lemon
   instant pudding
6 cups (combined) fresh, sliced
   fruits
1 (16-ounce) can crushed
   pineapple, undrained
1 (8-ounce) can Mandarin oranges,
   undrained

½ bag miniature
   marshmallows
Chopped nuts
1 large container Cool Whip
2 bananas

Pour dry pudding mix into a large bowl. Add fruits (such as peaches, strawberries, grapes, apricots, cantaloupe, melon), pineapple, oranges, marshmallows, nuts, and Cool Whip, reserving a portion of the Cool Whip for garnish. Cover and chill salad overnight.

   Just before serving, peel and cut bananas into bite-size pieces, and fold into pudding mixture. Top with dollops of reserved Cool Whip.

Utah Cook Book

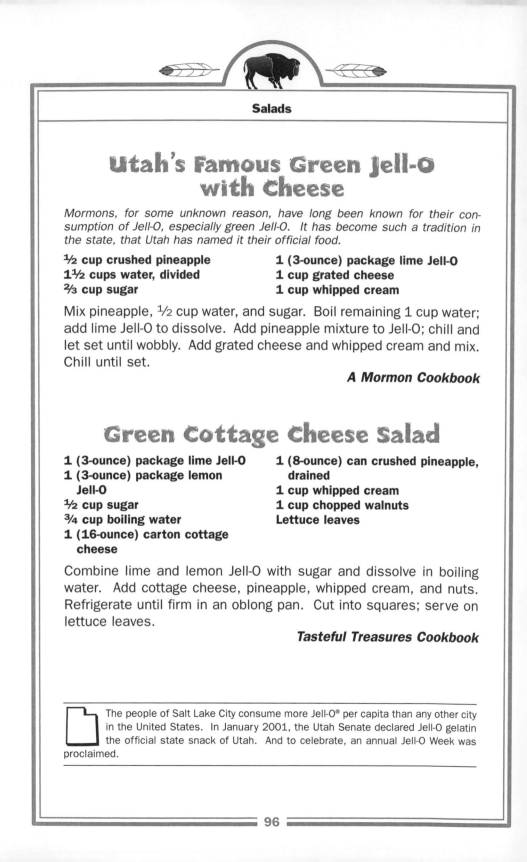

Utah's Famous Green Jell-O with Cheese

Mormons, for some unknown reason, have long been known for their consumption of Jell-O, especially green Jell-O. It has become such a tradition in the state, that Utah has named it their official food.

½ cup crushed pineapple
1½ cups water, divided
⅔ cup sugar

1 (3-ounce) package lime Jell-O
1 cup grated cheese
1 cup whipped cream

Mix pineapple, ½ cup water, and sugar. Boil remaining 1 cup water; add lime Jell-O to dissolve. Add pineapple mixture to Jell-O; chill and let set until wobbly. Add grated cheese and whipped cream and mix. Chill until set.

A Mormon Cookbook

Green Cottage Cheese Salad

1 (3-ounce) package lime Jell-O
1 (3-ounce) package lemon
  Jell-O
½ cup sugar
¾ cup boiling water
1 (16-ounce) carton cottage
  cheese

1 (8-ounce) can crushed pineapple,
  drained
1 cup whipped cream
1 cup chopped walnuts
Lettuce leaves

Combine lime and lemon Jell-O with sugar and dissolve in boiling water. Add cottage cheese, pineapple, whipped cream, and nuts. Refrigerate until firm in an oblong pan. Cut into squares; serve on lettuce leaves.

Tasteful Treasures Cookbook

The people of Salt Lake City consume more Jell-O® per capita than any other city in the United States. In January 2001, the Utah Senate declared Jell-O gelatin the official state snack of Utah. And to celebrate, an annual Jell-O Week was proclaimed.

Sun Bonnet Salad

1 (20-ounce) can crushed
   pineapple
½ cup lemon juice
1 cup sugar
2 envelopes unflavored gelatin

¼ cup cold water
1 cup chopped celery
1 cup grated cheese
1 cup whipped cream
1 cup chopped nuts (optional)

Bring pineapple, lemon juice, and sugar to a boil. Dissolve gelatin in ¼ cup cold tap water and immediately add to the above mixture. Let it cool completely before adding celery, grated cheese, whipped cream, and nuts. Chill till set. Serves 8.

Recipes Thru Time

Beet Salad

1 cup cooked diced or shoestring
   beets
1 (3-ounce) package strawberry,
   cherry, or raspberry gelatin

¾ teaspoon salt
1 cup boiling water or beet juice
1 cup crushed pineapple with juice
   (8-ounce can)

Drain beets, measuring liquid. Add water to make 1 cup. Dissolve gelatin and salt in boiling liquid. Add 4 ice cubes and stir until ice is melted. Chill until thickened. Add beets and crushed pineapple. Chill until set. Makes 6–8 servings.

DRESSING FOR BEET SALAD:

½ cup very thinly sliced green
   onions

⅔ cup chopped celery
½ cup sour cream

Fold vegetables into sour cream. Let stand to develop flavors. Serve about 1 tablespoon of dressing on each salad.

Lion House Recipes

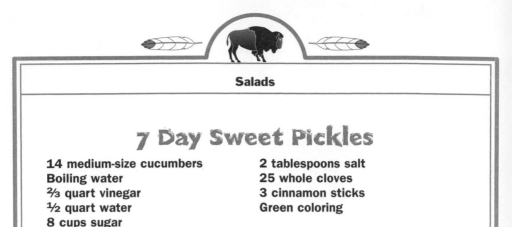

7 Day Sweet Pickles

14 medium-size cucumbers
Boiling water
⅔ quart vinegar
½ quart water
8 cups sugar

2 tablespoons salt
25 whole cloves
3 cinnamon sticks
Green coloring

Slice cucumbers, and in glass container, cover with boiling water each day for 4 days. Each day, pour water off and rinse cukes with cool water and rinse out container. On the 5th day, bring vinegar, ½ quart water, sugar, salt, cloves, cinnamon sticks, and coloring to a boil. Pour over cukes. For the next 2 days, reheat to boiling and pour over cukes. On the 7th day, pour into sterilized jars and seal tightly.

The Cowboy Chuck Wagon Cookbook

Spiced Cranberry Orange Relish

Great served with turkey, chicken, pork or duck. Delicious warmed over ice cream.

1 (12-ounce) bag fresh
cranberries
1 cup water
1 cup sugar
1 apple (Pippin, Granny Smith, or
Golden Delicious), cored and
cut into ½-inch dice
1 pear (Comice, D'Anjou, or Bosc),
cored and cut into ½-inch dice

Zest and juice of 1 orange
¼ teaspoon each: ground
cinnamon, ground cloves, and
ground nutmeg
2 tablespoons orange liqueur
(optional)

In a medium saucepan, bring the cranberries, water, and sugar to a boil. Lower heat to a simmer; add apple, pear, orange zest, orange juice, and spices. Simmer for 10 minutes until cranberries pop. Cool relish to room temperature. Refrigerate relish until ready to serve. Stir in the orange liqueur just before serving. Can be made several days in advance. Serves 6–8.

Savor the Memories

Vegetables

Mountain biking is an ideal way to see the arches, rock spires, gardens, canyons, pre-historic Native American ruins, and pictographs surrounding the Needles District of Canyonlands National Park.

Funeral Potatoes

Called "funeral potatoes" because after a funeral it is customary for family and friends to gather at the church for a light luncheon provided by the Relief Society Sisters (women of the congregation). This is the standard recipe used and is always a favorite.

6–8 potatoes, boiled
1 (10¾-ounce) can cream of
  chicken soup
¼ cup butter or margarine,
  softened, divided
1 pint sour cream

⅓ cup chopped green onions
½ cup shredded Cheddar
  cheese
2 tablespoons melted butter
½ cup crushed cornflakes

Slice or cube potatoes into greased baking dish. Mix together soup, ¼ cup margarine, sour cream, onions, and cheese, and pour over potatoes. Combine melted butter with cornflakes and top casserole. Bake at 350° for 45 minutes. Serves 12.

A Century of Mormon Cookery, Volume 1

Whipped Potatoes with Olive Oil and Parmesan

2 pounds russet potatoes, peeled
  and cubed
¾ cup canned chicken broth,
  hot

6 tablespoons olive oil
¾ cup grated Parmesan cheese
½ cup chopped fresh chives
Salt and pepper to taste

Bring a large pot of water to a boil. Add potatoes and cook until tender. Drain. Transfer to large bowl; add broth. Beat potato mixture with an electric mixer until smooth. Gradually beat in oil, then Parmesan cheese, adding more broth if too thick. Stir in chives. Season with salt and pepper. Garnish with additional grated cheese.

JLO Art of Cooking

Dutch Oven Potatoes by Don

1 stick (½ cup) butter
2 medium onions, chopped
6 large potatoes, sliced
Salt and pepper to taste
2 tablespoons seasoned salt
½ cup salsa

1 (10¾-ounce) can Cheddar
  cheese soup
½ can water
Chopped green onions or broccoli
  (optional)

Grease a 12-inch Dutch oven; add butter and arrange ¼ of the onions on bottom. Put ¼ of the sliced potatoes on the onions. Sprinkle with seasonings. Mix salsa and soup with water and pour ¼ of it over the potatoes. Repeat layers until all onion and potatoes are used ending with soup and salsa mixture. You can sprinkle chopped green onions or broccoli on top for color, if desired. Cook in your Volcano with 10 briquettes, or in a 350° oven for 25–30 minutes.

Log Cabin Dutch Oven

Dutch Oven Potatoes

¼ pound bacon
3 onions, sliced or diced

Sliced potatoes to fill (10- to
  12-inch) Dutch oven

Fry bacon in Dutch oven until nearly crisp. Add onions and sauté 2–3 minutes. Add potatoes and mix together very well. Cover and remove from heat. Completely cover lid with coals; heap 'em up. Bake for 45–50 minutes or until tender.

Dutch Oven Gold

In 1912, Lester Wire, of Salt Lake City, invented an electric traffic light that used red and green lights.

Potato Fans

8 medium red potatoes   **Paprika**
Cold water

Peel potatoes if you wish. Cut a thin slice from one side for a base. Place, base down, in a large spoon and cut into slices down to the spoon, but not through the base. Place cut potatoes in cold water for 30 minutes. Drain. Place in Dutch oven and lightly spray with nonstick cooking spray. Bake at 350° for about one hour, 10–12 coals on bottom, 18–22 on lid.

Note: Cut both ways for an interesting variation. Sprinkle with paprika for extra browning.

Dutch Oven Delites

Tomatoes Baked in Sour Cream

4 tomatoes, sliced   **1 teaspoon sugar**
1 red onion, sliced   **Salt and pepper to taste**
1 cup sour cream, divided   **Bread crumbs**

In casserole dish, make layers alternating stacks of tomato and onion slices, and a dab of sour cream. Keep repeating until casserole dish is full. Sprinkle sugar, salt and pepper on top. Top with remaining sour cream. Sprinkle bread crumbs on top. Bake at 350° for one hour.

Recipes & Remembrances

Over seventy percent of Utah's population are members of the Church of Jesus Christ of Latter-day Saints, better known as the Mormons.

Ratatouille

½ eggplant, peeled and cut
  into chunks
1 cup sliced zucchini
1 green pepper, cut into chunks
1 large onion, cut into chunks
2 stalks celery, cut diagonally
2 shallots, finely chopped
  (optional)

1 clove garlic, minced
2–3 tablespoons chopped fresh
  parsley
⅛ teaspoon ground pepper
2 cups chunked fresh tomatoes or
  diced canned tomatoes

Combine all ingredients, except fresh tomatoes, in a large pot. Cover and cook over low heat for about 20 minutes. Uncover and cook 15 minutes more over moderate heat, stirring with spoon to prevent scorching. Add the tomatoes, heating through, but not permitting tomatoes to become mushy. Serve hot or cold. Serves 6.

Note: This dish is easily varied by adding additional seasonings as desired, such as canned salsa, Italian seasoning, oregano, basil, or any combination.

No Green Gelatin Here!

Escalloped Eggplant

1 small to medium eggplant
1 egg, slightly beaten
½ cup chopped onion

⅛ teaspoon pepper
10–12 saltines, crushed
3 slices bacon, cut in halves

Peel eggplant and cut into cubes. Cover with water and boil until just barely tender. Drain well. Add beaten egg, onion, pepper, and saltines. Mix well and pour into a greased baking dish. Place bacon on top and bake at 350° for 30–40 minutes until brown around the edges and bacon is cooked. If a large eggplant is used, add a little more onion and saltines. Can also add more bacon.

Family Favorites from the Heart

Stuffed Spaghetti Squash

¼ pound hamburger
1 small onion, finely chopped
½ green pepper, finely chopped
½ cup sliced mushrooms
1 (16-ounce) can stewed
  tomatoes
½ teaspoon basil
½ teaspoon oregano
1 tablespoon seasoned salt, or
  ¼ teaspoon salt and
  ⅛ teaspoon pepper
1 teaspoon garlic powder
1 medium spaghetti squash, cut in
  half and cleaned
Shredded white cheese

Mix all ingredients, except squash. Fill cleaned squash with mixture. Bake in a 12-inch warmed and oiled Dutch oven (10 briquettes on bottom, 15 on top) or 350° in your oven for 35 minutes or until you can smell it. Sprinkle the tops with white cheese and return to the fire for 5 more minutes to melt the cheese. Cut squash in halves; serves 4 people.

Log Cabin Campfire Cookn'

Squash Casserole

4 chicken breasts
2 pounds squash, diced (3 cups
  yellow and 3 cups zucchini)
¼ cup chopped onion
1 (10¾-ounce) can cream of
  chicken soup
1 cup sour cream (optional)
1 cup shredded carrots
1 (8-ounce) package seasoned
  stuffing mix
½ cup margarine, melted

Cook chicken and cut into cubes. In saucepan cook squash and onion in lightly salted water until tender. Drain. Combine soup and sour cream and stir in uncooked carrots. Fold squash and diced chicken into soup mixture. Combine stuffing and margarine. Spread layer of stuffing on top of vegetable-chicken mixture. Bake at 350° for 25–30 minutes.

Favorite Recipes from Utah Farm Bureau Women

Stuffed Yellow Summer Squash

Anyone who has grown yellow summer squash in their gardens knows that every once in a while you get busy with your summer fun and turn around twice, and darn those small tender squashes have grown too large and tough to eat. Don't put them in your compost pile; fix this recipe!

2 large yellow squash	**8 mushrooms, diced**
8 Ritz Crackers	**1 tablespoon chopped parsley**
½ cup grated Cheddar cheese	**Salt and pepper to taste**
½ small yellow onion, diced	**½ tablespoon minced garlic**
¼ stick butter, diced	**¼ stick butter**
1 medium tomato, diced	

Boil squash in pot ⅓ full of water until slightly tender, but still very firm. Don't overcook or they will be too hard to handle.

In mixing bowl crumble Ritz Crackers, then add Cheddar cheese, onion, diced butter, tomato, mushrooms, parsley, and seasonings. Preheat oven to 350°. Remove cooked squash from the pot; cool in cold water. When cool, cut squash in half and scrape out seeds, adding seeds to the cracker mixture.

With the ¼ stick butter, butter the bottom of a 9x13-inch pan; place cut squash in pan. Stuff each half of the squash with the mixture. Bake for 30 minutes at 350°. Serves 4.

Recipes & Remembrances

Sunshine Casserole

6 cups sliced zucchini
2 teaspoons salt
1 (10¾-ounce) can cream of
   chicken soup
1 cup sour cream
1 cup shredded carrots

¼ cup minced fresh onion
1 (8-ounce) package herb stuffing
   mix
½ cup butter or margarine,
   melted

Cook squash 5 minutes in boiling water and add salt. Combine soup, sour cream, and carrots. Fold in drained squash and onion. Mix stuffing mix with butter and spread half on bottom of casserole dish. Add vegetable mixture and top with remaining stuffing. Bake at 400° for 30 minutes.

How to Enjoy Zucchini

Impossible Garden Pie

2 cups chopped zucchini
1 cup chopped tomato
½ cup chopped onion
⅓ cup grated Parmesan cheese
1½ cups milk

¾ cup biscuit mix
3 eggs
½ teaspoon salt
¼ teaspoon pepper

Lightly grease a 10-inch pie plate. Sprinkle zucchini, tomato, onion, and cheese in pie plate. Beat remaining ingredients until smooth, 15 seconds in blender on high speed or 1 minute with hand beater. Pour into pie plate. Bake in preheated 400° oven about 30 minutes, or until golden brown and knife inserted in center comes out clean. Let stand for 5 minutes. Garnish with tomato and zucchini slices, if desired. Any leftover pie may be refrigerated. Serves 6.

How to Enjoy Zucchini

Cheese-Topped Zucchini

3 medium zucchini	Oregano
1 medium onion, diced	1 cup tomato sauce
Oil	Mozzarella slices
Salt and pepper to taste	Parmesan cheese

Slice zucchini in halves lengthwise. In large skillet, sauté onion until tender in small amount of oil. Add zucchini halves, cut-side-up; sprinkle with salt and pepper and a little oregano. Pour tomato sauce over zucchini. Cover and cook on medium heat until tender, about 10 minutes. Top zucchini with sliced mozzarella cheese; sprinkle with additional oregano and cook, covered, until cheese melts. Cover with Parmesan cheese and serve.

Favorite Recipes from Utah Farm Bureau Women

Hearty Harvest Casserole

2 large onions, cut and separated into rings ¾ inch thick	2 medium zucchini, cut into 1½-inch chunks
1 each: medium green and red peppers, cut into 1-inch strips	1 pound green beans, snapped in half
1 cup sprouted barley, partially cooked (save 1 cup water)	½ head cauliflower florets
1 cup barley water from above	2 cloves garlic, crushed
4 tablespoons vegetable broth mix	1 tablespoon salt
3 medium carrots, cut into chunks	¼ teaspoon black pepper
2 large tomatoes, peeled and quartered	1 teaspoon paprika
	¼ cup chopped parsley

Steam-fry onions and green peppers. Combine all ingredients in a casserole dish. Cover. Bake at 350° for one hour. Barley should be tender. Serves 12.

Back to the House of Health

Pan-Grilled Vegetables

Crisp grilled vegetables studded with savory herbs complement most any meal! Though great prepared over a charcoal grill, it's easy to do in the kitchen at any time of year with the aid of a ridged grill pan.

2 small zucchini	1 tablespoon minced rosemary
2 medium carrots	1 garlic clove, minced
2 Japanese eggplants	½ tablespoon freshly ground
1 tablespoon minced sage	black pepper
1 tablespoon minced thyme	¼ cup olive oil

Trim and slice each of the vegetables lengthwise into ¼-inch slices. Whisk the herbs, garlic, and pepper with the olive oil. Place the veggies in a shallow dish, and drizzle with the herb mixture. Heat a ridged grill pan over medium-high to high heat. Place veggies in a single layer in the pan and cook, turning once, until just softened and nicely marked on both sides. Serves 2.

Aromatherapy in the Kitchen

Mediterranean Grilled Veggies

1 (8-ounce) package fresh mushrooms	2 small bell peppers (1 red, 1 green), cut into chunks
1 medium onion, cut into wedges	2 cups cherry tomatoes

MARINADE:

6 tablespoons extra virgin olive oil	1 tablespoon soy sauce
2 tablespoons balsamic vinegar	2 garlic cloves, crushed
	¼ cup chopped fresh basil

Prepare all the vegetables. Whisk together Marinade ingredients. In a large bowl, toss vegetables in Marinade and marinate for 1 hour. Put veggies, except tomatoes, in a grilling basket or on skewers. Grill, brushing with Marinade and turning several times, for 15 minutes. Add tomatoes and grill 5 minutes longer, or until veggies are as tender as desired.

Cherished Recipes

Mushrooms and Onions

Great with steak, or as a vegetable side dish.

1 pound fresh mushrooms, washed
  and sliced
4 tablespoons butter
¼ teaspoon salt

Dash pepper
2 tablespoons dried parsley
2 tablespoons dried onion
¼ cup water

Place the mushrooms on an 18-inch square of double layered aluminum foil. Dot with butter and sprinkle with salt, pepper, parsley, and onion. Pour water over all. Fold foil securely so that no juices can escape. Refrigerate and take along, or cook immediately over low coals, turning often, or on a grill about 15 minutes. Serves 6.

Vacation Cooking: Good Food! Good Fun!

Hot and Spicy Onion Rings

This batter can also be used to make onion blossoms, if you have a blossom cutter.

1 egg
1 cup milk
1 cup flour
1 teaspoon salt
1 teaspoon ground red pepper

¼ teaspoon oregano
⅛ teaspoon cumin
Oil for deep-fat frying
2 large onions, sliced thick, then
  separated into rings

Combine egg, milk, flour, and seasonings and mix until the batter is smooth. Heat about 2 inches of oil in the Dutch oven. This will take about 16–20 coals (350°–375°) at bottom heat only. Dip the onion slices into the batter, then fry them in the hot oil, a few at a time. Turn them over to cook both sides, then remove with a slotted spoon and drain on paper towels. Serve with ketchup, ranch dressing, or horseradish sauce. Serves 4–6.

The Beginner's Guide to Dutch Oven Cooking

Horseradish Carrots

**4 cups carrot sticks that have
    been scrubbed or peeled**
¼ cup reserved water
2 tablespoons grated onion
2 tablespoons horseradish

½ cup mayonnaise
1 teaspoon salt
¼ teaspoon pepper
¼ cup buttered bread crumbs

Cook carrots in water to cover until just tender; drain, reserving ¼ cup water. Place carrots in shallow 1-quart baking dish. Mix remaining ingredients (including reserved water), except the crumbs. Pour over carrots; sprinkle with crumbs. Bake at 375° for 20 minutes or until heated through with the top lightly browned.

Ladies' Literary Club Cookbook

Sausage and Cabbage

This one always gets good reviews at the Kohler's Dutch oven workshops, even though it's so simple to make.

1 large head of cabbage
½ stick butter
Seasoned salt, salt, and pepper

1 large Polish sausage
Water

Clean and wedge one large head cabbage (remove core); place in a 12-inch Dutch oven. Season to taste with butter, seasoned salt, salt, and pepper. Place Polish sausage on top of cabbage; add small amount of water to bottom of Dutch oven and steam until tender over medium coals from bottom only, approximately 30–45 minutes. Excellent served with corn bread.

World Championship Dutch Oven Cookbook

The Uinta Mountains, named after the Ute Indians, are the only major East-West axis mountains in North America.

Chinese Spinach

1 pound fresh spinach
2 tablespoons salad oil
2 tablespoons soy sauce
½ teaspoon sugar

2 tablespoons finely chopped
onion
1 (8-ounce) can water chestnuts,
drained and sliced

Wash and pat spinach leaves dry. Tear into bite-size pieces. In large saucepan, simmer spinach with a small amount of water for 3 minutes; drain thoroughly. Heat oil, soy sauce, and sugar in skillet; add spinach and onion. Cook and toss until spinach is well coated, 2–3 minutes. Stir in water chestnuts. Makes 4 servings.

Lion House Recipes

Nutmeg Spinach Soufflé

1 pound fresh spinach
2 tablespoons margarine
2 tablespoons all-purpose flour
1 teaspoon salt
1 cup milk
4 eggs, separated

¼ cup chopped onion
⅛ teaspoon nutmeg
¼ teaspoon cream of tartar
3 tablespoons grated Parmesan
cheese

Wash spinach; cook in small amount of salted water. Drain and press out all excess water; chop spinach. Melt margarine in saucepan; add flour and salt and blend. Gradually add milk and stir until thickened. Gradually add beaten egg yolks. Stir in spinach, onion, and nutmeg. Beat egg whites and cream of tartar until stiff. Fold into spinach mixture. Pour into greased soufflé dish. Sprinkle with Parmesan cheese. Bake at 375° for 50 minutes or until set. Makes 6 servings.

Lion House Entertaining

Broccoli Casserole

2 (10-ounce) packages frozen
  broccoli
1 cup chopped celery
1 (10¾-ounce) can cream of
  mushroom soup

1 cup sour cream
Buttered bread crumbs
Grated Cheddar cheese

Boil broccoli until tender; drain. Cook celery in separate pan until tender; combine with broccoli. Mix with soup and sour cream. Pour into casserole and top with buttered bread crumbs and cheese. Bake at 350° for 30 minutes.

Cherished Recipes

Spicy Green Beans

½ cup soy sauce
¼ cup sesame oil
Crushed red pepper flakes
1 clove garlic, minced
Garlic salt
2 tablespoons black bean garlic
  sauce

1 tablespoon granulated sugar
¼ teaspoon fresh ginger, peeled
  and grated
1 pound fresh green beans,
  snipped

Combine all ingredients except beans. Set aside. Boil or blanch green beans. Marinate beans for at least one hour in spicy dressing. Serve at room temperature.

JLO Art of Cooking

Calico Beans

½ pound bacon, chopped
1 pound hamburger
1 large onion, chopped
1 cup ketchup
1 tablespoon dry mustard
1 tablespoon vinegar
½ cup molasses (optional)

2 teaspoons salt
¾ cup brown sugar
1 (29-ounce) can pork and beans
1 (15-ounce) can garbanzo beans
1 (15-ounce) can kidney beans
1 (16-ounce) package frozen baby lima beans

Fry bacon in pot. Add hamburger and onion. Cook 7–10 minutes. Add rest of ingredients and mix well. Cover and bake for one hour at 350°. Use 6–8 coals on bottom, 14–18 on top.

Championship Dutch Oven Cookbook

Baked Bean Casserole

1 pound bacon
1 onion, chopped
1 green pepper, chopped
1 (1-pound, 13-ounce) can pork and beans
1 (15-ounce) can kidney beans
1 (15-ounce) can lima beans with ham

1 (8-ounce) can chunk pineapple
1 (15-ounce) can whole onions
1 cup ketchup
1 cup brown sugar
3 tablespoons molasses
4–6 tablespoons Worcestershire sauce

Cut bacon in pieces and fry. Add onion and pepper to bacon and cook until tender. Add remaining ingredients and bake 2½–3 hours in a 325° oven. This casserole will keep for reheating or can be frozen to be used later. Yields 12 servings.

Dude Food

Best in the West Beans

1 (16-ounce) can butter beans
1 (16-ounce) can pinto beans
1 (16-ounce) can pork and beans
½ pound ground beef
10 slices bacon, chopped
½ cup finely chopped onion
⅓ cup brown sugar
⅓ cup sugar

¼ cup ketchup
¼ cup spicy hot BBQ sauce
2 tablespoons Dijon mustard
2 tablespoons dark molasses
½ teaspoon salt
½ teaspoon pepper
½ teaspoon chili powder

Drain butter beans and pinto beans and combine with pork and beans. In large saucepot, brown beef, bacon, and onion; drain. Add beans and remaining ingredients; mix well. Put into large casserole dish and bake, uncovered, for one hour at 350°. Enjoy!

Family Favorites from the Heart

Pasta, Rice, Etc.

Oddly shaped stone pillars and knobs (known as goblins or hoodoos) populate Goblin Valley State Park. Visitors may wonder if they're in Utah or on Mars! This unusual space-like landscape was featured in the film Galaxy Quest.

Chuck Wagon Noodles

1 egg
½ teaspoon salt (optional)

2 tablespoons water or milk
1–1¼ cups whole-wheat flour

Generously flour your working surface. Combine all ingredients and add enough flour to make dough stiff. Place dough on floured surface and roll out until very thin. Cut into strips about ¼ inch wide and let dry for about 2 hours. Drop into boiling soup or boiling, salted water, and cook uncovered about 10 minutes. Makes 3 cups cooked noodles.

Note: You may substitute white flour for wheat, or use half wheat and half white.

The Cowboy Chuck Wagon Cookbook

Stuffed Manicotti

½ cup chopped onion
1½ pounds hamburger
1 box large shell pasta or
   manicotti shells
2 eggs, slightly beaten
1 cup chopped spinach
4 tablespoons parsley

½ teaspoon salt
¼ teaspoon pepper
2 slices French bread, soaked in
   ½ cup milk
1 (26-ounce) jar spaghetti sauce
1 cup mozzarella cheese
Parmesan cheese

Brown onion and hamburger. Parboil shells about 6 minutes; set aside. Mix all ingredients, except shells, spaghetti sauce, and cheeses. Stuff shells with meat filling. Pour ½ spaghetti sauce in bottom of a 9x13-inch pan. Place stuffed shells, leaving room for shells to expand, and cover with remaining sauce. Sprinkle mozzarella cheese on each shell. Cover and bake for 30 minutes in 350° oven. Uncover and sprinkle with Parmesan cheese. Cook 10 minutes.

A Century of Mormon Cookery, Volume 2

Macaroni and Cheese

1 (8-ounce) package macaroni
  (2 cups cooked)
1¼ cups sharp Cheddar cheese,
  cut into ½-inch cubes or strips
2 tablespoons butter

¾ teaspoon salt
¼ teaspoon pepper
2 cups milk
Paprika

Cook macaroni according to package directions. Drain macaroni and layer with cheese in a 12 x 7½ x 2-inch casserole dish. Dot with butter; sprinkle with seasonings, then pour milk over the top. Bake at 350° for 40 minutes or until crust is golden brown. Sprinkle the casserole with paprika to serve. Serves 6–8.

Recipe by Rodney H. Brady
Five-Star Recipes from Well-Known Latter Day Saints

Vegetable Lasagne

1 pound lasagna noodles
2 green peppers, chopped
2 large onions, chopped
¾ pound sliced mushrooms
5 carrots, grated
1½ tablespoons oil
1 quart diced tomatoes
1 quart tomato sauce

¾ teaspoon oregano and basil,
  combined
⅛ teaspoon black pepper
2 pounds cottage cheese
1 pound mozzarella cheese,
  grated
5 ounces Parmesan cheese

Boil noodles until just tender. Remove from heat and hold. In Dutch oven sauté raw vegetables in oil until tender. Add tomatoes, sauce, and spices. Simmer 10–15 minutes. Remove half to bowl. Cover what's left in Dutch oven with ⅓ noodles. Spoon some of the cottage cheese on and spread; sprinkle mozzarella over. Place remaining half of vegetables on top, layer with another ⅓ noodles, then half the remaining cottage cheese and mozzarella. Repeat noodles and cheeses until gone. Top with Parmesan. Bake one hour at 350° until hot and bubbly.

Championship Dutch Oven Cookbook

Chicken Alfredo

Fast, fabulous, and rich!

6 ounces dried bow tie pasta
2 tablespoons olive oil or butter
½ pound chicken tenders or
** boneless, skinless chicken**
** breasts cut in strips**
2 green onions, chopped
1 tablespoon butter
¾ cup sliced fresh mushrooms
** (optional)**

1 tablespoon fresh thyme or 1
** teaspoon dried**
½ tablespoon garlic powder
2 cups heavy cream
¾ cup grated Parmesan or
** Romano cheese**
½ teaspoon salt
½ teaspoon pepper
⅛ cup toasted pine nuts (optional)

Cook pasta according to package directions. Drain and set aside. In a large skillet, heat olive oil or butter over medium heat. Add chicken and stir-fry about 5 minutes or until cooked through. In a separate pan, sauté green onions in 1 tablespoon butter until tender. Add mushrooms (if desired), thyme, and sautéed onions to chicken. Add garlic powder, cream, cheese, salt, and pepper. Simmer about 30 minutes, stirring occasionally, until chicken is cooked and tender. Serve over pasta. Top with pine nuts. Makes 2 servings.

The Essential Mormon Cookbook

Penne Pasta with Gabby's Fresh Mushroom-Meat Sauce

A crispy cold tossed salad and a loaf of crusty-warm Italian bread and you've got a wonderful meal—oh, yes, a red beverage of your choice will really make it complete.

12 ounces penne pasta
1 pound extra lean ground beef
½ pound lean ground pork
1 tablespoon olive oil
½ pound fresh mushrooms, sliced
1 small zucchini, thinly sliced
1 small red bell pepper, finely chopped
4–5 pieces of sun-dried tomatoes, thinly sliced
2–3 cloves garlic, pressed or minced

1 quart thick spaghetti sauce (homemade is best)
¼ cup bold dry red wine (Burgundy)
3 tablespoons sweet basil, finely chopped, or 1 tablespoon dried
Salt and freshly ground pepper to taste
2 cups shredded mozzarella cheese
1 cup shredded fresh Parmesan cheese

Cook pasta until just barely tender; drain well.

In a large skillet, brown beef and pork in olive oil. Remove meat from pan and add mushrooms, zucchini, bell pepper, dried tomatoes, and garlic to drippings. Sauté this mixture 4–5 minutes over high heat, stirring often. Return meat mixture to pan and stir in the sauce, wine, basil, salt and pepper. Let this mixture come to a simmer, then remove from heat.

Lightly spray a large, shallow baking dish. Layer half of the penne pasta into the dish, then half of the sauce mixture, followed by half of the cheeses. Repeat layers, then bake in a preheated 325° oven for 60 minutes. Serves 6–8.

Enjoy! Again and Again

Risotto Giardino

The main ingredient in risotto is arborio rice, a short-grain starchy rice prized for its ability to absorb liquid and create a rich, creamy consistency in any of its many versions, combining savory liquids and fresh ingredients.

2 tablespoons butter	½ cup julienned carrots,
1 tablespoon olive oil	blanched
¾ cup chopped onion	½ cup julienned zucchini
1 cup uncooked arborio rice	½ cup fresh green beans,
3 cups chicken stock	blanched
¼ cup dry white wine	¼ cup grated Parmesan cheese
¾ cup chopped fresh tomatoes	Salt and pepper to taste
1 cup small unmarinated	
artichokes	

Heat butter and olive oil in a medium saucepan over medium-low heat. Add onion and cook until light brown. Add rice. Cook for 5 minutes or until liquid is absorbed, stirring constantly.

Heat chicken stock in a saucepan. Add ¼ cup at a time to the rice, cooking until broth is absorbed after each addition and stirring constantly. Add wine, tomatoes, artichokes, carrots, zucchini, and green beans. Cook until rice is al dente and liquid is absorbed. Stir in the cheese, salt and pepper. Serves 4.

Always in Season

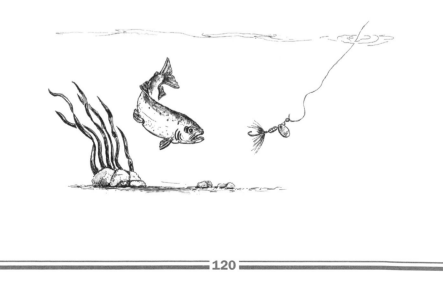

Penne alla Siciliana

1 pound imported penne pasta
1 tablespoon minced garlic
¼ cup fresh basil leaves
¼ cup fresh oregano leaves
¼ cup fresh parsley
¼ cup fresh mint leaves
2 pounds Roma tomatoes,
  cored and coarsely chopped
½ teaspoon salt
¼ teaspoon ground black
  pepper
½ cup extra virgin olive oil
½ cup shredded Parmesan
  cheese

Cook pasta al dente, then rinse under cold water to stop cooking process. Drain and set aside in a large bowl.

In a food processor, place garlic, herbs, tomatoes, salt, and pepper. Pulse on and off 5 times. You want the mixture to look like a salsa, not puréed. The tomatoes should have some texture and the herbs should be chopped. Add oil and pulse on and off once. Pour sauce over the pasta and toss well. Taste for seasoning. Toss in the shredded cheese. Serves 8.

Savor the Memories

Rich Raw Tomato Sauce

This is a wonderfully fresh-tasting raw tomato sauce that goes great over pasta. It is also a wonderful dipping sauce, and can be served cold or warmed, but not cooked.

3–5 sun-dried tomatoes
4 fresh, firm tomatoes, chopped
½ cup chopped fresh basil
1 teaspoon dried onion
1 teaspoon roasted garlic
1 teaspoon salt

Put all ingredients in food processor and blend to desired consistency. Store in airtight container in refrigerator for up to 3 days.

Variation: Instead of the fresh basil and roasted garlic, just use ¼–⅓ cup Garlic Galore Pesto. This is a lovely nondairy pesto that is also great on wraps. It is found in most large health food stores.

Back to the House of Health

Angel Hair Pasta with Shrimp

12 ounces fresh or frozen shrimp, peeled and deveined
1 cup chopped onion
2 cloves garlic, minced
1 tablespoon olive or cooking oil
¼ cup white cooking wine or water
1 tablespoon snipped fresh basil
1½ teaspoons snipped fresh oregano
1 teaspoon instant chicken bouillon granules
1 teaspoon cornstarch
⅛ teaspoon pepper
6 ounces dried angel hair pasta, cooked
2 medium tomatoes, peeled, seeded, and chopped
¼ cup snipped parsley
¼ cup grated Parmesan cheese

Thaw shrimp, if frozen. In a large saucepan, cook the onion and garlic in hot oil until onion is tender. Combine the cooking wine or water, basil, oregano, bouillon granules, cornstarch, and pepper. Add to saucepan. Cook and stir until bubbly.

Add shrimp to liquid mixture in saucepan. Cover and simmer about 3 minutes, or until shrimp turn pink.

Meanwhile, cook pasta in boiling water for 2 minutes, until it is al dente. Stir tomatoes into shrimp mixture and heat through. To serve, toss pasta with parsley. Spoon shrimp mixture over pasta. Sprinkle with Parmesan cheese. Serves 4.

Recipe by Janet Lee Chamberlain
Five-Star Recipes from Well-Known Latter Day Saints

In 1847, a small choir sang on what is now Temple Square in Salt Lake City, marking the beginning of the Mormon Tabernacle Choir. Since then, the choir has grown to 325 unpaid members. The choir has performed in numerous countries and has released more than 150 albums.

Broccoli Pilaf

2 cups long-grain rice
1 onion, chopped
1 cup chopped celery
2 cups coarsely chopped broccoli

4 bouillon cubes
4 cups water
½ cup slivered almonds

In Dutch oven, lightly toast rice over 20–25 coals or low heat. Add onion and cook 4–5 minutes more. Add other ingredients and bring to a boil. Remove all but 8 coals from bottom and 6–8 on lid. Cook for 20 minutes or until water is absorbed.

Dutch Oven Delites

Mexicali Rice

This is a salsa rice that is a great complement to a Mexican dinner.

3 tablespoons olive oil, divided
1 onion, chopped
1 clove garlic, minced
½ cup diced celery
¼ cup diced bell pepper
2 large tomatoes, coarsely
chopped
2 serrano chiles, seeds and
stems removed, chopped

2 tablespoons chopped fresh
cilantro
1 teaspoon fresh lemon juice
½ teaspoon oregano
1 teaspoon salt
3–4 cups cooked rice

Put half the olive oil in a skillet or electric frypan, and sauté the onion and garlic until onion softens. Then add the rest of the ingredients and steam-fry until veggies are bright and still somewhat crisp. Add 3–4 cups cooked rice and the rest of the olive oil. Mix well and serve warm.

Back to the House of Health

Ultimate Jambalaya

3 tablespoons unsalted butter
1 pound smoked sausage cut in
  ¼-inch slices
1 pound smoked ham, diced
1 pound boneless, skinless
  chicken breasts cut into
  bite-size pieces
2 bay leaves
2 tablespoons Cajun seasoning
  (low salt)

1 cup chopped onion, divided
1 cup chopped celery, divided
1 cup chopped green bell pepper,
  divided
1½ tablespoons minced garlic
½ cup tomato sauce
1 cup peeled, chopped tomatoes
2½ cups chicken stock or broth
1½ cups uncooked, long grain rice
1 teaspoon gumbo filé

Remove all the racks from your Ultimate Dutch Oven and spray oven with nonstick vegetable spray. Melt butter in Dutch oven over medium heat (10 or 11 briquettes). Add sausage and ham. Cook until meat starts to brown, stirring frequently and scraping oven bottom well. Add chicken and continue cooking until chicken is brown, stirring frequently and scraping bottom of oven as needed.

Stir in bay leaves, Cajun seasoning, and ½ cup each onion, celery, green pepper, and all the garlic. Stir frequently. Cook until vegetables start to soften. Stir in tomato sauce and cook about one minute, stirring often. Stir in remaining onion, celery, and green pepper, and add tomatoes. Stir in stock and rice, mixing well. Bring to a boil, stirring occasionally.

Reduce heat and simmer, covered, over very low heat (8 or 9 briquettes) until rice is tender but still chewy, about 30 minutes. Stir well, remove bay leaves, add filé, and let stand uncovered 5 minutes before serving.

Ultimate Dutch Oven Cookbook

Meats

Glen Canyon National Recreation Area is home to Lake Powell, the second largest man-made reservoir in the United States. (Lake Mead in Nevada is the largest.) Lake Powell is 186 miles long, has 1,960 miles of shoreline, and took seventeen years to reach the full planned sea level of 3,700 feet above sea level.

Honey Apricot Ham

1 precooked ham
⅛ cup honey
½ teaspoon ground cloves
2 (12-ounce) jars apricot
  marmalade

1 teaspoon mustard powder
½ tablespoon Worcestershire
  sauce

Score face of ham with diagonal lines making diamonds approximately 1½ inches in size and ½ inch deep. Place ham in Dutch oven to fit, with 12 coals on bottom and 14 coals on top. Mix together remaining ingredients; baste over ham. Cover and cook for approximately 1–1½ hours until done, basting with mixture every 20 minutes.

Note: If desired, delete ground cloves and add whole cloves by spiking them into the middle of each diamond. This adds a delicious and pleasing effect to the cooked dish.

A Complete Guide to Dutch Oven Cooking

Pork Chop Suey

1 pound pork, sliced thin
1 medium onion, sliced
3 ribs celery, sliced
2 cans sliced water chestnuts
3 cubes chicken bouillon
¼ cup soy sauce

8 ounces sliced mushrooms
1 pound bean sprouts
2 cups water, divided
5–6 tablespoons cornstarch
¼ pound Chinese peas (in pods)

Lightly cook pork in Dutch oven, then add onion and celery and cook 3–5 minutes. Add rest of ingredients, except cornstarch and 1 cup water. Cook and stir until veggies are tender. Mix cornstarch and remaining cup of water and add slowly to Dutch oven, stirring constantly until thickened. Serve with hot rice.

Dutch Oven Delites

Pork Chops and Sliced Apples

Kids love this recipe.

6 pork chops
2½ cups sliced apples
2 tablespoons flour
2 tablespoons brown sugar

¼ teaspoon salt
½ teaspoon cinnamon
⅓ cup boiling water

Brown pork chops on all sides and place in oven-proof baking dish. Combine all ingredients (except water) and pour over chops. Then pour boiling water over top. Cover and bake at 300° for 2 hours.

JLO Art of Cooking

Bunkhouse Pork Chops in Ranch Sauce

8 pork chops
1½ cups water, divided
2 tablespoons brown sugar
¼ cup chopped onion
1 teaspoon garlic powder

1 tablespoon seasoned salt
¼ cup flour
½ cup sour cream
3 tablespoons ketchup

Place chops in 12-inch Dutch oven. Add 1 cup water, brown sugar, onion, garlic powder, and seasoned salt. Simmer for 1 hour and 30 minutes in 350° oven. Add flour to remaining ½ cup water and mix with sour cream and ketchup. Pour over chops and return to heat. Heat thoroughly without boiling. Chops will be very tender. Use 10 briquettes on bottom and 15 on top, or 12 in Volcano with damper closed half way (briquettes will last 2 hours).

Log Cabin Dutch Oven

Approximately 700 American Bison roam Antelope Island, the largest of the Great Salt Lake's ten major islands. The present herd is descended from twelve bison placed on the island in 1893.

Skillet Pork Chops

3 tablespoons flour
5 tablespoons Parmesan cheese, divided
1½ teaspoons salt
½ teaspoon dill weed
¼ teaspoon pepper
6 or 7 pork chops
1 tablespoon oil
2 medium onions, sliced
⅓ cup water
3 medium zucchini, sliced
½ teaspoon paprika

In a large plastic bag, combine flour and 2 tablespoons Parmesan cheese, salt, dill weed, and pepper. Place pork chops in bag and shake to coat. Shake off excess flour in bag; reserve. Heat oil in a skillet over medium heat; fry and brown pork chops on both sides. Reduce heat; place onion slices on chops. Add water to skillet, cover, and simmer for 15 minutes. Place zucchini slices over onion slices. Mix remaining Parmesan cheese with reserved flour in bag; sprinkle over zucchini, put paprika over that, and simmer for 25 minutes or until chops are nice and tender. Excellent served over rice.

Log Cabin Holidays and Traditions

Grandpa Dick's Hawaiian Pork

1 pound lean pork, cubed
2 tablespoons apple juice
2 tablespoons soy sauce
2 eggs, lightly beaten

2 tablespoons cornstarch
2 tablespoons flour
Oil for frying

Mix pork with apple juice, soy sauce, eggs, cornstarch, and flour. Heat oil in 10-inch Dutch oven to 350°. Separate pork pieces and deep-fry until well done and crisp on the edges. Remove to a pan covered with paper towels. Keep warm. Remove oil from Dutch oven. Serves 5–6 hearty meals with Vegetables and Sauce over rice.

VEGETABLES:

1 tablespoon oil
2 medium onions, cut into
  quarters
2 medium bell peppers, cut into
  strips

1 clove garlic, minced
1 (4-ounce) can water chestnuts
1 ounce slivered almonds

Heat oil in Dutch oven and sauté onions, green peppers, garlic, water chestnuts, and slivered almonds over high heat (350°) for 5 minutes, mixing well.

SAUCE:

⅓ cup sugar
1 tablespoon apple juice
4 tablespoons soy sauce
4 tablespoons ketchup
2 tablespoons vinegar

1 teaspoon garlic powder
1 tablespoon cornstarch mixed
  with ⅓ cup water
2 (8-ounce) cans pineapple
  tidbits

Add all Sauce ingredients, except cornstarch and pineapple tidbits, to vegetables and bring to a boil. Thicken with cornstarch mixture, stirring constantly; add fried pork and pineapple, mix well, and serve immediately with rice.

A Complete Guide to Dutch Oven Cooking

Sweet and Sour Pork

½ teaspoon salt
¼ teaspoon pepper
¼ cup powdered sugar
3 cups cubed pork
1–2 tablespoons oil
¼ cup water
2 tablespoons butter
1 cup finely chopped onion

1 (8½-ounce) can diced bamboo
  shoots, drained
1 (10-ounce) package frozen
  peas
3 tablespoons lemon juice
¼ cup soy sauce
Cooked rice or noodles

In a small bowl, combine salt, pepper, and powdered sugar. Coat pork cubes with mixture. Heat oil in wok. Add pork and stir-fry for about 10 minutes or until evenly browned. Reduce heat and add water. Cover and simmer for 30 minutes or until pork is tender. Push pork up side of wok. Add butter; when melted, add onion and bamboo shoots; stir in pork. Push mixture up on the side of the wok and add frozen peas, lemon juice, and soy sauce; cook for 2 minutes. Mix all together. Serve with rice or noodles.

Log Cabin Presents Lewis and Clark

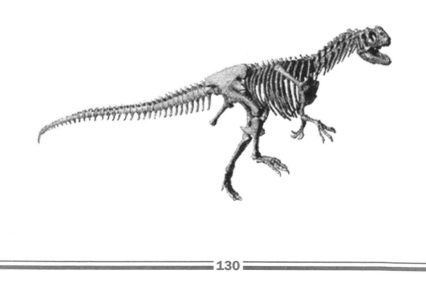

Jane's Juicy Pork Pot Roast (or Ribs)

2 teaspoons salt
1 teaspoon pepper or to taste
¼ teaspoon thyme
¼ teaspoon oregano
¼ teaspoon fennel (optional)
4 pounds boneless pork roast or boneless spareribs

1 cup flour
3 tablespoons oil or shortening
1 cup chicken broth
1½ cups apple juice or cider
2 cloves minced garlic
½ teaspoon nutmeg

Remove all racks from your Ultimate Dutch Oven and spray your oven with nonstick vegetable spray. In a small bowl combine salt, pepper, thyme, oregano, and fennel. Rub spice mixture all over the roast. Now dredge the roast in flour until it is completely covered, rubbing it in well.

Heat Dutch oven over high heat (12–15 briquettes) and add oil. Brown roast on all sides. Once meat is browned, remove from heat and remove meat from oven. Put in bottom rack and put meat back in oven on top of bottom rack. Add chicken broth, apple juice, garlic, and nutmeg to oven and cover. Simmer over low heat (8 or 9 briquettes) for 3–4 hours. When done remove the meat and make gravy from the drippings.

Ultimate Dutch Oven Cookbook

The largest quarry of Jurassic Period dinosaur bones ever discovered was found in the 200,000-acre Dinosaur National Monument. About 350 million tons of fossils, including full skeletons and remains of some dinosaur species that were previously unknown, were excavated. The visitor center at Dinosaur Quarry, seven miles north of Jensen, displays more than 2,000 dinosaur bones and dinosaur replicas.

Porky Pineapple Spareribs

Great gourmet dish and excellent with Dutch oven potatoes or rice.

1 (20-ounce) can pineapple
  chunks, drained (reserve juice)
¼ cup vinegar
½ cup flour
1 teaspoon salt
¼ teaspoon pepper
4 pounds boneless pork
  spareribs

½ cup ketchup
¼ cup molasses
1 large green pepper, chopped
  fine
1 large onion, chopped fine

Warm and oil a 12-inch Dutch oven. Put reserved pineapple juice, vinegar, flour, and seasoning in oven and simmer until bubbling. Put ribs in oven; cover and cook at 350° for 50 minutes. Remove lid and stir ribs to baste with juices. Add ketchup and molasses and cook until ribs are tender, another 10–20 minutes. Add pineapple chunks, green pepper, and onion. Return to heat for 10 minutes to heat through.

Log Cabin Dutch Oven

Country-Style Ribs and Kraut

3 pounds (12) spareribs
2 tablespoons oil or bacon
  grease
¼ teaspoon salt
⅛ teaspoon pepper

2 large onions, sliced
1 clove garlic, minced
½ cup hot water
2 pounds or 3 large cans
  sauerkraut

Place ribs in greased 12-inch Dutch oven. Add salt, pepper, onions, garlic, and water. Simmer on low heat (325°) for ½ hour. Remove from heat and add sauerkraut. Cover and simmer 15–20 minutes until warm through. Serves 5–6. Use 10 briquettes on bottom and 15 on top, or 12 briquettes for Volcano.

Log Cabin Dutch Oven

Barbecue Sauce for All Meats

1 cup ketchup
¼ cup vinegar
2 tablespoons Worcestershire
  sauce
½ teaspoon liquid smoke

½ cup or more chopped onion
½ cup chopped celery
1 cup chopped tomatoes
¼ cup chopped green pepper
  (optional)

Put all ingredients in pan or Dutch oven and simmer until all vegetables are well done. You can add the meat to the sauce and continue to cook until the meat is done, or place the meat in another pan and cover with enough sauce to taste. You can also spice up your leftovers with the sauce by simmering the meat in it to flavor and taste.

Log Cabin Grub Cookbook

Western Style Barbecue Sauce for a Crowd

Great for spareribs, beef, or pork.

2 quarts ketchup
2 cups cider vinegar
½ cup dry mustard
½ cup Tabasco sauce
1½ tablespoons black pepper
½ cup chili powder

1 cup brown sugar
2 cups tomato juice
¼ teaspoon garlic powder
2 tablespoons salt
30 pounds ribs or rump roasts

Combine all ingredients of sauce. Brown meat in oven at 450° for 20 minutes. Pour in the sauce. Bake covered at 300° for 4–5 hours or until meat begins to fall apart. Serves 50.

Recipes Thru Time

Heavenly Barbecue Sauce

This barbecue sauce is great for ribs and chicken. Also adds flavor to canned pork and beans.

1 cup ketchup	**½ teaspoon Ac'cent**
¼ cup lemon juice	**1 clove garlic**
2 tablespoons brown sugar	**¼ teaspoon cayenne pepper**
1 tablespoon soy sauce	**½ teaspoon pepper**
1 tablespoon horseradish	**¼ teaspoon oregano**
1 tablespoon grated onion	**¼ teaspoon Tabasco**
1 teaspoon salt	

Mix all ingredients together ahead of time so that spices are able to blend well. When doubling the recipe, do not fully increase the horseradish, salt, Tabasco, and cayenne, or sauce will be too hot.

No Green Gelatin Here!

Teriyaki Sauce

This has always been one of my favorite sauces. I use this to marinate meat dishes. Until the time I decided to write this recipe book, I had always made it with a pinch of this and a "glug, glug" of that. But writing down the recipe requires more precision. The following is a very good marinating sauce.

1 (10-ounce) bottle teriyaki sauce	**1 tablespoon liquid smoke**
1 (14-ounce) bottle hickory smoked barbecue sauce	**1 teaspoon Worcestershire sauce**

Blend all ingredients together. Pour over meat and let stand at least one hour. Use some of the mixture for moisture in cooking the meat. The flavor increases the longer it cooks, so test it often.

Let's Cook Dutch

Barbecued Beef Ribs

4–5 pounds beef ribs
1 teaspoon dry mustard
1 teaspoon onion powder
¼ teaspoon garlic powder
2 tablespoons soy sauce
1 tablespoon vinegar

1 cup ketchup
1 tablespoon Worcestershire
  sauce
2 tablespoons brown sugar
1 tablespoon molasses

Boil ribs for 40 minutes before baking in Dutch oven. This will reduce fat.

Mix remaining ingredients to make barbecue sauce. Place ribs in oven and bake at 375°, 10–14 coals under, 18–22 on lid for 40 minutes if raw, or 10 if boiled. Brush well with sauce and continue cooking for 15–20 minutes, brushing with sauce every few minutes.

Dutch Oven Delites

Sunday Dinner

1 (4- to 5-pound) chuck roast,
  frozen
8 carrots, peeled and cut into
  large chunks
10 potatoes, peeled and
  quartered

1 large onion, peeled and sliced
1 (10¾-ounce) can cream of
  mushroom soup

Make a liner out of heavy-duty aluminum foil so that you can wrap the dinner. Put roast in the middle of the foil-lined pan; put carrots on one end and potatoes on the other. Place onions on top and pour undiluted soup over the onions. Wrap foil loosely over food. Or use large roasting pan with cover. Bake at 325° for 4 hours.

Patty's Cakes and Things

Bar-B-Que Beef Sandwiches

Because you will be using this for sandwiches, an economy cut of meat will be fine. They have a good flavor, and with a little extra cooking time, will come out fine when they are cut up.

¼ cup vegetable oil or
  margarine
1 roast (¼-pound per sandwich)
Salt, pepper, and Ac'cent to
  taste

1 large bottle hickory-flavor
  barbecue sauce
1 onion, chopped

Use a 10- to 12-inch Dutch oven, depending on size of roast. Make your oven level over medium coals. Pour in oil. Brown roast on all sides, then add salt, pepper, and Ac'cent to taste. Cover, add heat to the top, and let simmer, checking every 15 minutes or so. Depending on the size and shape of the roast, in about an hour it should be ready for you to take the meat off the bone, if any, pulling in strips. Remove all excess fat. While doing this, let the juice from the roast simmer slowly. Using a spoon, dip out any extra grease, then pour in the barbecue sauce and onion to thicken the juice that was in the oven. It may take the whole bottle of sauce.

You can now add the meat you have prepared to the flavorful mixture of juice and sauce. Simmer for about 30 minutes to let the meat absorb the flavor. I think it makes the best barbecue sandwiches. I hope you agree.

Let's Cook Dutch

Capitol Reef National Park protects a 100-mile-long bulge in the earth's crust. This bulge was created over millions of years from an ancient underground fault. Popular geologic formations created by the bulge include Capitol Dome, Hickman Bridge, and Cathedral Valley. Designated a national monument in 1937 and a national park in 1971, the park is located ten miles east of the town of Torrey, and thirty-seven miles west of the town of Hanksville.

Dutch Oven Pot Roast with Sour Cream and Mushroom Gravy

3 teaspoons bacon grease or
  vegetable oil
1 (3- to 4-pound) roast beef
1 beef bouillon cube
1 cup boiling water
4 teaspoons ketchup
1 teaspoon Worcestershire
  sauce

1 small onion, chopped
½ clove garlic, minced
2 teaspoons salt
½ teaspoon pepper
1 teaspoon celery salt
4 teaspoons flour
1 (4-ounce) can mushrooms
1 cup sour cream

In a Dutch oven on top of the stove, put bacon grease or vegetable oil. Brown roast on all sides. Dissolve bouillon cube in boiling water. Add to roast. Combine ketchup, Worcestershire sauce, chopped onion, garlic, salt, pepper, and celery salt. Stir well and add to roast. Put the lid on and cook in the oven at 250° for 2–2½ hours, until meat is tender. Remove from oven.

Take meat from Dutch oven. Blend flour into liquid to make gravy. Add mushrooms and stir in the sour cream. Slice beef and serve with gravy over it. Good eating!

If camping, do it the same way, just don't let the fire get too hot. Also, if cooking a big roast for a lot of people, you will need to increase the ingredients to cover the extra people. Judge for yourself what amount you will need. Cook extra if you have big eaters. They will all want second helpings.

Doin' Dutch Oven: Inside and Out

Cola Roast

1 (3-pound) beef roast	**2 (12-ounce) cans cola (diet cola**
1 envelope dry onion soup mix	**cannot be substituted)**

Place roast in greased 4- to 5-quart slow cooker. Sprinkle with soup mix. Pour cola over all. Cover and cook on LOW heat 7–8 hours. Makes 4–6 servings.

101 Things To Do With a Slow Cooker

Grandma's Pot Roast

3–4 pounds beef chuck roast	**2 medium onions, cut into**
2 cloves garlic, minced	**wedges**
Salt and pepper to taste	**8 potatoes, cut into wedges**
Oil	**2 stalks celery, cut into 2-inch**
1 cup water	**pieces**
1 bay leaf	**6 carrots, cut into 2-inch pieces**

Rub the outside of roast with garlic and season with salt and pepper. Brown roast in large frying pan with a small amount of oil until well browned. Place roast in roasting pan. Add water and bay leaf to frying pan that the meat was browned in and cook until water boils. Pour water into roasting pan. Cover and roast at 325° for 35–40 minutes. Place onions, potatoes, celery, and carrots around the meat and cook until vegetables are done. Use drippings from meat and thicken with flour and water to make gravy. Spoon gravy over meat and vegetables.

Favorite Utah Pioneer Recipes

Perfect Prime Rib

12–15 large cloves garlic
1 sweet onion
½ stick butter
1 teaspoon salt
2 teaspoons black pepper
2 teaspoons white pepper

1 teaspoon cayenne pepper
1 tablespoon coarsely ground oregano
1 teaspoon coarsely ground thyme
1 prime rib roast (with rib bones)

Preheat oven to 300°. Finely chop garlic and onion. In large skillet, sauté garlic and onion in butter. Set aside. In medium bowl, combine all seasonings. Using a large carving knife, remove fat cap from roast, leaving it attached slightly at one end. Pour some of the onion and garlic mixture here, and also coat the rest of the roast with it. Then liberally coat the entire roast with seasonings, pressing into the meat with your fingers and palms. Replace the fat cap. Depending on the roast, you may want to tie it back together with string. Brown roast in a very hot skillet, 1–2 minutes per side. Place in open roasting pan and cook 35 minutes per pound for medium rare, more or less to taste.

Hint: The roast will continue to cook a bit after you remove it from the oven, so be careful of cooking time.

Pleasures from the Good Earth

Gabby's No-Peek Prime Ribber

The secret to this preparation is the method of roasting, as you will see.

**1 prime rib beef roast, 4–7 ribs
long (large or small end; small
end has least waste)**
Worcestershire sauce to taste
Fresh minced garlic to taste

Sweet Hungarian paprika
**Seasoned or freshly ground
pepper to taste**
Flour to coat the roast

The weight of this roast does not matter, as long as it is between 4 and 7 ribs long. Rub the Worcestershire, garlic, paprika, and pepper over the outside of the entire roast (bone side, too). Dust with flour, then set meat on roasting rack inside a roasting pan.

Bake in a preheated 500° oven for 5 minutes for each pound (you must know the exact weight of the roast) if you want rare meat, 5½ minutes per pound for a more medium to well-done roast. After this roasting period, turn the oven off, but don't you dare open the oven door! If fact, the oven door must not be opened for exactly 2 hours. Now, open it up, place the meat on a warmed platter, and carve away. Serves 6–12.

Oh, this is so good, especially if you have chosen a Certified Angus Beef roast.

Enjoy! Again and Again

The Seagull Monument located on Temple Square in Salt Lake City stands as a memorial to the flocks of California gulls that saved the crops of the early Saints in the Salt Lake Valley. During the summer of 1848, a flock of gulls descended upon and for two weeks ate the Rocky Mountain crickets that were destroying the crops. The Seagull Monument was designed and created by Mahonri M. Young, a grandson of Brigham Young. The monument was dedicated on October 1, 1913, by President Joseph F. Smith. The California gull, Larus californicus, was selected as the state bird of Utah by an act of the legislature in 1955.

Beef Stroganoff

1 cup chopped onion
2 cloves garlic, chopped
2 cups chopped fresh mushrooms,
  or 2 (8-ounce) cans
3 tablespoons butter or
  margarine, divided
1 pound sirloin or round steak

1 package dry onion soup mix
2 (10¾-ounce) cans cream of
  mushroom soup
½ cup ketchup
1 pint sour cream
Cooked noodles or rice

Brown onion, garlic, and mushrooms in 2 tablespoons butter or margarine. Take out of pan. Add 1 tablespoon butter or margarine to pan. Cut 1 pound sirloin or round steak in very thin strips. Brown well; season to taste. Add onion soup mix to the meat; add a little water. Mix in mushroom soup and onion mixture, and simmer for one hour, then add ketchup. Pour in the sour cream just before ready to serve. Serve over cooked noodles or rice. Serve 6.

Dude Food

Stroganoff

½–1 pound hamburger
1 onion, chopped, or dry onion
  soup mix
1 (10¾-ounce) can cream of
  mushroom soup

2 cups water
2 cups uncooked noodles
1 cup sour cream

Cook hamburger until browned. Add onion or onion soup mix, mushroom soup, and water. Bring to a boil and add the noodles. Reduce heat to low and let simmer for 10–15 minutes. Stir in sour cream and serve immediately. Serves 2–4.

Quick & Easy Cooking

Beef Parmesan

3 pounds lean beef (½–¾
  inches thick)
¼ cup evaporated milk
Fine bread crumbs, about 1 cup
2 tablespoons bacon drippings,
  more if needed
1 medium onion, diced
¾ pound mozzarella cheese
½ cup grated Parmesan cheese,
  divided

½ teaspoon salt, or to taste
¼ teaspoon freshly ground
  pepper
¼ teaspoon thyme
½ teaspoon garlic powder
1 quart tomato preserves, or 2
  (8-ounce) cans tomato sauce
  and 1 (16-ounce) can stewed
  tomatoes

Cut meat into serving-size pieces. Pound to tenderize. Dip meat in evaporated milk, then coat with bread crumbs. Brown in hot bacon drippings. Remove meat and sauté onions in drippings. Remove onions, and arrange meat in one layer in a 14-inch Dutch oven. Place a slice of mozzarella cheese on each piece of meat. Sprinkle ½ of the Parmesan cheese over the top.

In a separate bowl, combine the rest of the ingredients except remaining Parmesan cheese. Pour over meat. Sprinkle remaining Parmesan cheese over the top. You may wish to add one tablespoon chopped parsley. Cook with 10 on bottom, 18 coals on top for 45 minutes, or until meat is tender.

Friends of Old Deseret Dutch Oven Cookbook

Sirloin Tips of Beef

1–1½ pounds sirloin tips
1½ teaspoons salt
1 teaspoon pepper
1 teaspoon garlic powder
Flour (½ cup or so)
2–3 tablespoons shortening

1 cup chopped onions
1 cup chopped celery
1 cup sliced carrots
1 cup cooked tomatoes
Water to cover
Cooked rice or noodles

Dredge meat in seasoned flour. Brown in shortening in 350° oven along with onions. Add celery, carrots, and tomatoes. Cover with water and cook 2 hours or until meat is tender. Serve over rice or noodles. Serves 6.

Dude Food

Bessie Steaks & Gravy

4 bacon strips, ¼ inch sliced
4 cloves garlic, diced
¼ cup diced onion
6 (6-ounce) boneless steaks
2 onions, cubed
2 cups fresh mushrooms

6 potatoes, cubed
3 (10¾-ounce) cans cream of
   mushroom soup
1 tablespoon pepper
½ tablespoon seasoned salt
½ tablespoon garlic powder

With 8 coals on bottom and 10 on top of 12-inch Dutch oven, cook bacon. Add garlic and diced onion. Sauté for 4 minutes. Add steaks and lightly brown on each side. Add cubed onions, mushrooms, and potatoes on top of steaks. Add soup and seasonings. Mix together. Cook with 10 coals on bottom and 14 on top for 1 hour.

A Complete Guide to Dutch Oven Cooking

Blackberry-Glazed Pepper Steaks

GLAZE:

¼ cup red wine vinegar   ½ cup blackberry jam

Heat vinegar and jam in small saucepan over medium heat. Stir well until jam is melted. Remove from heat.

1 tablespoon freshly ground   4 (8- to 10-ounce) boneless
  pepper   steaks
                                      Fresh blackberries for garnish

Sprinkle pepper on steaks and grill over medium heat until done to your preference. Spread with Glaze and garnish with fresh berries.

All That Jam

Pepper Steak

1 pound lean beef steak (round   1 cup sliced onion
  or sirloin)   1 green pepper, sliced
2–3 teaspoons paprika   ½ cup sliced celery
1 clove garlic, crushed   ½ cup sliced mushrooms
1 small slice fresh gingerroot   ¼ cup water
  (optional)   2 tablespoons cornstarch
1 tablespoon plus ¼ cup soy   1 large fresh tomato, cut in
  sauce, divided   wedges
2 tablespoons butter   Cooked rice
1½ cups beef broth

Slice beef very thin and marinate with mixture of paprika, garlic, gingerroot, and 1 tablespoon soy sauce for ½–1 hour. Brown meat in butter in large skillet. Add broth and simmer for 30 minutes. Lightly stir-fry vegetables in small amount of hot oil and add to beef.

Blend ¼ cup soy sauce, water, and cornstarch. Add to meat mixture and simmer until thick and clear. Add fresh tomato wedges. Heat through. Serve over rice.

Favorite Recipes from Utah Farm Bureau Women

Ginger-Honey Flank Steak

2 tablespoons butter, softened
½ cup honey
¼ cup stone-ground mustard
½ teaspoon powdered ginger

⅛ teaspoon cayenne pepper
1 (2-pound) flank steak or London broil
Salt and black pepper

Preheat oven to broil. Make a thick paste of the butter, honey, mustard, ginger, and cayenne pepper. Rub top of steak with half of seasoning paste. Broil 5 minutes for medium rare, or longer, depending on your taste. Turn steak and top with remaining mixture. Add salt and pepper to taste; broil 5 minutes or longer, depending on your preference. Slice across the grain. Serve cold or at room temperature.

How to Win a Cowboy's Heart

Hobo Dinner

18-inch-wide heavy-duty aluminum foil
2 carrots, peeled and thinly sliced
2 medium potatoes, peeled and thinly sliced

2 onions, sliced
1 pound ground beef, shaped into 4 patties
1 teaspoon salt
½ teaspoon pepper

Cut 4 squares of foil. Divide vegetables into 4 equal portions. Layer with half the carrots, potatoes, and onions. Then add the ground beef and layer on the remaining carrots, potatoes, and onions. Season with salt and pepper. Seal tightly, and cook on a bed of hot coals for 15 minutes on each side. Serves 4.

Note: Chicken breast fillets or fish fillets may be substituted for ground beef patties.

Roughing It Easy at Girls Camp

Beef Pot Pie

½ pound bacon
1½ pounds stew meat
1 onion, diced
½ pound carrots, sliced
1 pound peas (frozen may be used)
5–6 medium potatoes, cubed
4 stalks celery, sliced

1 cup water
2–3 drops Tabasco sauce
2 beef bouillon cubes
⅓ cup soy sauce
2 tablespoons Worcestershire sauce
Cornstarch to thicken

In Dutch oven, fry bacon, add meat and onion, and brown well. Add remaining ingredients, except cornstarch. Simmer until tender. Thicken with cornstarch and remove to bowl. Put one pie crust in bottom of oven, add filling, and top with remaining crust. Bake at 350° for 35–45 minutes. Use 6–9 coals on bottom, 12–16 on top. Serves 8–12.

CORNMEAL PIE CRUST:

2¼ cups flour
¾ cup yellow cornmeal
½ teaspoon salt
¾ cup cold butter or margarine, cut into small pieces

2 large eggs
3–4 tablespoons cold water
1 egg white for glaze

Mix flour, cornmeal, and salt. Cut in butter with pastry cutter. Beat eggs with 3 tablespoons water and add to flour mixture until it sticks together. Add more water if needed. Divide into 2 balls, ⅔ and ⅓. Cool or refrigerate for 30 minutes. Pat ⅔ into bottom and sides of Dutch oven and add filling. Roll out remaining ball to cover top. Cut 2–3 slits in top crust. Brush with egg white. Bake at 350° for 35–45 minutes.

Dutch Oven Gold

Hungarian Goulash

2 pounds beef for stew, cut into 1-inch cubes
1 medium onion, sliced
1 small clove garlic, finely chopped, or ⅛ teaspoon instant minced garlic
¼ cup shortening
1½ cups water
¾ cup ketchup
2 tablespoons Worcestershire sauce
1 tablespoon packed brown sugar
2 teaspoons salt
2 teaspoons paprika
½ teaspoon dry mustard
Dash cayenne red pepper
¼ cup cold water
2 tablespoons flour
Cooked noodles

In a 10-inch Dutch oven, cook and stir beef, onion, and garlic in shortening until beef is browned. Drain off any excess grease. Stir in 1½ cups water, ketchup, Worcestershire sauce, brown sugar, salt, paprika, mustard, and red pepper. Heat to boiling; reduce heat. Cover and simmer until beef is tender, 2–2½ hours.

Shake ¼ cup cold water and the flour in tightly covered container; stir gradually into beef mixture. Heat to boiling, stirring constantly. Boil and stir 1 minute. Serve over hot noodles. Makes 6–8 servings.

Dutch Oven Secrets

Aunt Phoebe's Goulash

This is one of my dad's favorite meals. "There's nothing better than a bowl of hot goulash on a cold day."

1 cup cooked elbow noodles	1 tablespoon Worcestershire
1 pound ground beef	sauce
1 onion, diced	1 tablespoon mustard
1 quart stewed tomatoes	Salt and pepper to taste
1 quart tomato juice	1 cup grated cheese

Boil noodles in 3 cups water until tender; do not drain. In separate pan, brown ground beef and onion. Stir together tomatoes and juice, Worcestershire sauce, mustard, salt and pepper, and bring to a boil. Add meat and noodles and simmer for 5 minutes. Stir in cheese. Serves 6.

The Cowboy Chuck Wagon Cookbook

Dinner in a Pumpkin

2 tablespoons oil	2 teaspoons oregano
2 pounds hamburger	2 teaspoons minced garlic
½ cup chopped ham	1 teaspoon vinegar
2½ teaspoons salt	⅓ cup chopped green olives
1 teaspoon pepper	1 (8-ounce) can tomato sauce
2½ tablespoons diced onion	½ cup cooked rice
1 green pepper, chopped	1 (10-inch) pumpkin

Combine all ingredients except pumpkin and cook in large fry pan until tender. Cut lid off pumpkin and clean out. Place meat mixture inside pumpkin. Place on a cookie sheet and bake for one hour. Serve the meal from the pumpkin. Scooping out some of the baked pumpkin gives you a vegetable with your meal.

Log Cabin Holidays and Traditions

Campfire Beef Skillet Supper

2 pounds hamburger
1 medium onion, diced
4 tablespoons steak sauce or
  Worcestershire
2 (10-ounce) packages frozen
  green beans

2 (10¾-ounce) cans cream of
  celery soup
2 (4-ounce) cans mushroom
  pieces, drained
Garlic croutons or crushed Ritz
  Crackers

In a 10- or 12-inch skillet or a 12-inch Dutch oven which has been warmed and lightly greased, fry hamburger and diced onion. When fully cooked, drain off excess grease and add sauce of your choice. Add green beans, soup, and mushrooms. Stir enough to mix. Heat to a simmering boil; cover for 10 minutes. Sprinkle with croutons or crushed crackers just before serving.

Log Cabin Campfire Cookn'

Sloppy Joe Biscuit Bake

1 medium onion, chopped
2 pounds lean ground beef
2 (1.3-ounce) packages Sloppy
  Joe seasoning mix

2 (6-ounce) cans tomato paste
2 cups water
1 (16-ounce) package prepared
  refrigerator biscuits

Heat a 12-inch Dutch oven over 9 hot coals. Brown onion and ground beef. Add seasoning mix, tomato paste, and water, stirring well, and bring to a boil. Separate individual biscuits and place on top of the meat mixture. Cover with Dutch oven lid and place 15 hot coals on top. Cook, covered, for 15–20 minutes, or until biscuits are browned and cooked through.

Or at home, preheat oven to 350°. In a large skillet, brown onion and ground beef; pour off drippings and add seasoning mix, tomato paste, and water, stirring well; bring to a boil. Transfer mixture to an oven-safe dish if the handle of your skillet is not oven-safe. Separate individual biscuits and place on top of meat mixture. Bake in preheated oven 15 minutes, until biscuits are browned and cooked through. Serves 4–6.

Recipes for Roughing It Easy

Tamale Casserole

1 pound lean ground beef
1 medium onion, chopped
Salt, pepper, garlic, and onion
　salt to taste
½–1 (4-ounce) can green
　chiles
8 prepared tamales

2 cans chili con carne
1 small can sliced olives
1 cup shredded cheese
Shredded lettuce
Chopped tomatoes
Salsa
Sour cream

Brown hamburger and onion; drain. Add salt, pepper, garlic, and onion salt to taste. Add green chiles. Cut tamales lengthwise; line the bottom of oblong cake pan that has been lightly greased. Pour hamburger mixture over tamales. Spoon chili con carne over mixture. Put olives and cheese on top. Bake at 375° for 30 minutes. Add lettuce and tomatoes on top. Serve with salsa and sour cream.

Ladies' Literary Club Cookbook

Tamale Pie

2 cups quick hominy grits
4 cups boiling salted water
1 small onion, diced
1 small bell pepper, diced
1 pound ground beef

Salt to taste
1 teaspoon chili powder
3 (8-ounce) cans tomato sauce
1 (4-ounce) can sliced olives

Cook hominy grits in boiling water until a thick mush. Spread half the grits over the bottom of a greased casserole dish. Sauté onion and pepper. Add meat, salt, and chili powder; cook until almost done. Add tomato sauce; pour onto grits. Top with remaining grits. Dot with olives. Bake at 350° for about one hour.

Family Favorites from the Heart

Taco Pie

2 pounds ground beef
¾ cup chopped onion
1 (1¼-ounce) package taco
　seasoning mix, divided
1 (16-ounce) can refried beans
2 tablespoons brown sugar
1 teaspoon soy sauce
1 teaspoon Worcestershire
　sauce
⅓ cup ketchup
1 teaspoon vinegar

½ teaspoon dry mustard
½ cup margarine or butter
2 cups milk
2¾ cups instant mashed potato
　flakes
1 cup shredded sharp Cheddar
　cheese
1½ cups shredded lettuce
Dairy sour cream
1 medium tomato, chopped
1 small can chopped olives

In bottom of a 12-inch Dutch oven, brown ground beef and onion. Drain fat. Stir in all but 2 tablespoons taco mix, beans, brown sugar, soy sauce, Worcestershire sauce, ketchup, vinegar, and dry mustard. Cook and stir until bubbly. Remove from pan. Set aside.

Melt margarine in bottom of oven. Add milk and remaining 2 tablespoons taco mix. Remove from heat and stir in potato flakes. Press this mixture into bottom of Dutch oven. Place taco filling inside crust. Bake at 350° for 30–35 minutes (3–5 coals on bottom, 16–20 coals on top). When baking is done, top with cheese, lettuce, sour cream, tomatoes, and olives. Serve.

Dutch Oven Gold

Utah native Russell Lowell Maughan thrilled crowds and drew national headlines when he made the first coast-to-coast airplane flight in a day. At 3:59 a.m., June 23, 1924, he took off from Mitchell Field in New York in a Curtiss Hawk and landed in San Francisco at 9:46 p.m.

Layered Mexican Hat

1 pound ground chuck
2 tablespoons chili powder
1 teaspoon ground cumin
½ teaspoon oregano
Dash of garlic powder
8 corn tortillas

1 large onion, chopped
1 large can chopped green
  chiles
12 ounces grated Cheddar
  cheese
Picante sauce

Brown beef in skillet. Mix chili powder, cumin, oregano, and garlic powder with beef. Soften tortillas in microwave (about 20–25 seconds). In deep, greased casserole dish, begin with one tortilla. Top with portions of beef, onion, green chiles, cheese, and picante sauce. Continue stacking in layers as suggested. Top the last tortilla with cheese and a bit of picante sauce.

Bake in 350° oven for 20–25 minutes, or until cheese is bubbly. Cut into pie-shaped pieces for serving.

Pleasures from the Good Earth

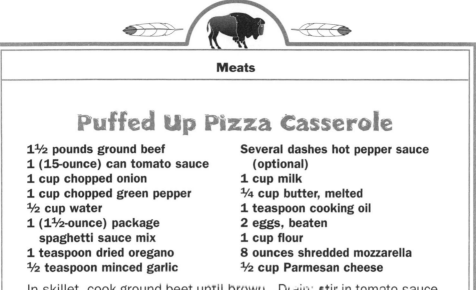

Puffed Up Pizza Casserole

1½ pounds ground beef
1 (15-ounce) can tomato sauce
1 cup chopped onion
1 cup chopped green pepper
½ cup water
1 (1½-ounce) package
  spaghetti sauce mix
1 teaspoon dried oregano
½ teaspoon minced garlic
Several dashes hot pepper sauce
  (optional)
1 cup milk
¼ cup butter, melted
1 teaspoon cooking oil
2 eggs, beaten
1 cup flour
8 ounces shredded mozzarella
½ cup Parmesan cheese

In skillet, cook ground beef until brown. Drain; stir in tomato sauce, onion, green pepper, water, spaghetti sauce mix, oregano, minced garlic, and hot sauce. Reduce heat, cover, and let simmer 10 minutes.

Meanwhile, in mixing bowl, beat milk, melted butter, oil, and eggs for 1 minute on medium speed. Add flour and beat 2 more minutes. Batter will be thin. Turn meat mixture into 9x13x2-inch baking pan and add flour mixture; sprinkle with mozzarella and Parmesan cheese. Bake at 400° for 30 minutes or until puffed and golden. Let stand 10 minutes. Makes 10 servings.

Favorite Recipes from Utah Farm Bureau Women

Onion Meatballs

2 (18-ounce) packages frozen
  cooked meatballs
1 (12-ounce) jar beef gravy
1 envelope dry onion soup mix

Combine all ingredients in greased 3½- to 4-quart slow cooker. Cook on LOW heat 3–4 hours. Meatballs can be served on a platter with toothpicks as appetizers, or on toasted hoagies with provolone cheese as sandwiches. Makes 4–6 servings.

101 Things To Do With a Slow Cooker

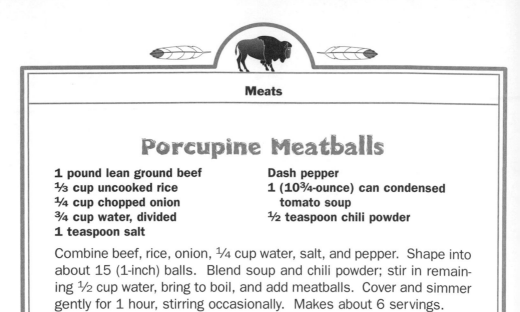

Porcupine Meatballs

1 pound lean ground beef
⅓ cup uncooked rice
¼ cup chopped onion
¾ cup water, divided
1 teaspoon salt

Dash pepper
1 (10¾-ounce) can condensed
   tomato soup
½ teaspoon chili powder

Combine beef, rice, onion, ¼ cup water, salt, and pepper. Shape into about 15 (1-inch) balls. Blend soup and chili powder; stir in remaining ½ cup water, bring to boil, and add meatballs. Cover and simmer gently for 1 hour, stirring occasionally. Makes about 6 servings.

A Century of Mormon Cookery, Volume 1

Meat Loaf in an Onion

4 large onions, peeled and halved
1 pound lean ground beef
1 egg
¼ cup cracker crumbs

¼ cup tomato sauce
½ teaspoon salt
⅛ teaspoon pepper
½ teaspoon dry mustard

Cut off root at the bottom end of the onion so that removal of the center is easy. Cut onions in half horizontally and remove center part of onion, leaving a ¾-inch thick shell. The removed center of the onion can be diced and combined with ingredients or used later. In a 1-gallon plastic zipper bag, combine ground beef, egg, cracker crumbs, tomato sauce, salt, pepper, and dry mustard, and mix by squeezing. Divide meat mixture into 4 portions and roll into balls. Place in the center of the 4 onion halves. Put onions back together. Wrap each onion in foil. Cook over a bed of hot coals for 15–20 minutes per side or in 350° oven for 45–50 minutes, or until ground beef and onions are cooked. Serves 4 as lunch or dinner.

Recipes for Roughing It Easy

Linda Thomas' Spaghetti Italian Sauce

1 pound lean ground hamburger
3 links hot Italian sausage
1 small onion, diced
1 tablespoon red wine vinegar
2 tablespoons oregano
1 tablespoon parsley flakes
2 tablespoons sugar
2 tablespoons fresh minced
  garlic

1 (14½-ounce) can Italian stewed
  tomatoes
1 (15-ounce) can tomato sauce
1 jar Ragu Garden Style Sauce
1 (6-ounce) can tomato paste
1 pound fresh mushrooms,
  sliced

Cook hamburger and sausage; drain excess grease. Add onion, vinegar, and spices; mix well. In separate large pot, combine stewed tomatoes, tomato sauce, Ragu, tomato paste, and mushrooms. Add meat mixture and simmer for several hours. The longer it simmers, the better it is.

Tasteful Treasures Cookbook

German Hamburgers

2–3 pounds lean hamburger
½ cup finely chopped onion
½ cup finely chopped green
  pepper
½ sleeve saltine crackers
Salt, pepper, and garlic salt to
  taste

1 large egg
½ cup water
2 (10¾-ounce) cans tomato
  soup

In large bowl, combine hamburger, onion, green pepper, crackers, salt, pepper, garlic salt, and egg. Form into small hamburger shapes, and brown on both sides in Dutch oven or large skillet; remove from pan. Add water and tomato soup to pan; return patties to soup mixture and cover. Simmer, covered, until patties are completely cooked through, usually 60–90 minutes.

Pleasures from the Good Earth

Roasted Leg of Lamb with Raspberry Glaze

1 (5- to 6-pound) leg of lamb
2 cloves garlic, slivered
⅓ cup seedless red raspberry
  jam (reserve 2 tablespoons for
  sauce)
3 tablespoons dry white wine

2 teaspoons Dijon mustard
¼ teaspoon rosemary leaves
¼ teaspoon crushed black
  pepper
1 cup beef broth
1 tablespoon cornstarch

Using the tip of a knife, make small slits evenly over leg of lamb and insert garlic slivers into each. In small bowl, mix together jam, wine, mustard, rosemary leaves, and pepper. Brush lamb with ¼ cup sauce mixture and place fat-side-up in roasting pan. Bake at 350° for 20–25 minutes per pound for medium rare (160° internal temperature). For more well-done meat, add 5 minutes per pound. Pour remaining sauce over lamb during last 40 minutes of cooking time. Remove lamb to warm platter and let stand 15 minutes.

Meanwhile, pour lamb drippings into saucepan. Remove excess grease. Mix broth, cornstarch, and reserved 2 tablespoons red raspberry jam and whisk into drippings. Cook over medium heat, continuing to whisk until sauce thickens. Serve gravy hot with sliced lamb. Makes 6–8 servings.

Favorite Recipes from Utah Farm Bureau Women

Poultry

PHOTO © FRANK JENSEN, STATE OF UTAH DIVISION OF TRAVEL DEVELOPMENT.

A golden spike marked the May 10, 1869, completion of the transcontinental railroad between the Central Pacific and Union Pacific Railroads. The event is re-enacted every year at the site now designated Golden Spike National Historic Site, located about thirty-two miles west of Brigham City.

Conestoga Chicken

12 slices bacon (6 full slices,
  6 quartered)
6 skinless, boneless chicken
  breasts
2 garlic cloves, diced
1 stick butter
1 (16-ounce) can chicken broth
2 cups long-grain brown rice
2 cups fresh mushrooms

2 tablespoons sage
½ tablespoon pepper
½ tablespoon onion powder
1 tablespoon Worcestershire
  sauce
2 cups fresh broccoli florets
2 (10¾-ounce) cans cream of
  mushroom soup

With 12 coals on bottom and 12 coals on top, cook bacon in 12-inch Dutch oven. Remove whole slices; drain grease, leaving quartered bacon in oven.

Pound chicken slightly until thin and workable to roll. Place one slice of bacon on each breast. Roll, securing with toothpick. Add garlic and butter to quartered bacon. Sauté until butter is melted; add chicken rolls, and brown both sides. Remove chicken and set aside.

Add chicken broth, rice, mushrooms, sage, pepper, onion powder, and Worcestershire sauce to oven. Stir lightly to blend together. Place chicken on top of rice. Place broccoli florets around and in between chicken. Place dollops of cream of mushroom soup around oven. Cover and let cook for 30–45 minutes until done.

A Complete Guide to Dutch Oven Cooking

Martha Maria Hughes Cannon was elected Utah State Senator on November 3, 1896, becoming the first woman ever elected to the United States Senate.

Please Everyone Chicken

1 pound bacon, cut into ¼-inch
   strips
¼ cup very small diced celery
2 cups sliced fresh mushrooms
½ cup diced onion
2 teaspoons seasoned salt
½ teaspoon onion powder
½ tablespoon pepper
½ teaspoon mustard powder

8 skinless, boneless chicken
   breasts
3 (10¾-ounce) cans cream of
   chicken soup
1 (10¾-ounce) can cream of
   mushroom soup
12 potatoes, sliced ¼ inch thin
3 cups sour cream
6 ounces stuffing (optional)

With 12 coals on bottom and 12 on top, cook bacon in 12-inch Dutch oven. Drain grease. Add celery, mushrooms, and onion. Sauté until onion is transparent. Add all seasonings. Place chicken in oven and cook until chicken becomes white. Add soups, potatoes, and sour cream. Stir ingredients together. Cook with 12 coals on bottom and 12 on top for about 30–40 minutes. About 15 minutes before serving, add the dry stuffing to the top, if desired, and lightly mix into soup mixture. Cover until stuffing is ready.

A Complete Guide to Dutch Oven Cooking

Door Slammer Chicken

2 (8-ounce) bottles Russian
   dressing
1 (12-ounce) bottle apricot jam

1 package instant onion soup
   mix
8 chicken breasts, skinless

Mix dressing, jam, and soup mix and pour over chicken. Bake in 12-inch Dutch oven at 350° oven for about 1½ hours. For 350° oven, use 10–12 briquettes on bottom and 15–16 on top. Replenish your briquettes as needed to maintain the 350° temperature.

Log Cabin Dutch Oven

Baked Pignoli Chicken

3 tablespoons butter and olive oil combined

6 chicken breasts, preferably boned and skinned

1 cup seasoned flour (flour, paprika, garlic powder, salt and pepper)

½ pound fresh mushrooms, sliced

1 can cream of mushroom soup (light)

½ cup dry white wine

½ cup chicken broth

2 tablespoons finely chopped fresh parsley

¼ teaspoon dried thyme

¼ cup toasted pignoli (pine) nuts

Sweet Hungarian paprika

6 cups cooked long-grain rice (or brown rice, if desired)

In a large fry pan, heat butter and oil combination over medium-high heat. Dredge each breast in seasoned flour mixture and place in the hot pan. Brown the breasts on each side, then remove and place in a sprayed shallow baking dish, skinned side up.

In the same skillet, brown the mushrooms in the pan drippings (add more butter, if too dry). Spoon the browned mushrooms over the breasts. Add the soup to the same pan, then whisk in the wine, broth, parsley, and thyme, and heat through. Sprinkle the pignoli nuts and paprika over the mushrooms and chicken. Spoon the sauce over all. Cover and bake in a preheated 350° oven for 20 minutes, then uncover and bake an additional 20–25 minutes. Serve over rice. Serves 6.

Enjoy! Again and Again

Chicken alla Cucina

2 tablespoons butter
1 tablespoon olive oil
1 medium onion, diced
1 tablespoon chopped garlic
1½ pounds boneless, skinless chicken breasts, cut into 1-inch pieces
2 tablespoons flour
1 (15-ounce) can artichoke hearts, drained and coarsely chopped

2 cups chicken broth
1 cup dry white wine
½ cup julienne-cut sun-dried tomatoes
1 teaspoon dried oregano
1 teaspoon dried basil
1 teaspoon salt
½ teaspoon ground black pepper

In a large skillet, heat butter and olive oil. Add onion; sauté for at least 2–3 minutes or until softened. Add garlic and chicken pieces. Sauté until chicken is cooked through. Stir in flour until incorporated in the chicken pieces. Add artichokes, chicken broth, white wine, sun-dried tomatoes, oregano, basil, salt, and pepper. Cover; simmer for 10 minutes, stirring often. Taste for seasoning. Serve over steamed rice, polenta, or orzo pasta. Serves 4–6.

Savor the Memories

Creamy Italian Chicken

4 frozen boneless, skinless chicken breasts
1 envelope dry Italian salad dressing mix

1 (10¾-ounce) can condensed cream of chicken soup

Combine all ingredients in greased 3½- to 4-quart slow cooker. Cover and cook on HIGH heat 6–8 hours or on LOW heat 10–12 hours. Makes 4 servings.

101 Things To Do With a Slow Cooker

Munsterrela Chicken Breast

8 boneless, skinless chicken
  breasts
3 eggs, beaten
2 cups bread crumbs
½ pound fresh, sliced
  mushrooms

½ pound Muenster cheese,
  grated
½ pound mozzarella cheese,
  grated
1 cup chicken broth

Dip chicken breasts in beaten eggs, then roll in bread crumbs. Brown in buttered skillet. Place in a 14-inch Dutch oven; top with mushrooms and grated cheeses. Pour broth over chicken and bake for 45 minutes to 1 hour or until golden brown. Use 10–12 briquettes on bottom and 10–12 on top. Serves 8.

Dutch Oven and Outdoor Cooking, Book Two: Homespun Edition

Grilled Chicken Teriyaki and Rice

1 (20-ounce) can pineapple
  chunks
½ cup soy sauce
1 tablespoon molasses
2 tablespoons brown sugar
¼ cup oil
3 tablespoons cider vinegar

1 teaspoon garlic powder
6 chicken breasts, boned and
  skinned
1 green bell pepper, cut into
  julienne strips
Cooked rice

Drain pineapple chunks and reserve liquid. Combine pineapple juice with soy sauce, molasses, brown sugar, oil, vinegar, and garlic powder. Marinate chicken breasts in the refrigerator in this mixture for at least 6–8 hours.

Drain liquid; grill chicken on barbecue. Slice into strips; add pineapple chunks and green peppers. Serve over cooked rice. Makes 6 servings.

Lion House Entertaining

Chicken Cordon Bleu with Cheese Sauce

CHEESE SAUCE:

¼ cup flour
⅓ cup mild Cheddar cheese
Dash of white pepper
½ can cream of chicken soup

½ teaspoon chicken bouillon
¾ cup milk
¾ teaspoon Dijon mustard

Combine all ingredients. Stir well. Heat until thickened, continuing to stir.

CHICKEN CORDON BLEU:

5 boneless, skinless chicken
  breasts
5 slices Swiss cheese

5 thin slices ham
¼ cup margarine, melted
2 cups crushed cornflakes

Pound out chicken breasts with meat hammer until breasts are all about the same thickness. Place about one tablespoon Cheese Sauce inside of chicken, then Swiss cheese and ham. Roll with small end inside; secure with toothpicks. Roll in melted margarine, then cornflakes. Cook at 350° in a 12-inch Dutch oven for about 45–55 minutes. Serve with sauce on the side or over the top.

Friends of Old Deseret Dutch Oven Cookbook

Kennecott Copper Mine, the world's largest man-made excavation and first open-pit mine, is located twenty-eight miles southwest of Salt Lake City. The mine is two and one-half miles across, and three-quarters-mile deep—so big, it can be seen from space shuttles in outer space. In open-pit mining, ore is mined from the surface using large mechanical shovels to remove the surface rock and dig out the ore. Kennecott is the second-largest copper producer in the United States—providing approximately fifteen percent of the country's copper needs. Copper is Utah's state mineral.

Chicken Breasts in Sauce

8 boneless, skinless chicken
  breasts
8 thick slices Swiss cheese
¼ cup water

1 (10¾-ounce) can cream of
  chicken soup
½ cup butter, melted
2 cups stuffing mix

Arrange chicken in the bottom of a Dutch oven. Put a slice of cheese on top of each breast. Mix water and soup together well and pour over the chicken. Drizzle with butter and sprinkle stuffing mix on top. Bake about 350° for about one hour, or until tender.

Dutch Oven and Outdoor Cooking, Y2K Edition

Ken's Apricot Almond Chicken

This is a delicious recipe.

1 pound bacon, ¼ inch sliced
2 cups diced onions
3 cloves garlic, diced
6–8 skinless, boneless chicken
  breasts
1 teaspoon mustard powder
1 (48-ounce) jar apricot or orange
  marmalade
1 (6-ounce) container frozen
  orange juice concentrate

1 (6-ounce) package sliced
  almonds
2 tablespoons Worcestershire
  sauce (optional)
2 tablespoons onion powder
1 tablespoon garlic powder
Pinch of chili powder

With 12 coals on bottom and 12 on top of 12-inch Dutch oven, cook bacon. Remove grease and sauté onions and garlic for 3 minutes. Add chicken and brown. Add all other ingredients, stirring from the bottom to mix bacon, garlic, and onion. Cover and cook until done. Stir occasionally to keep ingredients mixed. Cook for approximately 30 minutes.

A Complete Guide to Dutch Oven Cooking

Gnocchi with Chicken and Portobellos

2 boneless, skinless chicken
 breast halves
2 garlic cloves, crushed
1 teaspoon lemon pepper
¼ cup plus 1 tablespoon basil
 oil*, divided
4 pearl or Roma tomatoes,
 quartered

¼ pound asparagus tips
¼ cup chopped basil
1 tablespoon sherry vinegar
1 pound gnocchi**
2 portobello mushrooms (about 6
 ounces total)
Shaved Parmesan

In a shallow dish, rub chicken with crushed garlic, lemon pepper, and ¼ cup basil oil, and let marinate chilled for 20 minutes.

Toss tomatoes, asparagus, and basil with sherry vinegar and 1 tablespoon basil oil in a glass bowl and set aside, covered with plastic wrap at room temperature.

Bring a large pot of water to a gentle boil, and cook gnocchi until they float. Drain and drizzle with a little basil oil to prevent sticking. While gnocchi are cooking, heat a skillet over medium-high heat. Place chicken in pan, sear on both sides, then reduce heat to medium. Cut mushrooms into half-inch slices and brush with any chicken marinade that is left in the dish. Cook mushrooms alongside chicken until they are soft and browned, and until chicken is cooked through.

Remove chicken and mushrooms to a cutting board. Increase heat to high and sauté tomato and asparagus mixture for 5 minutes, or until asparagus is just tender to the bite. Toss tomato mixture with gnocchi and divide into large shallow bowls. Slice chicken breasts into half-inch slices, fan chicken and mushrooms over the gnocchi, and garnish with shaved Parmesan. Serves 2.

*Basil oil is available in special food stores, or better yet, make your own (put a few basil leaves in vegetable oil).

**Gnocchi (dumplings) can be found frozen or vacuum-packed in specialty food stores and some supermarkets.

Aromatherapy in the Kitchen

Baked Chicken and Rice

Chicken and Dutch ovens seem to go together. This is an easy, but tasty version.

1 cup uncooked rice
1 chicken
1 package dry onion soup mix
1 (15-ounce) can chicken broth

1 (10¾-ounce) can cream of
mushroom soup
Water

Pour rice into a 10-inch Dutch oven. Place cut-up chicken parts on top of rice. Sprinkle onion soup mix on top of the chicken. Dilute chicken broth and cream of mushroom soup with 1 soup can water. Pour this mixture over the chicken and bake with 5 coals on bottom and 10 coals on top for at least one hour.

World Championship Dutch Oven Cookbook

Dutch Oven French Dressing Chicken

1 frying chicken, or 12–15 legs
  and thighs
Oil
1 large bottle French dressing

1 package dry onion soup mix
1 medium-size jar apricot jam or
  orange marmalade

If using frying chicken, cut into serving-size pieces. Remove skin from chicken. In a 12-inch Dutch oven, add oil to bottom and a layer of chicken. Pour some French dressing over and sprinkle with some of the onion soup mix. Spread with part of the jam. Place another layer of chicken on top and repeat above process until oven is full. Indoors, cook, covered, at 300° for one hour, checking with fork for tenderness. If outdoors, use 6–8 briquettes on bottom and 16–18 on top. It will cook in about one hour, also. Use juice from chicken to pour over rice as a side dish.

Doin' Dutch Oven: Inside and Out

Nipponese Chicken

½ cup flour
½ teaspoon ginger
½ teaspoon nutmeg
Dash of salt and pepper
2 chickens, cut up and skinned
¼ cup butter
2 (8-ounce) cans chunk
   pineapple
2 (11-ounce) cans Mandarin
   oranges

⅔ cup soy sauce
2 tablespoons cornstarch
1 cup sugar
2 tablespoons vinegar
½ teaspoon garlic powder
2 tablespoons prepared mustard
2 medium onions, chopped
1 cup diced green pepper

Mix flour, ginger, nutmeg, and dash of salt and pepper. Flour chicken and fry in butter in hot Dutch oven until browned. Drain pineapple and oranges; reserve juices. Mix juices with soy sauce and cornstarch, then add sugar. Add vinegar, garlic powder, mustard, and chopped onions. Pour around chicken, stirring and basting 20–25 minutes, covered. Add diced green pepper, pineapple, and oranges. Cover and cook until chicken is tender.

Championship Dutch Oven Cookbook

Smothered Yardbird

1 cup flour
2 teaspoons poultry seasoning
½ teaspoon garlic powder, or to taste
½ teaspoon onion powder
1 frying chicken cut into 8 pieces
½ cup buttermilk
1 cup vegetable shortening or oil for frying

2–4 baking potatoes
2 carrots, peeled (optional)
1 onion, sliced thin and separated
1 (10¾-ounce) can cream of mushroom soup
1 (10¾-ounce) can cream of chicken soup
1 soup can water
Salt and pepper to taste

Preheat oven to 300°. Combine flour, poultry seasoning, garlic powder, and onion powder. Dip each chicken piece in buttermilk and coat well with flour mixture. Melt shortening over medium-high heat until hot and water sprinkled in the pan sizzles. Shake extra flour from chicken and fry 3–4 pieces at a time until lightly browned on all sides. Transfer pieces to a large baking pan (a chicken roaster is perfect).

Slice potatoes and carrots about ¼–½ inch thick and fry quickly in the same oil until outsides are crisp, but not cooked all the way through. Remove with slotted spoon and add to chicken in roaster. Pour out all but 2 tablespoons of the oil, add onion, and cook until just soft. Combine soups, water, and seasoning; add to pan and stir until mixed and warm. Pour soup and onion over chicken and vegetables. Bake for 2½–3 hours, until meat is tender and gravy is bubbling.

Note: You may choose to cover the chicken in the oven if it will be unattended for much of the cooking time or if the gravy starts to develop a tough surface. Cover for half of cooking time, or occasionally simply stir the meat down into the gravy.

How to Win a Cowboy's Heart

Dutch Oven Chicken Creole

2 eggs
1 cup milk
1 frying chicken, or pieces of
  your choice
1 cup flour
¼ cup bacon grease or
  vegetable oil

1 large onion, chopped
1 large green pepper, chopped
Garlic powder to taste
Salt and pepper to taste
1 (14½-ounce) can stewed
  tomatoes

Mix eggs with milk for batter. Cut chicken into serving pieces or use specific pieces. Dip pieces in batter, then in flour. When Dutch oven is hot, add bacon grease or vegetable oil and brown all the chicken as quickly as you can. Keep the Dutch oven on high until all the chicken is browned. Drain off extra grease.

Now place layers of chicken in Dutch oven alternately with layers of onion and pepper. Season with garlic powder and salt and pepper to taste. Repeat layers until all chicken, onion, and pepper are used. Pour tomatoes over all; check seasoning.

Indoors, bake at 325°–350° in your oven for 1–1½ hours. The more pieces you cook, the more time it will take, but you should be done in about 1½ hours. Outdoors, keep most of the heat on top as you are baking. It might take a little longer, but it should cook in 1½ hours, also. Keep an eye on it.

Doin' Dutch Oven: Inside and Out

Green Chicken Enchiladas

FILLING:

1 cup grated Cheddar cheese

2 cups grated Monterey Jack cheese

2 cups cubed, cooked chicken

½ medium onion, chopped

½ cup sliced black olives

1½ cups sour cream

2 tablespoons chopped parsley

¾ teaspoon freshly ground pepper

In a large bowl, mix together cheeses, chicken, onion, olives, sour cream, parsley, and pepper, and set aside.

SAUCE:

2 tablespoons butter

2 tablespoons all-purpose flour

½ cup milk

1½ cups chicken broth, divided

1 (10-ounce) package frozen spinach, cooked, drained, and coarsely chopped

⅔ cup sour cream

4 tablespoons chopped green chiles

½ medium onion, chopped

1 clove garlic, minced

¾ teaspoon cumin

In a sauté pan, heat butter over low heat. Add flour and cook for a few minutes, stirring constantly. Stir in milk and add ½ cup chicken broth. Bring to a boil. Boil for one minute, stirring constantly. Add remaining 1 cup chicken broth; cook and stir until hot and thickened; add spinach, sour cream, green chiles, onion, garlic, and cumin.

1 (18-ounce) package flour tortillas

Additional shredded cheese for garnish

Lime and tomato slices for garnish

Dip each tortilla into Sauce, coating both sides. Spoon about ¼ cup Filling onto each tortilla and roll up. Place seam-side-down in an ungreased 9x13-inch baking dish. Pour remaining sauce over enchiladas and bake uncovered at 350° for about 20 minutes or until bubbly. Garnish with shredded cheese and lime and tomato slices. Serve. Serves 6–8.

JLO Art of Cooking

Deon's Chicken Pies

Bake these tasty pies and freeze for future eating.

1 (3-ounce) package cream cheese, softened
4 tablespoons butter, softened, divided
⅛ teaspoon salt
⅛ teaspoon pepper
2 tablespoons finely chopped onion
1 tablespoon finely chopped celery
1 small bottle pimento, drained and chopped
2 tablespoons milk
3 cups diced cooked chicken
2 (8-ounce) cans crescent rolls
1 cup seasoned bread crumbs
⅛ teaspoon garlic powder

Lightly grease a cookie sheet; set aside. Preheat oven to 350°. In a small bowl, combine cream cheese, 2 tablespoons butter, salt, pepper, onion, celery, pimento, and milk; stir with wooden spoon until well blended. Add chicken. Open crescent rolls and separate the dough, keeping 2 triangles together to form a square, for a total of 8 squares. Press the perforations to seal the holes. In the center of each square, place about ½ cup chicken mixture. Pull the 4 corners together and twist top to seal pie.

Melt remaining 2 tablespoons butter. Combine bread crumbs with garlic powder. Brush each pie with butter and sprinkle with crumbs. Place on greased cookie sheet and bake 20 minutes until lightly browned. Serve immediately, or can be kept frozen for up to 2 weeks. To reheat, cook at 325° for 10–15 minutes, or wrap in foil and place on medium coals for 10 minutes. Serves 4.

Vacation Cooking: Good Food! Good Fun!

There have been several television series filmed in Utah: *Touched by an Angel, Death Valley Days, Gunsmoke, Everwood, Cover Me* and *The Lone Ranger.*

Texas Ranch Casserole

12 (6-inch) corn tortillas
3 cups diced, cooked chicken
1½ cups chopped onion
1½ cups chopped green pepper
2 cups shredded Cheddar cheese
1 teaspoon chili powder
½ teaspoon garlic powder

2 (10¾-ounce) cans condensed
cream of chicken soup, undiluted
1 (28-ounce) can crushed
tomatoes
6–8 drops Tabasco
1 (4-ounce) can chopped green
chiles, drained

Heat oven to 350°. Grease 9x13-inch baking pan; line with tortillas, overlapping as necessary and extending slightly above the rim of the pan. Layer over the tortillas, the chicken, onion, green pepper, and cheese. Sprinkle with chili and garlic powders. Drop dollops of undiluted condensed soup on top. Combine crushed tomatoes, hot sauce, and green chiles, and spoon on top of soup. Bake about 45 minutes, until bubbly and heated through. Let stand 15 minutes before cutting and serving. Serves 8–12.

Ladies' Literary Club Cookbook

Hot Creamed Chicken in a Puff Pastry

1 cup finely diced onion
2 cloves garlic, minced
2 tablespoons clarified butter
8 cups diced chicken
1 teaspoon chopped fresh thyme

4 cups chicken stock
1 pint heavy cream
Salt and pepper to taste
20 baked puff pastries

Sauté onion and garlic in clarified butter until translucent; do not let brown. Add diced chicken and thyme and cook until done. Add chicken stock and cream and bring to a boil; let reduce to a thick consistency. Add salt and pepper to taste. Spoon into puff pastries and serve immediately. Makes 20 servings.

Note: Chicken stock can be replaced by a good quality chicken base. Do not use bouillon cubes—they contain too much salt.

Lion House Weddings

Chicken Pastry Pillows

3 cups cubed, cooked chicken
  breasts
1 (8-ounce) package cream
  cheese, softened
½ stick butter, softened

1 cup chopped mushrooms
¼ cup chopped onion
1 package Pepperidge Farm Pastry
  Sheets

Combine cooked chicken, cream cheese, butter, mushrooms, and onion in a bowl. Thaw pastry sheets according to package instructions. Roll out a bit thinner and cut into 8 rectangles per sheet. Place ¼ cup chicken mixture onto each rectangle (reserving ½ cup for sauce). Fold over and seal with fork. If pastry dries out, wet your fingers and stick together. Prick each pastry pillow with a fork and place on cookie sheet. Bake at 350° for 20–25 minutes. Remove from oven and cover with Mushroom Sauce.

MUSHROOM SAUCE:

1 (10¾-ounce) can cream of
  mushroom soup
1 cup milk
½ cup water

1 chicken bouillon cube
1 beef bouillon cube
½ cup chicken mixture

Mix all ingredients in saucepan until heated through. You may thicken sauce with flour or cornstarch, if desired.

Making Magic

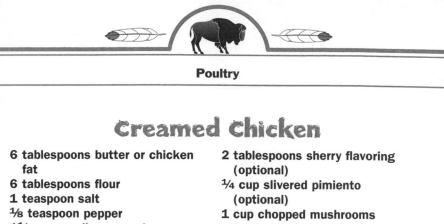

Creamed Chicken

6 tablespoons butter or chicken fat
6 tablespoons flour
1 teaspoon salt
⅛ teaspoon pepper
1½ cups well-seasoned chicken broth
1 cup cream or top milk
1 cup cubed cooked chicken

2 tablespoons sherry flavoring (optional)
¼ cup slivered pimiento (optional)
1 cup chopped mushrooms (optional)
½ cup slivered green pepper (optional)

Melt butter in saucepan and blend in flour, salt, and pepper. Cook over low heat until bubbling. Remove from heat. Stir in chicken broth and cream. Bring to a boil and boil one minute, stirring constantly. Stir chicken in gently. Just before serving, add sherry flavoring, pimiento, mushrooms, and green pepper, if desired. Serve hot in patty shells, pastry cases, biscuit rings, or timbale cases, or over toast points, noodles, fluffy rice, etc. Makes 6 servings.

Family Favorites from the Heart

Chicken in a Nest

¼ cup (½ stick) margarine
½ cup chopped onion
½ cup chopped celery
¼ cup unsifted flour
1 teaspoon salt

⅛ teaspoon pepper
1½ cups chicken broth
½ cup heavy cream
3 cups cubed, cooked chicken

Melt margarine in large saucepan. Add onion and celery; sauté over low heat until tender. Stir in flour, salt, and pepper and cook several minutes over low heat. Remove from heat; gradually stir in broth and cream. Cook over low heat, stirring constantly, until mixture comes to a boil. Add chicken. Cook, stirring, until heated through. Serve mixture in Potato Nests.

POTATO NESTS:

1 egg, beaten
3 cups thick mashed potatoes

2 tablespoons margarine, melted

Add egg to mashed potatoes and mix until blended. Drop mixture by spoonfuls onto greased baking sheets, using ½ cup for each nest. Spread each mound into a 3½-inch circle, shaping sides with spoon. Brush with margarine. Bake at 425° for 15 minutes, or until potatoes are light brown. Makes 6 servings.

Family Favorites from the Heart

Utah is a Ute Indian word meaning "people of the mountains."

Chicken Flips

FILLING:

¼ cup chopped onion
¼ cup sliced celery
2 tablespoons margarine
1 (10¾-ounce) can cream of
    chicken soup

¼ cup milk
2 cups diced chicken

In small saucepan, cook onion and celery in margarine until tender. Add soup and milk. Stir in chicken. Heat through.

BATTER:

2 eggs, beaten
¼ cup flour
2 tablespoons Parmesan cheese
1 teaspoon chives

1 teaspoon parsley flakes
Dash salt and pepper
2 cups shredded zucchini,
    drained

In medium bowl, combine eggs, flour, cheese, chives, parsley, salt and pepper. Add zucchini and mix well. Drop Batter on griddle; flatten slightly. Cook on both sides until brown. Spoon on Filling and fold over.

How to Enjoy Zucchini

Dutch Oven Chicken Wings Supreme

Chicken wings are a good snack and they can be a special treat. If you like wings, you will love these. I think they are the best I have ever tasted.

1 cup or more flour
Seasonings you like, to taste
6–12 chicken wings per person

2 tablespoons vegetable oil or
bacon grease

Depending on how many you are going to cook, select the right size Dutch oven. If you are doing it inside on the stove, select the right size burner, too, so that the Dutch oven will sit on the outside of the burner on its 3 legs. Now you are ready to start.

Put flour and seasonings in a paper bag. Add chicken wings a few at a time and shake them in the bag so the seasoned flour will cover them. With a set of tongs, remove chicken from sack and shake off excess flour. Repeat until all wings are floured.

Heat Dutch oven on medium high; add vegetable oil or bacon grease. When hot, brown all the wings, one layer at a time, until all are brown. You can pile them on one side of the oven or use a separate oven to keep them warm on another burner. When all chicken wings are brown, put them in the Dutch oven in layers. Be sure there is at least ¼ inch of oil in the bottom of the Dutch oven to insure the sauce not burning. Pour the Special Sauce over them.

Indoors, put Dutch oven in oven with lid on and bake at 300° for 45 minutes or until tender to the fork. Try not to overcook them or they will fall apart. They still taste great, but are hard to pick up. Outdoors, be sure to have most of your heat on top. Also, stir the wings approximately every 10 minutes to insure even cooking.

SPECIAL SAUCE:
¼ cup soy sauce
½ cup sugar
½ cup vinegar
1 cup barbecue sauce

¼ cup water
2 tablespoons Tabasco sauce
(optional)

Blend all together in a large cup or bowl to pour over wings after they are browned and before they go into the oven. If you like them hot, add Tabasco sauce.

Doin' Dutch Oven: Inside and Out

Cornish Hens and Orange Sauce

¾ cup honey
¾ cup orange marmalade
3 Cornish hens

Salt and pepper to taste
½ teaspoon seasoned salt
1 orange, sliced

Mix honey and marmalade together. Heat a 14-inch Dutch oven to about 450°. Wash hens and season. Place orange slices inside each hen and put on a rack in the Dutch oven. Cover and bake with top and bottom heat for 45 minutes to an hour. As the hens begin to brown, remove coals to prevent burning. Glaze hens with honey mixture about 20 minutes before they are done. When done, remove oranges from hens and throw away. Glaze again just before serving.

Dutch Oven and Outdoor Cooking, Y2K Edition

Orange Turkey

1 (12- to 14-pound) turkey
1 cup salt
1 cup sugar
1 (12-ounce) can orange juice
  concentrate

3 cans water plus enough water
  to cover turkey
1 (6-ounce) can orange juice
  concentrate mixed to directions

Place thawed turkey in a large bag or in a bowl large enough to hold the turkey. Mix salt, sugar, and 12-ounce can of orange juice concentrate with 3 cans of water. Pour over turkey and add enough additional water to cover turkey. Tie bag up and shake turkey around to completely mix water and orange juice mixture together. Place in the fridge for about 24 hours.

Remove turkey from brine and place over the cone of the Ultimate Roaster. Place oven on a Camp Chef burner over low heat for about 30 minutes. Add 1 cup orange juice to the bottom of oven. As liquid evaporates, add more orange juice throughout cooking. Turkey will need to cook for about 5–8 minutes per pound. Remove turkey when it reaches a temperature of 165°–175°.

Ultimate Dutch Oven Cookbook

Dutch Oven Roast Turkey à la Bob

I have always wanted to cook a turkey in the Dutch oven, but because they are too big for the oven, I had to settle for half a turkey. The butcher will be happy to cut a turkey in half for you. After you have tried it, you will be glad for the other half to enjoy again. Everyone who has eaten it says that a Dutch oven-cooked turkey is the best.

¼ cup vegetable oil or bacon
  grease
½ small turkey, 6–8 pounds

Salt and pepper
1 cup water

Let turkey defrost before you cook It. Level a 14- to 16-inch Dutch oven on the heat and add oil. When hot, put turkey in and salt and pepper to taste. Brown on all sides until good and brown. Add water, put the lid on the oven, add coals to the top, and let it simmer. Check it about every 20 minutes, stirring the juice, and turn the turkey over each time so both sides will have the flavor and not be dry as most oven-cooked turkeys are. Also add additional water, if needed. It will take about 2½ hours to cook an 8-pound turkey, 3 hours for 10–12 pounds, but it will be the best turkey you ever tasted.

Test for doneness by sticking with a fork. Serve while warm and use juice in oven as a special treat, pouring it over the meat and potatoes or rice.

Let's Cook Dutch

My Turkey Dressing

This is good and easy.

2 cups chopped celery
2 cups chopped onions
2–3 tablespoons margarine or
  butter
2 cans cream of mushroom soup
1 soup can water

10 cups toasted bread cubes
1 teaspoon poultry seasoning
1 teaspoon sage
Salt and pepper to taste
Turkey

Sauté celery and onions in butter until done, but not brown. Add soup and water. Blend well. To the bread cubes, add the seasonings. Mix well, then add celery and onion mixture. Mix well, adding more seasonings to suit your taste. If dressing is a little dry, add a little more water. Stuff turkey. Allow about 1 cup of dressing for each pound of turkey. Cook according to turkey recommendations.

To make gravy, simmer gizzard, heart, and neck in a quart of water until tender. Cut all meat fine and add back to liquid. Drain juices from the cooked turkey and add to liquid. Mix ½ cup flour with ½ cup cold water and mix well; add to boiling liquid. Season to taste.

Dude Food

Seafood

The Snowbird Tram takes skiers to the top of Hidden Peak (11,000-foot elevation) in just seven minutes. Skiers can enjoy Snowbird and adjoining Alta Ski Area on a single pass.

Halibut à la Orange

1 orange
Zest from orange
1 cup orange juice
4 teaspoons cornstarch

3 green onions, chopped
1 teaspoon chicken bouillon
1½–2 pounds halibut, thawed

Zest orange, then peel, section, and chop. Place all ingredients, except fish, in oven over 30 briquettes. Cook, stirring often, until thickened and bubbly. Remove from heat. Remove most of sauce and place fish in oven. Pour sauce over fish and bake at 350° for 15–25 minutes or until fish is flaky. Use 10–12 coals under, 18–22 on lid. Serve with sauce spooned on fish.

Dutch Oven Delites

Halibut Supreme

A treasure of the sea.

2 pounds fresh halibut pieces
¼ cup plus 1 tablespoon
   butter, divided
¼ cup flour
2 cups milk
¼ teaspoon salt

¼ teaspoon Worcestershire sauce
3 tablespoons chopped onion
1 cup grated Cheddar cheese
Buttered bread crumbs (1 cup
   crumbs plus 2 tablespoons
   melted butter)

Place halibut in salted boiling water. Simmer, covered, about 20 minutes or until flaky. Drain well and set aside.

In a medium saucepan, make white sauce by melting ¼ cup butter, then stirring in flour until well combined. Add milk, salt, and Worcestershire, stirring constantly over medium heat until the mixture comes to a boil. Continue cooking at a boil for about 2 minutes, until thickened. Remove from heat; set aside.

Sauté onion in 1 tablespoon butter for about 5 minutes, or until tender. Add to white sauce. Layer halibut, cheese, and sauce in greased 2½-quart baking dish, ending with sauce on top. Top with buttered bread crumbs. Bake at 325° for about 30 minutes. Makes 4–6 servings.

The Essential Mormon Cookbook

Spice-Rubbed Halibut

¾ pound halibut, cut into
  1-inch-thick pieces
½ teaspoon coriander
½ teaspoon ground cumin

½ teaspoon curry powder
¼ teaspoon ground ginger
¼ teaspoon salt
⅛ teaspoon cayenne

Rinse fish and pat dry. In a small bowl, mix spices. Rub fish with spice mixture. Set pieces slightly apart in an 8-inch-square pan. Broil 6 inches from heat for 3 minutes. With a wide spatula, turn fish over and broil until opaque, but still moist looking in center of thickest part, about 3–5 minutes.

SAUCE:

¼ cup orange juice
3 tablespoons rice vinegar
3 tablespoons apricot jam

1 tablespoon grated fresh ginger
1 tablespoon cornstarch

In a medium saucepan over medium heat, bring orange juice, vinegar, jam, and fresh ginger to a boil. Stir often until reduced to about ¼ cup; add cornstarch and simmer 10 minutes. With spatula, transfer fish to plates and spoon sauce over fish.

All That Jam

Creamy Baked Halibut Steaks

**4 halibut steaks, about ¾-inch
   thick**
Salt to taste
Pepper to taste
¾ cup thick sour cream
¼ cup dry bread crumbs

¼ teaspoon garlic salt
**1½ teaspoons chopped chives,
   fresh or frozen**
⅓ cup grated Parmesan cheese
1 teaspoon paprika

Place steaks, close fitting, in a shallow buttered baking dish. Sprinkle with salt and pepper. Mix together sour cream, bread crumbs, garlic salt, and chives, and spread over steaks. Sprinkle with Parmesan cheese and paprika. Bake, uncovered, at 400° for 15–20 minutes, or until fish flakes with a fork. Makes 4 large or 8 small servings.

Lion House Recipes

Roasted Salmon
with Cinnamon and Cumin

Your taste buds will surely come alive with the wonderful flavors in this dish. Let the spicy aromas work their magic to invigorate the senses and stimulate the appetite!

¼ cup orange juice
1 tablespoon lemon juice
4 (6- to 8-ounce) salmon fillets
2 tablespoons brown sugar

2 tablespoons grated orange zest
¾ teaspoon cumin
¼ teaspoon cinnamon
Salt and pepper to taste

Combine orange and lemon juices and pour over salmon in a marinating dish. Refrigerate for up to 2 hours.

Preheat oven to 400°. Combine sugar, orange zest, cumin, cinnamon, salt and pepper in a small bowl. Remove fish from the marinating dish and place in an oiled baking dish. Rub the sugar mixture over both sides of the salmon, and bake in the oven for approximately 10–15 minutes, until the salmon is just opaque. Serves 4.

Aromatherapy in the Kitchen

Herb's Salmon or Tuna Bake

DEVILED EGGS:

6 hard-cooked eggs
2 tablespoons mayonnaise

¼ teaspoon salt
¼ teaspoon dry mustard

Split eggs and remove yolk; mash with mayonnaise, salt, and dry mustard. Stuff egg whites with mixture. These eggs are good with any fish dish.

1 (1-pound) can salmon, or 2
  (7-ounce) cans tuna, drained
1 teaspoon lemon juice
¼ cup butter or margarine
¼ cup flour
½ teaspoon salt

2 cups milk
¾ cup shredded processed
  cheese
About 12 pitted ripe olives
1 cup crushed potato chips

Break fish in chunks and arrange in a 12-inch warmed and oiled Dutch oven. Sprinkle with lemon juice. Melt butter and blend in flour and salt. Stir in milk. Cook and stir till thickened, then stir in cheese. Pour half of cheese sauce over fish. Arrange Deviled Eggs and olives on top. Cover with remaining sauce. Sprinkle with potato chips. Bake at 350° for 25 minutes or until hot. Use your Dutch oven in your oven or cook with 10 coals on the bottom and 15 on top.

Log Cabin Presents Lewis and Clark

Salmon as a Gift

This dazzling and divine main dish is sure to get rave reviews.

HERB BUTTER:

2 tablespoons butter, softened   ½ teaspoon fresh thyme or
                                       ¼ teaspoon dried

Mix softened butter with thyme in a small bowl. Recipe can be doubled several times to accommodate larger groups on other occasions.

Parchment paper   1 small zucchini, thinly sliced
2 salmon fillets   4 baby carrots, thinly sliced
Juice of one lemon   ¼ small red onion, thinly sliced
Lemon pepper to taste   ¼ red pepper, thinly sliced
½ teaspoon crushed rosemary   Twine, for tying parchment paper
Salt and pepper to taste

Cut a 12x16-inch piece of parchment paper for each salmon fillet. Place each fillet in center of parchment paper.

Drizzle fresh lemon juice over salmon. Sprinkle lightly with lemon pepper, crushed rosemary, salt and pepper to taste.

Layer sliced vegetables on top of each salmon. Top each with approximately 1 tablespoon Herb Butter.

Wrap the above in the parchment paper and tie in a bow with twine. Place salmon packages on a cookie sheet and bake at 400° for about 15 minutes or until cooked through. Makes 2 servings.

The Essential Mormon Cookbook

The recipient of the world's first permanent artificial heart was Barney B. Clark, a 61-year-old retired dentist from Utah. The successful transplant operation was performed on December 2, 1982, at the University of Utah Medical Center in Salt Lake City. Dr. Robert Jarvik designed the aluminum-and-plastic artificial heart. Mr. Clark survived for 112 days.

Stuffing for Fish

½ stalk celery
½ dozen mushrooms
1 small onion
4 tablespoons butter
5 cups bread crumbs or diced
  dry bread
Dash of salt

Dash of granulated garlic
Squirt of lemon juice
2 eggs
Water
Crayfish (optional)
Melted butter combined with
  lemon juice

Dice celery, mushrooms, and onion, and lightly fry in butter. Add bread crumbs or bread, salt, granulated garlic, and lemon juice or juice of ½ lemon. Add eggs; mix and add water until you have the consistency of stuffing. You may add crayfish to the stuffing for a really nice accent, if desired.

Fill trout or salmon cavity with stuffing; truss if necessary. Baste fish with melted butter and lemon juice and grill, basting occasionally, till done (be sure to oil grate before placing). Be careful turning fish over.

The Practical Camp Cook

Fish Parmesan

1½ pounds filleted fish
Garlic salt
Pepper
½ teaspoon oregano

1 (8-ounce) jar marinara sauce
Grated mozzarella cheese
2 tablespoons Parmesan cheese

Season fish with garlic salt, pepper, and oregano. Put fish in baking dish. Pour marinara sauce over it. Sprinkle with cheeses and bake at 425° for 15 minutes. Serves 4.

30 Days to a Healthier Family

Grilled Fish

2 tablespoons olive oil	½ teaspoon salt
2 large fish fillets (½- to 1-inch thick)	⅛ teaspoon pepper

CAMP STOVE:

In a large skillet, heat oil; add fish and season with salt and pepper. Cook for 2½–4½ minutes on each side, or until fish flakes and is opaque. Serves 2.

GRILL:

Heat grill and brush with oil. When hot, add fish fillets and cook 2½–4½ minutes per side. To prevent fish from flaking and falling into the coals, place a strip of pierced, oiled foil on the grill and lay the fish on the foil. Be careful not to overcook. When fish flakes easily, it is fully cooked. Serves 2.

DUTCH OVEN LID:

Place the lid of a 12-inch Dutch oven upside down on a lid holder over 12–15 hot coals. Preheat the lid for 5 minutes. Brush oil on hot lid, add fish, and season with salt and pepper. Cook 2½–4½ minutes on each side, or until the fillets are evenly browned and flake easily. Serves 2.

Roughing It Easy at Girls Camp

Flaming Gorge National Recreation Area is home to Flaming Gorge Reservoir, which extends as far as 91 miles and has a total capacity of 3,788,900 acre-feet. At full elevation of 6,045 feet, it has a surface area of 42,020 acres. The reservoir is famous for its trout fishing.

Oven Fried Fish

It's hard to believe, but it's true. With this method there's no pot watching, no turning, and no odor. Try it!

¼ cup milk
2 teaspoons salt
Dash of dried thyme, tarragon, dill, or rosemary (or minced onion, garlic, or Tabasco)
½ cup packaged dried bread crumbs (or crushed corn or wheat flakes)

½ teaspoon paprika
Dash of dry mustard
Dash of chili powder
A little grated cheese
A little snipped parsley
1–2 pounds small fish or fillets or steaks
Salad oil or melted butter

Mix milk and salt with a dash of herbs or seasoning in shallow dish. In a second dish, combine bread crumbs or crushed flakes with paprika and mustard, chili powder, grated cheese, and snipped parsley. Start heating oven to 500°. Now, with one hand, dip each piece of fish into milk, then with other hand roll it in crumbs, arranging side-by-side, in greased shallow baking dish lined with foil. Drizzle a little salad oil or melted butter onto fish. Then bake 12–15 minutes or until golden and easily flakes with fork, but still moist. Serves 6.

A Century of Mormon Cookery, Volume 2

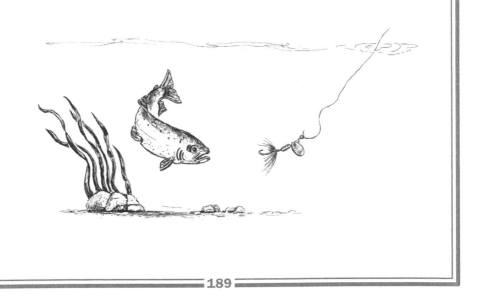

Shrimp Pesto Pizza

Okay, we know using a prepared pizza dough is cheating, but when time is of the essence, it sure comes in handy! Use freshly made pesto to really bring out the aromas and flavor of the basil. This pizza comes out looking as great as it tastes!

6 jumbo shrimp, halved lengthwise
¼ cup homemade basil pesto, divided
¼ cup sliced sun-dried tomatoes (packed in oil, drained, reserve oil)
3 garlic cloves, sliced

1 cup sliced mushrooms
¼ cup sliced roasted red bell pepper
1 prepared pizza shell
½ cup mozzarella cheese, divided
¼ cup fresh spinach leaves
2 tablespoons pine nuts

Toss shrimp with 1 tablespoon pesto and set aside. Drain about 2 teaspoons oil from the sun-dried tomatoes into a small skillet. Heat over medium-high heat and sauté the garlic, mushrooms, sun-dried tomatoes, and roasted pepper for 5 minutes. Remove from heat.

Place a pizza stone in the oven and preheat to 425°. Spread the remaining pesto over the pizza shell. Sprinkle with half the cheese. Top with sauté mixture, and sprinkle with half the remaining cheese. Place pizza on the stone and bake for 8–10 minutes. Remove from oven and arrange shrimp over the pizza.

Return to oven and bake for 3 minutes, or until the shrimp start to curl up. Remove from oven, and set the thermostat to broil. Sprinkle with spinach, pine nuts, and remaining cheese, and set under the broiler for 1–2 minutes, or until cheese is just bubbly. Remove from oven and let rest for 3–5 minutes before slicing. Serves 4.

Aromatherapy in the Kitchen

Wasatch Mountain State Park, in beautiful Heber Valley, is Utah's most developed state park. One of Utah's finest golf courses is found here. Soldier Hollow at the south end of the park was the 2002 Olympic Winter venue for biathlon and cross-country events.

Shrimp Newburg

This is my all-time favorite—easy and deliciously rich. Everyone loves it.

2 tablespoons onion, finely
 chopped
Butter
½ teaspoon curry powder
 (to taste)

1 (10¾-ounce) can cream of
 shrimp soup
1 cup sour cream
1 cup cooked shrimp
¼ cup lemon juice

In a 2-quart saucepan, sauté onions in a little butter until transparent. Add curry powder to taste. Stir in canned soup and sour cream, and cook gently over medium heat. Add shrimp and heat through, but do NOT let boil. Add lemon juice to taste. Serves 4–6.

Variation: Cream of shrimp soup is difficult to find. You may substitute cream of chicken soup, then add a drop of red food coloring and slightly more lemon juice. Lemon juice is the key to this recipe's delicious flavor. I also like to cook my own shrimp in seasoned water until barely done. It has more flavor than purchased cooked shrimp.

Recipe by Elaine Jack
Five-Star Recipes from Well-Known Latter Day Saints

Crustless Crab Quiche

4 eggs
1½ cups sour cream
½ cup grated Parmesan cheese
½ cup flour
⅛ teaspoon salt
4 drops Tabasco sauce

1 (6½-ounce) can crabmeat,
 drained
2 cups grated Swiss cheese
1 cup chopped fresh mushrooms
2 shallots, minced
2 tablespoons butter

Preheat oven to 350°. Combine eggs, sour cream, Parmesan cheese, flour, salt, and Tabasco sauce in a large bowl; beat with a whisk until smooth. Stir in crabmeat and Swiss cheese. Sauté mushrooms and shallots in butter until soft and add to mixture. Pour into ungreased 10-inch pie plate. Bake for 45 minutes or until knife inserted near center comes out clean. Cool 5 minutes before serving. Yields 6 servings.

A Pinch of Salt Lake Cookbook

The History of Latter-day Saints

Once an isolated people living in the remote geography of the American West, members of The Church of Jesus Christ of Latter-day Saints today number more than 12 million, worshiping in more than 26,000 congregations in 160 nations. In the United States, the faith known to some as "the Mormon church" is the fifth largest religious denomination.

The Church of Jesus Christ of Latter-day Saints was officially organized in 1830 but had its beginnings a decade earlier, when in 1820, Joseph Smith published the Book of Mormon, a translation of sacred records kept by ancient prophets living in the Americas between about 2200 B.C. and A.D. 421. Joining the Bible as a testament of Jesus Christ, the Book of Mormon includes an account of the Savior's ministry on the American continent following his resurrection in Palestine.

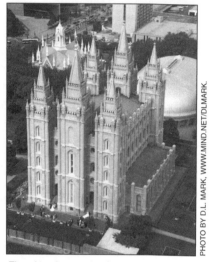

The six-spire granite Salt Lake Temple in downtown Salt Lake City took forty years to complete.

After the Church was organized in western New York, religious persecution forced the Latter-day Saints to move to Ohio, then to Missouri and later to Illinois. Following Joseph Smith's assassination in Illinois in 1844, the majority of Latter-day Saints followed Brigham Young on the historic 1,300-mile trek across the American frontier to the Valley of the Great Salt Lake.

Today the Church's ministerial outreach includes a humanitarian aid effort that encompasses the globe, an educational program that serves nearly half a million students worldwide (with Brigham Young University in Provo, Utah, as its flagship institution), the world famous Mormon Tabernacle Choir, and operation of the largest family history library in the world at its world headquarters in Salt Lake City, along with branch libraries in more than 4,000 locations.

Cakes

The Wasatch Mountains form a stunning backdrop to Salt Lake City. In a matter of minutes, you can go from city life to mountain biking in the summer or snow skiing in the winter.

Chocolate Cola Cake

CAKE:

2 cups flour
2 cups sugar
1 stick butter or margarine
½ cup oil
3 tablespoons cocoa
1 cup cola

1½ cups mini marshmallows
½ cup buttermilk
1 teaspoon baking soda
2 eggs
1 teaspoon vanilla

Mix flour and sugar in a large mixing bowl. In a pan, heat butter, oil, cocoa, and cola until boiling, stirring occasionally. Add marshmallows and stir until smooth. Pour heated mixture over flour and sugar and mix well. Add buttermilk, baking soda, eggs, and vanilla, and beat for 2 minutes. Pour batter into a greased and floured 9x13-inch cake pan. Bake at 350° for 30–40 minutes, or until toothpick comes out clean. Frost while warm.

FROSTING:

1 (1-pound) box powdered sugar
1 stick butter or margarine
3 tablespoons cocoa
6 tablespoons cola

½ cup chopped pecans or
   walnuts
1 teaspoon vanilla

Pour powdered sugar in a mixing bowl. In a pan, heat butter, cocoa, and cola until boiling. Pour heated mixture over powdered sugar; beat well. Add nuts and vanilla; stir. Spread on cake while still warm. Serve with ice cream.

JLO Art of Cooking

Arches National Park, located five miles north of the town of Moab, contains the world's largest concentration of natural stone arches. The 73,000-acre region has over 2,000 oddly eroded sandstone formations such as fins, pinnacles, spires, balanced rocks, and arches. A 40-mile, round-trip paved road leads to the major sights, including Balanced Rock, Skyline Arch, Double Arch, Fiery Furnace, and the park's most famous geologic feature, Delicate Arch.

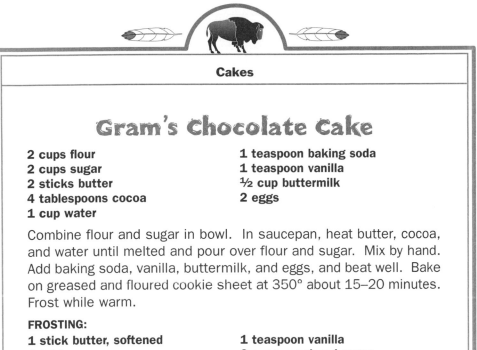

Gram's Chocolate Cake

2 cups flour
2 cups sugar
2 sticks butter
4 tablespoons cocoa
1 cup water

1 teaspoon baking soda
1 teaspoon vanilla
½ cup buttermilk
2 eggs

Combine flour and sugar in bowl. In saucepan, heat butter, cocoa, and water until melted and pour over flour and sugar. Mix by hand. Add baking soda, vanilla, buttermilk, and eggs, and beat well. Bake on greased and floured cookie sheet at 350° about 15–20 minutes. Frost while warm.

FROSTING:
1 stick butter, softened
4 tablespoons cocoa
6 tablespoons milk

1 teaspoon vanilla
2 cups powdered sugar

Combine all ingredients and beat well. Frost cake while still warm.

Family Favorites from the Heart

Cherry Chocolate Surprise Cake

1 (18¼-ounce) chocolate cake
 mix
1 (1-pound, 13-ounce) can cherry
 pie filling
1 (8-ounce) package cream
 cheese, softened

1 egg
3 tablespoons sugar
1 teaspoon vanilla
Whipped cream for topping

Prepare cake mix as directed on box. Pour prepared cake batter into a greased 12-inch Dutch oven. Spoon cherry pie filling in clumps over cake batter. In a small mixing bowl, cream together cream cheese, egg, sugar, and vanilla until smooth. Drop by table-spoons over top of cake. Place lid on oven. Bake, using 8–10 bri-quettes on bottom and 14–15 on top for 1 hour or until you can smell the cake. Serve warm with whipped cream as topping.

Log Cabin Presents Lewis and Clark

Chocolate Snowball

Doesn't it seem fitting that a ski area should serve snowballs for dessert?

CAKE:

12 ounces semisweet chocolate, chopped in ½-inch pieces

1 cup strong coffee, hot

1 cup sugar

¾ pound (3 sticks) unsalted butter, softened

6 eggs, lightly beaten

FROSTING:

1½ cups heavy cream

2 tablespoons sugar

½ teaspoon vanilla extract

15–20 fresh, edible purple flowers, for garnish

TO MAKE THE CAKE:

Preheat the oven to 350°. Line a medium (5- to 6-cup, about 8-inch diameter) stainless steel bowl with aluminum foil so the foil overlaps the bowl 3 or 4 inches.

Put the chocolate in a saucepan. Pour the coffee over, which will melt some of the chocolate. Place over medium-low heat; add the sugar and stir with a wire whisk to dissolve the sugar and any unmelted chocolate. Add the butter gradually, a dollop at a time, whisking until the butter is incorporated before adding the next dollop. This should take about 10 minutes. Remove from the heat.

Slowly whisk the beaten eggs into the chocolate mixture. Pour through a strainer into the foil-lined bowl. Discard any firm bits of egg that remain in the strainer. Bake 50–55 minutes, until the batter rises and a cracked top crust forms. The mixture will still jiggle, like molded gelatin. Resist the urge to bake it a little more; the butter and chocolate set up when chilled.

Let the cake cool. Fold the overlapping foil over the top and refrigerate at least 8 hours, keeping the cake in the bowl. It will keep for up to a week if refrigerated and well wrapped in plastic wrap. (It is best to store the cake in the bowl. Once it is cold, you can invert the dome onto a cardboard circle—but do not remove the foil wrapper. Wrap the foil-enclosed dome in plastic wrap.) The cake can also be frozen for up to a month; thaw in the refrigerator before frosting.

(continued)

(Chocolate Snowball continued)

TO FROST AND SERVE:

Remove the plastic wrap from the bowl. (If you have taken the cake out of the bowl for storage, invert it back into the bowl.) Pull the overlapping foil away from the cake. The cake will have fallen in the center; to make the top (or what will be the bottom of the cake) flat and even, press the raised outer edges down, or trim the extra height with a knife, reserving the scraps for indulgent snacks. Place a flat serving plate or cardboard circle over the bowl and invert. Gently remove the foil.

Whip the cream with the sugar and the vanilla until the cream comes to soft peaks that hold their shape. Put the cream into a pastry bag fitted with a large star tip. Pipe stars, covering the dome completely. If you wish, decorate with edible flowers or another garnish such as chocolate shavings or crystallized flowers. Makes 1 (8-inch) cake; serves 10–12.

Chocolate Snowball

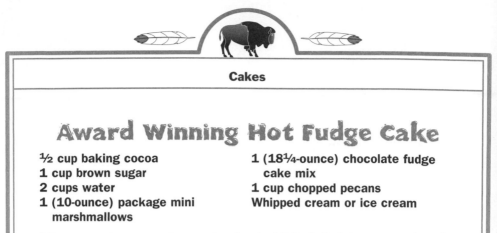

Award Winning Hot Fudge Cake

½ cup baking cocoa
1 cup brown sugar
2 cups water
1 (10-ounce) package mini
   marshmallows

1 (18¼-ounce) chocolate fudge
   cake mix
1 cup chopped pecans
Whipped cream or ice cream

Mix cocoa, brown sugar, and water in 12-inch Dutch oven and sprinkle marshmallows evenly on top. Make cake mix according to package instructions. Pour mixture over marshmallows and spread to cover completely. Sprinkle pecans on top. Put on lid. Place about 7 coals on bottom and 15 on top of Dutch oven. Bake for 30 minutes or until done. Serve warm, topped with whipped cream or ice cream.

Note: To make it even richer, try chocolate chips sprinkled on top before cooking.

Dutch Oven and Outdoor Cooking, Y2K Edition

Turtle Cake

1 (18¼-ounce) cake mix
   (yellow or butter)
1 pound caramels, melted
1 (14-ounce) can sweetened
   condensed milk

1 cup chopped pecans
1 cup chocolate chips

Prepare cake mix according to directions. Pour half of the cake batter in a 12-inch Dutch oven and bake at 350° for 20 minutes. Cake will not be done. Melt caramels and pour over the cake. Pour sweetened condensed milk on as well. Add remaining cake batter and cook for about 10 minutes longer. Top with pecans and chocolate chips. Return the cake to heat and finish baking until cake is done.

Dutch Oven and Outdoor Cooking, Book Two: Homespun Edition

Better Than Sex Chocolate Cake

¾ cup sour cream
4 eggs
½ cup water
½ cup oil
1 (18¼-ounce) box chocolate
  cake mix

1 (3-ounce) box instant chocolate
  pudding
1 cup semisweet chocolate chips
Powdered sugar

Heat oven to 350°. Beat sour cream, eggs, water, and oil together in a large bowl until thoroughly mixed. Add cake mix and pudding mix. Stir in chocolate chips. Place batter in a sprayed or greased and floured Bundt pan. Bake 45–55 minutes or until a fork insert ed into cake comes out clean. While still hot, invert cake onto a serving platter. When cool, sift powdered sugar over top of cake.

No Green Gelatin Here!

Candy Bar Cake

1 (18¼-ounce) German
  chocolate cake mix
4–6 large candy bars (the kind
  with peanuts and caramel inside)

¾ cup milk chocolate chips
Whipped cream or ice cream

Mix cake according to package directions, then pour half of the batter into oiled Dutch oven. Cover and cook using 16–22 coals (400°), with a ratio of 1 (bottom)/3 (top), for 15 minutes. After cake has cooked for 15 minutes, remove from heat. Chop candy bars into large pieces and sprinkle over cake along with chocolate chips. Use care not to break the crust of the cooked cake.

Gently pour the remaining cake mix over the top. Cover and return the oven to heat, then cook for an additional 25–35 minutes or until cake is done. Rotate lid and oven while cooking and check often. Serve with whipped cream or ice cream. Serves 8–12.

The Beginner's Guide to Dutch Oven Cooking

Scandinavian Almond Cake

6 eggs	1½ cups butter, melted
3 cups sugar	3 cups flour
2 tablespoons almond extract	¼ cup sliced almonds

In a large bowl, beat eggs with sugar. Add almond extract and melted butter and mix. Gradually add flour.

Prepare 12-inch Dutch oven by greasing and dusting with flour (or nonstick cooking spray). Place a round parchment paper on the bottom of the oven. Spread mixture evenly in the oven. Sprinkle top with sliced almonds. Bake 60–80 minutes with 6–8 coals under oven and 16–18 coals on top. Rotate oven and lid a quarter turn every 15 minutes. Cake is done when browned on top. Remove cake from oven. Garnish with powdered sugar, mint leaves, and strawberries.

Friends of Old Deseret Dutch Oven Cookbook

Whipping Cream Cake

Everyone needs a good pound cake recipe. This one, made with whipping cream, is extra moist. Serve it with spring strawberries or the first of the Bear Lake raspberries.

1 cup butter, softened	1 teaspoon lemon extract
3 cups sugar	Confectioners' sugar for
6 eggs	garnish
3 cups cake flour, sifted	Fresh berries of fruit for
1 cup heavy whipping cream	garnish
1 teaspoon vanilla extract	

Cream butter and sugar in a mixer bowl until light and fluffy. Add eggs, flour, and whipping cream and mix well. Stir in the flavorings. Spoon into a greased and floured Bundt pan. Bake at 325° for 1¼ hours or until cake tests done. Cool in the pan for several minutes. Invert onto a wire rack to cool completely. Garnish with confectioners' sugar and fresh berries. Serves 16.

Always in Season

Perfect Pecan Cake

CRUST:

2 cups crushed vanilla wafers　　　¾ cup butter, softened
1 cup chopped pecans

In a large mixing bowl, combine wafer crumbs and chopped pecans. Using a pastry cutter, cut in butter until crumbly. Divide mixture in half and press half evenly on the bottom of a greased and floured 10-inch Dutch oven. Set the other half aside.

CAKE:

2½ cups flour or cake flour　　　¾ teaspoon cinnamon
1 cup granulated sugar　　　　　¾ teaspoon allspice
¾ cup packed brown sugar　　　½ teaspoon ground cloves
1 teaspoon baking powder　　　½ teaspoon nutmeg
1 teaspoon salt　　　　　　　　½ cup buttermilk
1 teaspoon baking soda　　　　¼ cup butter
4 eggs　　　　　　　　　　　1 (16-ounce) can pumpkin

In a large mixing bowl, mix Cake ingredients until smooth. Divide mixture in half. Spread ½ on Crust and bake approximately 350° (6 charcoal briquettes on bottom and 14 on top) for 30–40 minutes until Cake tests done. Cool 5 minutes; remove from pan and cool completely. Repeat procedure with other half of Crust and Cake mixture.

FILLING:

4–6 cups powdered sugar　　　6 ounces cream cheese, softened
⅔ cup butter, softened　　　　2 teaspoons vanilla

Combine ingredients until light and fluffy. Spread between Cake layers and frost Cake.

TOPPING:

½ cup whipping cream　　　1 cup pecan pieces
1 cup sugar　　　　　　　¼ stick butter
1 egg　　　　　　　　　　1 teaspoon vanilla

Mix the cream, sugar, and egg in saucepan. Bring to a boil. Add pecan pieces and butter. Bring to a boil again. Remove from heat and add vanilla. Cool and drizzle over top of Cake. Garnish with cherry and pecans halves. Serves 8–10.

Note: You can use two 10-inch Dutch ovens to speed baking.

The Dutch Oven Resource

Tropical Getaway Cake

CAKE:

1 (18¼-ounce) yellow cake mix
3 eggs
½ cup vegetable oil
½ cup applesauce
1 small can Mandarin oranges, drained

Preheat oven to 350°. Mix together cake mix, eggs, oil, applesauce, and oranges until smooth, then pour into a greased 9x13-inch pan. Bake 30–35 minutes, or until golden brown. Allow Cake to cool.

GLAZE:

1 cup crushed pineapple with juice
3 tablespoons cornstarch
1 cup sugar

Prepare Glaze by mixing pineapple with juice, cornstarch, and sugar in a small saucepan. Cook over medium heat, stirring constantly until thick and clear. Pour over Cake.

TOPPING:

4 bananas, sliced
1 cup 1% milk
1 (3-ounce) box vanilla instant pudding
8 ounces whipped topping
⅓ cup flaked coconut

Right before serving, place sliced bananas on top of Glaze. Blend pudding mix and milk with wire whisk. Fold in whipped topping. Spread over bananas. Sprinkle coconut over top.

101 Things To Do With a Cake Mix

The first monument to be administered by the Bureau of Land Management, rather than the National Park Service, Grand Staircase-Escalante National Monument was designated in September of 1996. At 1.7 million acres, the Grand Staircase Monument is divided into three distinct sections: the Grand Staircase, the Kaiparowits Plateau, and the Canyons of the Escalante. The 800,000-plus acres of the Kaiparowits form the wildest, most arid, and most remote part of the Monument.

Peach Dessert Cake

1 cup cake flour	½ cup shortening
1 teaspoon baking powder	1 teaspoon grated lemon rind
¼ teaspoon salt	2 eggs, unbeaten
½ cup sugar	4 ripe peaches, peeled and sliced

Sift flour, baking powder, and salt together. Beat ½ cup sugar and shortening until light. Add lemon rind, then eggs, one at a time, beating well. Add flour mixture in fourths, beating after each addition. Spread half the batter in a greased 8x8-inch baking pan. Top with peaches, then remaining batter.

TOPPING:

⅓ cup sugar	¼ cup chopped walnuts or
½ teaspoon cinnamon	pecans

Combine sugar, cinnamon, and nuts; sprinkle over all. Bake 50 minutes at 350°. Cut into squares and top with whipped cream.

Utah Cook Book

Muffin Cake

2 cups flour	1½ cups shredded apples
1¼ cups sugar	½ cup chopped dates
2 teaspoons baking soda	¾ cup coconut
2 teaspoons cinnamon	½ cup chopped pecans
½ teaspoon salt	3 eggs, beaten
1½ cups finely shredded	1 cup oil or ½ cup milk
carrots	½ teaspoon vanilla

Combine flour, sugar, baking soda, cinnamon, and salt. Mix together carrots, apples, dates, coconut, pecans, eggs, oil, and vanilla. Add to dry ingredients; stir until moistened. Bake at 375° for 40–50 minutes (8–10 coals on bottom, 14–18 coals on top).

Dutch Oven Gold

Apple Pie Harvest Cake

3 tablespoons shortening
1 cup sugar
1 egg
½ cup chopped nuts
¾ teaspoon cinnamon
¾ cup nutmeg

½ teaspoon salt
½ teaspoon baking powder
1 teaspoon baking soda
1 teaspoon vanilla
1¼ cups flour
3 cups peeled and diced apples

Mix well, the shortening, sugar, and egg. Add all remaining ingredients and mix only enough to moisten flour. Spread in greased pie tin and bake for 40–45 minutes at 350°. This is a great dessert to serve warm and with whipped cream or ice cream.

Log Cabin Grub Cookbook

Raw Apple Cake

In Sweden this dish is called "Epplekaka," and is one of the best apple cake recipes I have tried.

½ cup brown sugar
1 cup sugar
2¼ cups flour
¼ teaspoon salt
2 teaspoons baking soda
2 teaspoons cinnamon

1 cup buttermilk or sour milk
2 eggs
½ cup softened butter
3 cups thinly sliced raw apples
   (leave skin if desired)
Topping

Mix dry ingredients in a large bowl. Beat buttermilk, eggs, and butter together for about 3 minutes; add to dry ingredients and stir until well blended. Fold in apples, then pour batter into a well-greased and floured 9x13-inch cake pan. Sprinkle with Topping, and bake for 45 minutes at 350°.

TOPPING:
¼ cup brown sugar
¼ cup sugar

½ teaspoon cinnamon
½ cup chopped nuts

Mix together until crumbly.

Favorite Utah Pioneer Recipes

Pineapple Upside-Down Cake

¼ cup butter or margarine
½ cup brown sugar
1 (20-ounce) can sliced
  pineapple

Maraschino cherries
1 (18¼-ounce) package yellow
  cake mix

In a medium (10-inch) or large (12-inch) Dutch oven, melt butter or margarine; sprinkle brown sugar across the melted butter and stir. Place pineapple slices in butter and brown sugar mixture with their sides touching; fit as many as possible. Place a maraschino cherry in the middle of each pineapple slice.

In a separate bowl, prepare cake mix according to instructions on box. Carefully pour cake batter on top of pineapple slices. Cover and cook about 45 minutes to 1 hour at 325°–375°; test with toothpick. Do not overcook on the bottom.

To remove cake, carefully slide a knife completely around the side. Using a round piece of cardboard (a pizza delivery box works well) cut to fit inside the Dutch oven, and covered with aluminum foil, place the covered cardboard on the cake and rapidly turn it over.

Backyard Dutch Oven

Luscious Lemon Cake

1 (18¼-ounce) package white
   cake mix
1 cup water
¼ cup sugar
2 eggs, beaten
2 tablespoons cornstarch
2 tablespoons sugar

Zest of 1 lemon
1 tablespoon butter
3 tablespoons fresh lemon juice
1 pint sweetened whipping cream,
   whipped
¼ cup white chocolate shavings

Grease and flour 2 (9-inch) cake pans. Set aside. Preheat oven and make cake according to package directions on cake mix. When cake is done, put on cake racks and cool completely. (Cake may be frozen for future use.) While cake is cooling, prepare lemon filling. Put water, ¼ cup sugar, and beaten eggs in a small saucepan. Mix cornstarch and 2 tablespoons sugar together in a small bowl. Slowly add to mixture in pan. Cook on medium heat, stirring constantly until thickened. When thickened, add lemon zest, butter, and lemon juice. Stir until butter is melted and mixture is well mixed and smooth. Remove from heat and let cool. Cover with plastic wrap while cooling.

When cake is cool, cut each layer in half to make 4 slices. Place a layer on a serving plate and spread with half of cooled lemon filling. Add second layer of cake and spread with whipped cream. Add third layer of cake and spread with remaining half of lemon filling. Top with fourth layer of cake. Frost sides and top of cake with whipped cream. Garnish with white chocolate shavings. Refrigerate until ready to serve. Serves 12–16.

Lion House Desserts

The original Utah state flag was adopted by the state legislature in 1896 and revised in 1913. The beehive on the shield stands for hard work and industry. The date 1847 is the year the Mormons came to Utah. A bald eagle, the United States national bird, perches atop the shield and symbolizes protection in peace and war. The sego lily is a symbol of peace, and a U.S. flag appears on each side, symbolizing Utah's support to the nation. The Utah state flag, as we know it today, was originally designed for the battleship Utah in 1912.

Sting of the Bee Cake

BIENENSTICH CAKE:

1 cup butter (no substitutes),
  softened
⅔ cup sugar
2 eggs

3 cups sifted flour
3 teaspoons baking powder
1 teaspoon salt
½ cup milk

Cream butter. Gradually add sugar, creaming well. Beat in eggs one at a time; beat until light and fluffy. Add sifted dry ingredients alternately with milk. Spoon batter into a well-greased 9-inch springform pan.

TOPPING:

½ cup butter
1 cup finely chopped almonds,
  blanched or unblanched

½ cup sugar
2 tablespoons milk
2 teaspoons vanilla

Melt butter; blend in chopped almonds, sugar, milk, and vanilla. Bring to a boil. Remove from heat and cool slightly. Spread carefully over batter. Bake at 375° for 50 minutes. Remove from oven and cool. Remove springform pan. Prepare filling.

BUTTER CREAM FILLING:

1 cup butter, softened
2 egg yolks
2 cups powdered sugar

2 teaspoons vanilla
½ cup raspberry jam

To softened butter, add egg yolks, powdered sugar, and vanilla; beat well. Split cake horizontally into 2 layers. Spread bottom layer with Butter Cream Filling. Top with raspberry jam. Very carefully replace top layer of cake. Cut into thin slices and serve. Makes 16–20 servings.

Lion House Recipes

Pioneer Carrot Cake

2 cups flour
2 teaspoons cinnamon
2 teaspoons baking soda
½ teaspoon salt
3 eggs
¾ cup vegetable oil
½ cup buttermilk

¾ cup sugar
2 teaspoons vanilla
1 cup crushed pineapple, drained
2 cups grated carrots
1½ cups flaked coconut
  (optional)
1 cup chopped nuts

Sift together flour, cinnamon, baking soda, and salt; set aside. Beat eggs; add oil, buttermilk, sugar, and vanilla. Mix well. Add flour mixture to egg mixture. Add pineapple, carrots, coconut, if desired, and nuts. Pour batter into a warmed and greased 12-inch Dutch oven and bake at 350° for about 55 minutes or until you can smell it. A toothpick will come out clean when inserted, and cake will pull away from sides of pan.

CREAM CHEESE FROSTING:

3 cups powdered sugar
12 ounces cream cheese,
  softened

1 teaspoon milk
1 teaspoon vanilla

Mix well and frost cake when cool.

Log Cabin Dutch Oven

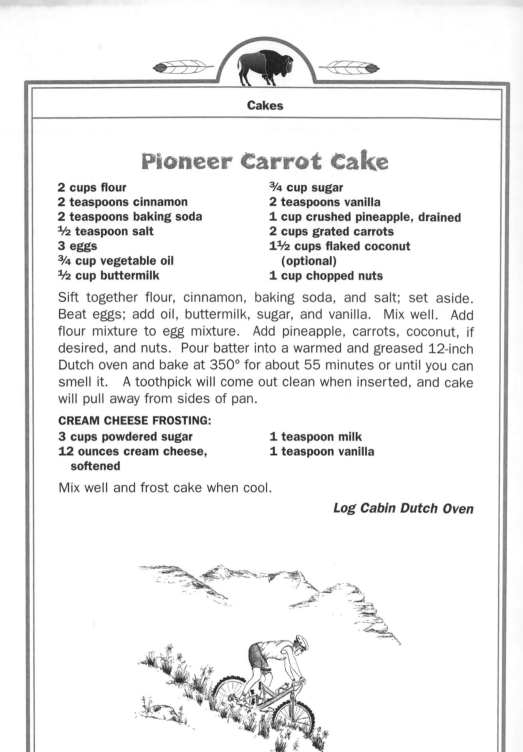

Cream Caramel Pecan Cheesecake

This cheesecake features a sensational toasted-pecan crust and caramel filling.

TOASTED-PECAN CRUST:

1 cup graham cracker crumbs	**¼ cup packed brown sugar**
¾ cup chopped pecans	**¼ cup butter, melted**

In a mixing bowl, combine crumbs, pecans, brown sugar, and melted butter. Pat onto bottom of an 8-inch springform pan.

2 (8-ounce) packages cream cheese, softened	**1 tablespoon vanilla**
¾ cup caramel topping, divided	**1½ cups sour cream**
3 eggs, beaten	**Pecan halves for garnish**

In a large mixing bowl, beat cream cheese until fluffy. Gradually beat in ½ cup caramel topping. Add eggs and vanilla, beating just until blended. Pour mixture into Toasted-Pecan Crust. Bake in 350° oven for 40–45 minutes, until center is set. Cool in pan 15 minutes.

Combine sour cream and remaining ¼ cup caramel topping; spoon over cheesecake. Loosen sides of cheesecake from pan with spatula. Cool 30 minutes more; remove sides of pan. Cool. Chill. Garnish with pecan halves before serving. Serves 8. Freezes well.

The Essential Mormon Cookbook

Located in the southwest corner of Utah, Quail Creek State Park's reservoir is a popular destination for fishing, boating, waterskiing, camping, and picnicking. Quail Creek boasts the warmest water in the state during summer.

Caramel Apple Pie Cheesecake

CRUST:

¾ cup all-purpose flour
½ cup self-rising flour
¼ cup sugar

½ cup butter, chilled, cut into
   pieces
2 egg yolks

Preheat oven to 375°. Lightly grease 9-inch springform pan. Sift flours into large bowl or food processor. Stir in sugar. Cut butter into flour with pastry blender or 2 knives or process in food processor for 40 seconds or so. Mix should resemble cornmeal. Add egg yolks and mix with a fork or your hands until dough forms. Press into bottom and 2 inches up side of prepared springform pan. Crust should be about ¼ inch thick; trim if necessary. Prick bottom and sides lightly with fork and refrigerate until ready to fill.

FILLING:

½ cup sugar
2 (8-ounce) packages cream
   cheese, softened

2 eggs
1 teaspoon vanilla

Beat sugar and cream cheese together until fluffy. Add eggs, one at a time, blending well after each addition. Add vanilla and beat on medium speed until smooth (1–2 minutes), scraping sides of bowl often. Spread over Crust.

TOPPING:

⅓ cup sugar
½ teaspoon ground cinnamon
⅛ teaspoon ground nutmeg

3–3½ cups sliced baking apples
   (then cut into 1-inch pieces)

Mix sugar, cinnamon, and nutmeg together. Sprinkle over apples; toss to coat. Arrange apples over Filling. Bake approximately 52 minutes, or until apples are tender and Filling is set. Cool completely. Refrigerate overnight to blend flavors.

When ready to serve, slice with sharp serrated knife and serve with warm Easy Caramel Sauce, whipped cream (spray can type), and chopped, roasted peanuts, or nuts of your choice.

(continued)

(Caramel Apple Pie Cheesecake continued)

EASY CARAMEL SAUCE:

1 stick real butter
1¼ cups firmly packed brown sugar

2 tablespoons light corn syrup
½ cup heavy whipping cream

Melt butter in a medium saucepan. Stir in the brown sugar and corn syrup. Bring to a boil, and stirring constantly, let boil for 1 minute or until sugar dissolves. Slowly stir in the whipping cream and return to a boil. Remove from heat. Sauce is now ready.

Only the Best

Lion House Cheesecake

1½ cups graham cracker crumbs
6 tablespoons plus 1 cup sugar, divided
6 tablespoons butter or margarine, melted
3 (8-ounce) packages cream cheese, softened

3 eggs
1¼ teaspoons vanilla, divided
1 tablespoon lemon juice
1 pint sour cream

In a medium bowl, thoroughly mix together graham cracker crumbs, 3 tablespoons sugar, and butter. Press firmly into a 10-inch deep-dish pie pan or springform pan, lining the bottom and sides. Set aside.

To make filling, place cream cheese in a large mixer bowl and beat well. Add 1 cup sugar a little at a time. Add eggs one at a time. Add ¾ teaspoon vanilla and lemon juice. Combine thoroughly. Pour filling into crust; fill to within ½ inch of top to allow room for topping. Bake 55–60 minutes at 300°. While cheesecake is baking, prepare topping.

To make topping, place sour cream in a small mixer bowl and whip; add remaining 3 tablespoons sugar gradually. Add ½ teaspoon vanilla. Pour topping over top of cheesecake and return to oven; bake for an additional 10 minutes. Allow to cool. Refrigerate until ready to serve. Makes 10–12 servings.

Lion House Weddings

Black Forest Cheesecake

2 cups Oreo cookie crumbs,
   rolled fine
3 (8-ounce) packages cream
   cheese, softened
1 cup sugar
3 eggs
¾ teaspoon vanilla

1 teaspoon almond extract
⅓ cup maraschino cherry juice
⅓ cup diced maraschino cherries
1 pint sour cream
3 tablespoons sugar
½ teaspoon vanilla
½ cup chocolate chips

Preheat oven to 300°. Crush Oreo cookies, including frosting centers, to make 2 cups of fine crumbs. Press evenly into bottom of a 10-inch springform pan.

Whip cream cheese in a mixer bowl; gradually add sugar; then add eggs one at a time. Stir in vanilla, almond extract, and maraschino cherry juice. Fold in maraschino cherries. Pour filling into crust. Bake 60 minutes.

Whip sour cream; add sugar and vanilla. Put half of sour cream topping on cheesecake; set remaining half aside. Melt chocolate chips and stir into the remaining sour cream topping. Then swirl this mixture into topping already on cheesecake. Return to oven and bake for 10 more minutes. Cool before removing sides from springform pan. Refrigerate until ready to serve. Makes 10–12 servings.

Lion House Desserts

Cookies and Candies

The 400- to 1,000-foot sandstone buttes, mesas, and pillars located in Monument Valley Navajo Tribal Park on the Utah/Arizona border were created as material eroded from the ancestral Rocky Mountains and was deposited and cemented into sandstone. Monument Valley has been featured in countless commercials and films, including John Wayne's Stagecoach.

PHOTO © FRANK JENSEN, STATE OF UTAH DIVISION OF TRAVEL DEVELOPMENT.

Wagon Wheel Cookies

FILLING:

1 cup water

1 cup sugar

1½ tablespoons lemon juice

2 cups chopped dates

1 cup chopped nuts

Cook Filling ingredients, except nuts, at medium heat, stirring until mixture thickens. Set Filling mixture aside to cool. When Filling mixture is cool, add nuts.

DOUGH:

1 cup shortening

2 cups brown sugar

3 eggs, well beaten

4 cups sifted flour

1 teaspoon baking soda

1 teaspoon vanilla

½ teaspoon salt

Beat together shortening, brown sugar, and eggs. Add flour, baking soda, vanilla, and salt. Mix until well blended. Divide Dough in half. Wrap each half in plastic wrap and chill for at least 30 minutes.

Roll each section of Dough into a rectangle. Spread with Filling and roll from long side. Wrap in plastic wrap and return to refrigerator for one hour.

Remove wrap and cut into ¼-inch slices. Place on greased cookie pan and bake at 350° for 10–12 minutes.

Recipes Thru Time

The Family History Library of the Church of Jesus Christ of Latter-day Saints in Salt Lake City houses the world's largest collection of genealogical information. The library has records of more than 2 billion names; 711,000 microfiche; and 278,000 books.

Pioneer Molasses Cookies
(Gingersnaps)

The pioneers used molasses because sugar was expensive and rarely available.

¾ cup butter	2 teaspoons baking soda
1 cup sugar	½ teaspoon salt
1 egg	2 teaspoons ground ginger
¼ cup dark molasses	¾ teaspoon ground cinnamon
2 cups flour	¼ teaspoon ground cloves

Cream butter and sugar. Beat until fluffy, and add egg and molasses. Stir together flour, baking soda, salt, ginger, cinnamon, and cloves, and blend into beaten ingredients. Form dough into balls, and roll in granulated sugar. Place on nongreased baking sheet, and bake at 350° for 10 minutes or until cookies have flattened and have cracks on top. Makes 5 dozen.

Recipes Thru Time

Church Windows

1 (12-ounce) package chocolate morsels	1 cup finely chopped pecans
½ cup butter or margarine	Flaked coconut
1 (10½-ounce) package multicolored mini marshmallows	

Melt chocolate and butter over low heat; cool. Add marshmallows and nuts to mixture. Shape into 2 rolls, 1½–2 inches in diameter. Roll each in coconut. Refrigerate. When rolls are thoroughly chilled, slice into wafers. The colored marshmallows make it look pretty.

Tasteful Treasures Cookbook

The Best of All Chocolate Chip Cookies

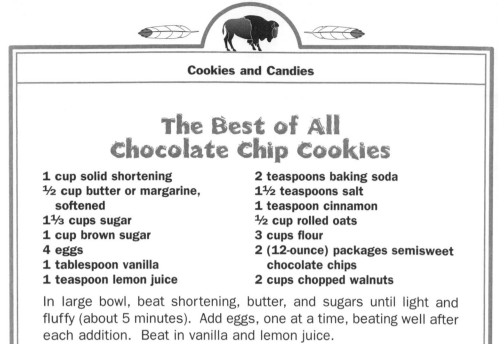

1 cup solid shortening
½ cup butter or margarine, softened
1⅓ cups sugar
1 cup brown sugar
4 eggs
1 tablespoon vanilla
1 teaspoon lemon juice

2 teaspoons baking soda
1½ teaspoons salt
1 teaspoon cinnamon
½ cup rolled oats
3 cups flour
2 (12-ounce) packages semisweet chocolate chips
2 cups chopped walnuts

In large bowl, beat shortening, butter, and sugars until light and fluffy (about 5 minutes). Add eggs, one at a time, beating well after each addition. Beat in vanilla and lemon juice.

In another bowl, stir together baking soda, salt, cinnamon, oats, and flour. Beat into creamed mixture until well combined; stir in chocolate chips and nuts.

For each cookie, drop a scant ¼ cup dough on a lightly greased baking sheet, spacing cookies about 3 inches apart. Bake in a 350° oven for 16–18 minutes or until golden brown. Transfer to racks and let cool. Makes about 3 dozen large cookies.

A Century of Mormon Cookery, Volume 1

Jumbo Double Chocolate Chip Cookies

This is my favorite of our jumbos. My willpower is vulnerable whenever these chocolate temptations are nearby—especially ones that are warm out of the oven.

½ pound (2 sticks) unsalted
   butter, softened
1 cup sugar
¾ cup firmly packed brown sugar
2 eggs
1 teaspoon vanilla extract
½ teaspoon instant espresso
   coffee powder

2 cups all-purpose flour
⅔ cup cocoa powder
1 teaspoon baking soda
1 teaspoon salt
¾ cup white chocolate morsels
½ cup semisweet chocolate
   morsels

Preheat oven to 325°. In a large bowl, using an electric mixer, cream the butter, sugar, and brown sugar until light and fluffy. Add the eggs, vanilla, and espresso powder. Mix well and scrape the sides and bottom of the bowl. Sift together the flour, cocoa powder, baking soda, and salt. Mix into the creamed butter, scraping again. Stir in the white and semisweet chocolate morsels.

Line 3 large baking sheets with parchment paper or oil them lightly with canola oil. Scoop the cookie dough into 12 large (⅓ cup) mounds, arranging them 4 to a sheet at least 3 inches apart. Bake until cookies are flat, 20–25 minutes. Makes 12 jumbo or 24 smaller cookies.

Chocolate Snowball

Hovenweep National Monument protects five prehistoric, Puebloan-era villages spread over a twenty-mile expanse of mesa tops and canyons along the Utah/Colorado border. The towers of Hovenweep were built by ancestral Puebloans, a sedentary farming culture that occupied the area from about A.D. 200 to A.D. 1300.

Wasatch Mountain Ranger Cookies

The Wasatch Mountains rise majestically from Salt Lake City and her sister cities, Ogden to the north and Provo to the south. The mountains form a geographical backbone to the populated adjacent land, which is often referred to as the Wasatch Front.

1 cup sugar	1 teaspoon baking soda
1 cup firmly packed brown sugar	Pinch of salt
	½ teaspoon baking powder
1 cup butter, margarine, or vegetable shortening, softened	1 teaspoon vanilla extract
	2 cups old-fashioned oats
2 eggs	2 cups rice crispies or cornflakes,
2 cups flour	or ¾ cup all-bran cereal

OPTIONS:

1 cup chopped walnuts or pecans	6 ounces milk chocolate chips
1 cup unsalted roasted peanuts	1 cup flaked coconut
6 ounces peanut butter chips	¾ cup golden raisins
6 ounces butterscotch morsels	

Preheat oven to 350°. In a large bowl, cream together the sugars and butter, then add eggs. Add remaining ingredients; fold in choice of cereal carefully. Choose any Options or combination of Options and add to dough. Spoon by tablespoons onto an ungreased baking sheet and bake for 12 minutes or until very lightly browned. Yields 6 dozen.

A Pinch of Salt Lake Cookbook

Melt-Aways

COOKIE:

1 cup butter, softened	⅓ cup powdered sugar
¾ cup sifted cornstarch	1 cup flour

Beat butter until very soft. Add cornstarch, sugar, and flour. Mix very well. Drop ½- to 1-inch balls onto ungreased cookie sheet. Bake at 350° for 10–12 minutes or until set and very lightly browned. Cool on wire rack in single layer, never stacked or overlapped.

FROSTING:

3 ounces cream cheese, softened	2 drops milk
1 teaspoon vanilla	2 drops food coloring
1 cup powdered sugar	

Combine all ingredients and beat until smooth. Drop a dab on top of each Cookie.

JLO Art of Cooking

Easy M&M Cookies

1 (18¼-ounce) white cake mix	⅓ cup vegetable oil
2 eggs	1¼ cups plain M&M's

Preheat oven to 350°. Mix together cake mix, eggs, and oil in a large bowl until mix is dissolved. Mix M&M's into dough. Drop balls of dough onto greased baking sheet. Bake 9–12 minutes, until golden brown. Remove from pan and cool.

101 Things To Do With a Cake Mix

Crazy Chocolate Caramel Cookies

1 (18¼-ounce) package chocolate cake mix	**2 eggs, slightly beaten**
½ cup oil	**Rolo candies**

Heat oven to 350°. In large bowl, combine cake mix, oil, and eggs. Blend well. Place a Rolo candy in the center of a piece of cookie dough. Roll the dough in a ball around the Rolo. Place on ungreased cookie sheet 2 inches apart. Bake 8–10 minutes. Cool 1 minute and remove from cookie sheet. Makes 4 dozen cookies.

Making Magic

English Toffee Cookies

1 cup brown sugar	**1 teaspoon vanilla**
1 cup butter, softened	**1 large Hershey's bar**
1 egg	**Chopped slivered almonds**
2 cups flour	

Cream sugar and butter. Stir in remainder of ingredients until blended and pat into 10x15-inch jellyroll pan. Bake at 350° 15–25 minutes until barely brown. Remove from oven. Break up Hershey's bar and put pieces on hot cookies and spread around as the chocolate melts. Sprinkle with almonds.

A Century of Mormon Cookery, Volume 2

Peanut Butter-Kiss Cookies

1 (18¼-ounce) yellow cake mix   ¾ cup peanut butter
2 eggs   1 package Hershey's Kisses
⅓ cup oil

Preheat oven to 350°. Mix together cake mix, eggs, and oil until mixture reaches brownie consistency. Mix peanut butter into the dough. Drop balls of dough onto a lightly greased pan. Place an unwrapped chocolate kiss in the center of each ball. Bake 10 minutes, or until light golden brown. Remove from pan and cool.

101 Things To Do With a Cake Mix

Child's Easy Peanut Butter Cookies

This cookie tastes like a peanut butter candy bar. Make without chocolate for a pure peanut butter experience.

1 cup peanut butter   3 squares semisweet chocolate,
1 cup sugar   coarsely chopped, or ½ cup
1 egg, beaten   chocolate chips

Mix together well. Roll teaspoonfuls of dough and place on cookie sheet. Mash with fork. Bake at 350° for 8 minutes. Yields 2 dozen.

Heritage Cookbook

More than 600 films and TV movies have been filmed in Utah. The top grossing movies filmed all or in-part in Utah include: *Butch Cassidy and the Sundance Kid, Indiana Jones and the Last Crusade, Forest Gump, Stagecoach, The Searchers, Dumb and Dumber, Back to the Future Part 3, Mission Impossible 2, Footloose, Fletch, Thelma and Louise, How the Grinch Stole Christmas, City Slickers 2, Austin Powers,* and *Maverick.*

Frosted Lemon Butter Cookies

An exquisite shortbread cookie, a lemon lover's joy.

COOKIE:

1 cup butter, softened
½ cup powdered sugar

⅔ cup cornstarch
1 cup flour

Cream butter and sugar. Stir in cornstarch and flour. Drop by teaspoonfuls on a cookie sheet. Bake at 325° for 15 minutes. Cool.

FROSTING:

¼ cup butter, melted
2 tablespoons lemon juice

Rind of one lemon, grated
2½–3 cups powdered sugar

Combine Frosting ingredients. Spread on cooled cookies. Yields 2½ dozen cookies.

Heritage Cookbook

Lemon Bars

CRUST:

2 cups flour
1 cup butter

½ cup powdered sugar
½ teaspoon salt

Cream together ingredients; pat into dripper pan (or cookie sheet) that has been greased and floured. Bake for 20 minutes at 350°.

TOPPING:

4 eggs, slightly beaten
2 cups sugar
½ teaspoon baking powder
4 tablespoons flour

1 tablespoon lemon juice
Grated rind of 1 lemon
Powdered sugar

Mix together all but powdered sugar; pour over hot Crust. Bake for 20 minutes at 350°. Remove from oven; sprinkle with powdered sugar.

Ladies' Literary Club Cookbook

Cream Cheese Squares

1 cup brown sugar
½ cup butter
2 cups Bisquick
¾ cup chopped walnuts
2 (8-ounce) packages cream
  cheese, softened

½ cup sugar
2 tablespoons lemon juice
1 tablespoon milk
1 teaspoon vanilla
2 eggs

Grease a 9x13-inch pan. Beat brown sugar and butter until fluffy. Stir in Bisquick and walnuts until mixture is crumbly. Reserve 2 cups of mixture; press remaining mixture in pan. Bake 12 minutes in 350° oven.

Mix cream cheese and sugar. Beat in remaining ingredients until smooth. Spread cheese mixture over baked crust. Sprinkle with reserved crumb mixture. Bake 30 minutes at 350°. Cool and cut in squares.

Dude Food

Cream Cheese Bars

CRUST:
1 (18¼-ounce) yellow cake mix   ⅓ cup oil
1 egg

Preheat oven to 350°. Mix together cake mix, egg, and oil until crumbly. Set aside 1 cup of Crust mixture for topping. Pat rest of dough lightly into a greased 9x13-inch pan. Bake 15 minutes.

FILLING:
1 (8-ounce) package cream
  cheese, softened
⅓ cup sugar

1 teaspoon lemon juice
1 egg

Beat together cream cheese, sugar, lemon juice, and egg until smooth. Spread evenly over baked layer. Sprinkle with reserved Crust mixture. Bake 15 minutes longer. Cool and cut into bars.

101 Things To Do With a Cake Mix

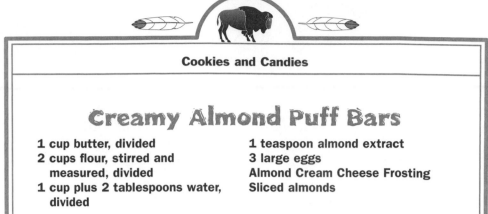

Creamy Almond Puff Bars

1 cup butter, divided
2 cups flour, stirred and
  measured, divided
1 cup plus 2 tablespoons water,
  divided

1 teaspoon almond extract
3 large eggs
Almond Cream Cheese Frosting
Sliced almonds

Cut 1 stick butter into 1 cup flour, as for pastry. Add 2 tablespoons water; mix with fork until ball forms. Divide. On large ungreased jelly-roll pan, pat each portion into a strip 3x12-inches, spacing strips about 3 inches apart.

In a saucepan, bring 1 cup water and other stick of butter to a boil. When butter is melted, stir in remaining flour all at once, and stir vigorously until mixture pulls away from sides of pan to gather into a smooth ball. Remove from heat. Add almond extract. Add eggs, one at a time, beating each into the dough until well incorporated and smooth. Divide dough in half and spread each half onto one pastry strip. Bake at 350° for one hour or until golden brown. Cool. Spread with frosting and top with sliced almonds. Slice diagonally.

ALMOND CREAM CHEESE FROSTING:
4 ounces cream cheese, softened
½ cup butter, softened

2½ cups powdered sugar
½ teaspoon almond extract

In large bowl, cream the cheese and butter until smooth. Gradually beat in the sugar and almond extract. Beat until of spreading consistency, adding a little evaporated milk, if necessary.

Only the Best

Cherry Chewbilees

1¼ cups flour
½ cup brown sugar
½ cup shortening
1 cup chopped walnuts, divided
½ cup flaked coconut
2 (8-ounce) packages cream
   cheese, softened

⅔ cup sugar
2 eggs
2 teaspoons vanilla
2 (21-ounce) cans cherry pie
   filling

Preheat oven to 350°. Combine flour and brown sugar. Cut in shortening with pastry blender till fine crumbs form. Add coconut and ½ cup nuts. Set aside ½ cup of crust mixture. Press remaining crust mixture in greased 9x13-inch pan. Bake 12–15 minutes till edges are slightly browned.

Beat cream cheese, sugar, eggs, and vanilla till smooth. Spread over crust. Bake 15 minutes more. Spread cherry pie filling on top. Combine remaining ½ cup nuts with reserved crust mixture; sprinkle over cherries. Bake 15 minutes to toast nuts. Cool. Refrigerate several hours before serving.

Recipes & Remembrances

Utah is the second largest tart cherry producing state in the nation and fifth in the nation in the production of sweet cherries. No other state ranks in the top five in both categories. About 2 billion cherries are harvested yearly, and approximately 4,800 acres of agricultural land is used for cherry production. The cherry became the official state fruit in 1997.

Split Seconds

⅔ cup sugar
¾ cup butter, softened
2 teaspoons vanilla
1 egg

2 cups flour
½ teaspoon baking powder
½ cup your favorite jam, divided

Preheat oven to 350°. In a large bowl, beat sugar and butter until light and fluffy. Add vanilla and egg; beat well. Lightly spoon flour into measuring cup and level off. Stir in flour and baking powder; blend well. On lightly floured surface, divide dough into 4 equal parts. Shape each into a roll 12 inches long by ¾ inch wide. Place on ungreased baking sheet. Using the handle of a wooden spoon or your finger, make a depression lengthwise down the center of each roll about ½ inch wide and ¼ inch deep. Fill each with 2 tablespoons jam. Bake for 15–20 minutes or until golden brown. Cool slightly. Cut diagonally into bars.

All That Jam

Marbelized Brownies

1 (8-ounce) bar German sweet
 chocolate
¾ cup margarine, softened,
 divided
6 eggs, divided
2 cups sugar, divided
1 cup plus 2 tablespoons flour,
 divided

½ teaspoon salt
1 teaspoon baking powder
3 teaspoons vanilla, divided
½ teaspoon almond extract
1 cup chopped nuts
6 ounces cream cheese, softened

Melt chocolate and 6 tablespoons margarine over low heat. Cool slightly. In bowl, beat 4 eggs until light colored; add 1½ cups sugar and beat well. Add 1 cup flour, salt, and baking powder. Blend in chocolate mixture, 1½ teaspoons vanilla, almond extract, and nuts.

In another bowl, combine cream cheese and remaining 4 table-spoons softened margarine; cream until smooth. Gradually add remaining ½ cup sugar; blend in 2 eggs, 2 tablespoons flour, and 1½ teaspoons vanilla. Lightly butter a 12-inch Dutch oven. Spread ½ of chocolate mixture in bottom. Spoon white batter over evenly. Spoon remainder of chocolate batter on top. Zigzag knife through batter to give marbelized effect. Bake at 350° for 40 minutes (6–8 coals on bottom, 12–16 coals on top).

Dutch Oven Gold

Ancient Native American rock art—called petroglyphs and pictographs—is common throughout Utah. Petroglyphs were pecked or incised into stone walls or boulders. Pictographs were painted on stone. Themes seem to vary widely from depictions of successful hunts to mythic figures considered to represent deities or ceremonial practices. Some depict scenes from domestic life. This rock art is protected by federal law and touching or removing it is prohibited.

Country Brownies

1 cup butter or margarine,
  melted
½ cup baking cocoa
2 cups sugar
4 eggs
1 teaspoon vanilla

2 cups flour
½ teaspoon salt
½ teaspoon baking powder
Real chocolate chips and chopped
  walnuts or pecans

Mix melted butter or margarine with cocoa in a mixing bowl. Add sugar and mix well. With wire whisk, beat in eggs one at a time. Add vanilla and dry ingredients. Stir only to mix; do not overstir. Spread in greased 12- or 14-inch Dutch oven, and sprinkle chocolate chips and nuts over batter. Cook with ⅓ heat on bottom and ⅔ heat on top of Dutch oven for 12 minutes, then remove oven from coals and cook from top only, 15–20 minutes longer, or until brownies are done (be careful not to overbake). Remove coals from lid and let brownies set up a few minutes before removing from oven.

Friends of Old Deseret Dutch Oven Cookbook

Good Easy Treat

2 pounds white or chocolate
  almond bark
1 cup chunky peanut butter

2 cups dry roasted peanuts
2 cups miniature marshmallows
3 cups Rice Krispies

Put white or chocolate almond bark in 200° oven and melt. Stir in remaining ingredients. Mix well and drop by teaspoons on wax paper. Makes 6 dozen treats.

Dude Food

Butterfinger Balls

1 pound powdered sugar
½ cup butter, softened
1 cup creamy peanut butter
3 cups rice crispies

4 squares sweet chocolate
Chopped nuts or crushed rice
  crispies

Mix sugar, butter, peanut butter, and rice crispies in a bowl and chill for one hour.

Remove from refrigerator and shape into 1-inch balls. Melt chocolate in a saucepan over low heat. Roll balls in it, then in nuts or crushed rice crispies. Store in cool place or refrigerator, covered.

Log Cabin Holidays and Traditions

English Toffee

1 stick margarine
1 stick butter
1 cup sugar

¼ cup water
1 cup chocolate chips
½ cup chopped nuts

Cook margarine, butter, sugar, and water on high heat, stirring constantly with a wire beater until it turns an amber color (or color of a brown paper bag) and smokes slightly. Pour candy into a buttered pan. Sprinkle chocolate chips on top, let melt, and spread on candy. Sprinkle with chopped nuts. Cool and break into small pieces.

Quick & Easy Cooking

Great Basin National Park's Wheeler Peak, with its 13,063-foot summit, is the site of one of the oldest bristle cone pine forests in the world. The park is located less than 20 miles over the Utah/Nevada border, straight west of Delta. Also located there is Lehman Cave, a large cavern with several "rooms" filled with stalagmites stalactities and other formations.

Caramels

Still a favorite Christmastime treat.

1 cup butter (must be real butter)
2 cups sugar

2 cups heavy cream, divided
Dash of salt
⅔ cup chopped nuts (optional)

Boil butter, sugar, and 1 cup of the cream for 25 minutes. Add remaining cup of cream and cook to firm-ball stage (between 244° and 248° on candy thermometer). Stir in salt and nuts, if desired, and pour into buttered pan. When cooled, cut into squares and wrap in wax paper, twisting the ends like candy wrappers.

Favorite Utah Pioneer Recipes

Great Salt Lake Taffy

Grandma used to say, "Cook it on a dry day, use a heavy pan, do not stir while cooking, don't undercook, and butter your hands."

1½ cups white vinegar
3 cups white sugar

¼ teaspoon baking soda
1 tablespoon butter or margarine

Combine vinegar and sugar in a heavy pan until sugar is dissolved. Cook over medium heat to soft-crack stage (between 270° and 290° on candy thermometer). Do not undercook. Remove from heat and add soda and butter. Pour onto greased platter to cool. When cool enough to handle, grease or butter hands, and pull until white. Cut into pieces and wrap in wax paper.

Recipes Thru Time

The Tabernacle organ in the Tabernacle Temple in Salt Lake City was built from timber located in the Parowan and Pine Valley mountains, 300 miles south of Salt Lake City. Originally powered by hand-pumped bellows and later by water power, the organ is now powered by electricity. It has been renovated and enlarged several times. With its 11,623 pipes, the organ has 206 ranks of voices, and the console has five manuals, or keyboards. The Tabernacle organ is considered to be one of the finest organs in the world.

Rocky Road Candy

½ stick (¼ cup) butter or
  margarine
1 (6-ounce) package semisweet
  chocolate pieces

3 cups miniature marshmallows
½ cup chopped nuts

In a saucepan, melt butter and chocolate pieces over low heat. Remove from heat; stir in marshmallows and nuts just until coated with chocolate. Spoon onto wax paper or into buttered pan. Chill until set, about 30 minutes. Makes about 24 pieces.

A Century of Mormon Cookery, Volume 1

Trail-Side Granola Mix

3 cups rolled oats (oatmeal)
1 cup wheat germ
½ cup olive oil or vegetable oil
½ cup honey or molasses
1 tablespoon vanilla
1–2 cups raisins, dried currants,
  or other assorted dried fruits

½ cup unsweetened coconut
2 ounces whole sesame seeds
½ cup nuts (almonds or cashews
  are best)
½ cup hulled sunflower seeds

Thoroughly mix all ingredients except fruit and nuts. Spread evenly on cookie sheet and toast for 1 hour, stirring every 15 minutes. Remove from heat and add fruit and nuts. As mixture cools, stir periodically. Serve with milk or yogurt or eat plain as a snack. Store in airtight container.

A Mormon Cookbook

Miracle Caramel Corn

This is made in a brown paper grocery bag.

2 gallons popped corn (1 cup
  unpopped)
1 stick butter
2 cups brown sugar

½ cup white corn syrup
1 tablespoon water
Pinch baking soda

In large double-strength grocery bag (or 2 bags, one inside the other), place popped corn. Bag should be about ⅓ full. Roll down edges of bag to the inside about 2 inches. Melt butter in saucepan. Add brown sugar, corn syrup, and water. Mix and place on medium heat. Stir constantly and bring to a hard boil. Add pinch of soda, remove immediately from heat, and pour syrup over popped corn in bag. Close bag at top, carefully shake, then knead the bag with both hands, over and over until the corn is well coated with syrup. The bag will get soggy, but if sturdy, should last.

Like magic, the corn will be thoroughly coated. Form into balls or leave in clusters. Serve immediately or place in containers for storage. May be frozen for several weeks, if desired.

A Century of Mormon Cookery, Volume 2

Pies and Other Desserts

Ancestors of the modern Pueblo Indians inhabited the Four Corners area from about A.D. 200 to A.D. 1300. They built rectangular masonry dwellings and large apartment complexes that were tucked into cliff faces or situated on valley floors.

Margarita Pie

1 cup crushed graham crackers	2 cups vanilla ice cream,
3 tablespoons powdered sugar	softened
⅓ cup plus ¼ cup frozen	Fresh strawberries
margarita mix, thawed, divided	Whipped cream
2 cups lime sherbet	

Mix cracker crumbs, sugar, and ¼ cup margarita mix. Press against the bottom and an inch up the side of a 10-inch Dutch oven. Mix sherbet and ⅓ cup margarita mix together. Mix in softened ice cream and spread evenly. Follow directions for Frozen Desserts below.

Cut strawberries in half and put on top of dessert just before serving; top each piece with whipped cream. Make this after breakfast and bury it until after dinner for a great surprise.

FROZEN DESSERTS:

You can make any frozen dessert in your Dutch oven easily—simply follow the recipe and make in the Dutch oven as you would at home in a regular dish. To freeze the dessert, dig a pit in the ground. Put a clean garbage bag in the hole and pour ice in the bottom of the bag and set your Dutch oven on top of the ice. Top with more ice and twist the bag closed and cover with dirt. Leave until you're ready to eat! Don't forget where you buried dessert; if necessary, mark you buried treasure! This doesn't take a lot of ice; one bag should be plenty; just experiment with it and see what works best for you.

Dutch Oven and Outdoor Cooking, Y2K Edition

Orange Chiffon Pie

This recipe was originally written for fresh tangelos. If you can get them, substitute their juice and grated rind for the orange juice and rind.

1 package unflavored gelatin
½ cup sugar
Dash of salt
4 eggs, separated
¾ cup orange or tangerine juice
  (fresh or frozen)
½ cup lemon juice

½ teaspoon grated lemon rind
½ teaspoon grated orange or
  tangerine rind
⅓ cup sugar
1 (9-inch) pie crust, baked
Whipped cream

Thoroughly mix gelatin, ½ cup sugar, and salt in a saucepan. In a bowl, beat egg yolks and fruit juices together. Stir into gelatin mixture. Cook and stir over medium heat just until mixture comes to boiling point. Remove from heat. Stir in grated rinds. Chill, stirring occasionally, until partially set.

In a separate bowl, beat egg whites, gradually adding ⅓ cup sugar. Continue beating just till stiff peaks form. Fold in cold gelatin mixture. Pile into baked pie crust. Chill 3 hours or overnight. To serve, garnish with whipped cream. Yields 1 (9-inch) pie.

Heritage Cookbook

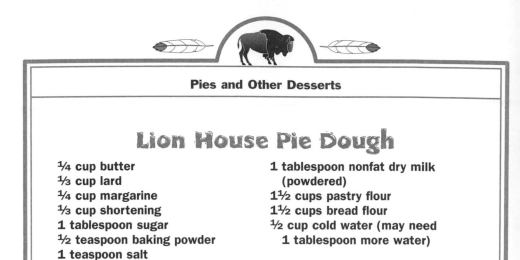

Lion House Pie Dough

¼ cup butter
⅓ cup lard
¼ cup margarine
⅓ cup shortening
1 tablespoon sugar
½ teaspoon baking powder
1 teaspoon salt

1 tablespoon nonfat dry milk
   (powdered)
1½ cups pastry flour
1½ cups bread flour
½ cup cold water (may need
   1 tablespoon more water)

In a mixer, cream together butter, lard, margarine, and shortening. In a bowl, mix sugar, baking powder, salt, and dry milk powder together. Then add to the creamed butter mixture and mix briefly. Add pastry flour and beat until it is blended. Add bread flour and mix slightly. Pour water in and beat again only until water is incorporated.

Divide dough into 2 or 3 balls. Roll out on floured board. Line pie pan with dough and cut off excess dough. For baked pie shells, flute edges. Prick holes in bottom with fork and bake at 425° for 12–15 minutes or until light golden brown. For fruit pies and other pies that bake in the crust, fill pie shell and follow instructions for particular pie recipe you are using. Yields 2–3 pie shells.

Note: All-purpose flour can be used instead of the combination of bread and pastry flour. The crust can also be made using the traditional pie crust method: by hand-cutting fats into the dry ingredients.

Lion House Desserts

Utah's passage to statehood was long and eventful because of the Mormon's early belief in polygamous marriage and their self-exile from the rest of country. It took almost fifty years for lawmakers to admit Utah as an official member of the Union. During that time Mormon leaders officially outlawed polygamy. In the autumn of 1895 a constitution was approved, which included granting women the right to vote. Several months later, on January 4, 1896, Utah was admitted as the 45th state in the Union.

Coconut Custard Pie

1¼ cups milk
½ cup half-and-half cream
¼ cup sugar
¼ teaspoon nutmeg
¼ teaspoon cinnamon

¼ teaspoon vanilla
⅛ teaspoon salt
3 eggs, slightly beaten
½ cup flaked coconut
Unbaked 9-inch pie shell

Combine all ingredients except coconut. Blend well. Cook on low heat or in double boiler until mixture boils, stirring constantly. Place coconut in pie shell. Pour mixture over coconut until shell is full. Bake at 400° for one hour, or until knife inserted comes out clean.

Lion House Recipes

Politician's Pie

Great recipe to take to a party or dinner!

CRUST:
1 cup flour
1 stick margarine, softened

1 cup chopped nuts

Combine ingredients until crumbly. Press into 9x13-inch pan. Bake at 350° for 15 minutes and cool.

FILLING:
1 (8-ounce) package cream
  cheese, softened
1 cup powdered sugar
1½ cups Cool Whip
1 (3.4-ounce) box vanilla instant
  pudding

1 (3.4-ounce) box chocolate
  instant pudding
3 cups milk
Cool Whip for topping
Hershey's bar, grated

Cream together cream cheese, powdered sugar, and Cool Whip. Spread on cooled Crust. Mix together puddings and milk until semi-thick. Spread on top of cream cheese mixture. Top with Cool Whip and grated Hershey's bar. Chill and serve. Serves 12–15.

Family Favorites from the Heart

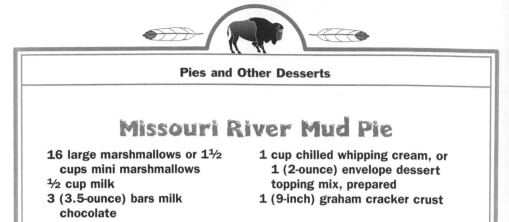

Missouri River Mud Pie

16 large marshmallows or 1½
  cups mini marshmallows
½ cup milk
3 (3.5-ounce) bars milk
  chocolate

1 cup chilled whipping cream, or
  1 (2-ounce) envelope dessert
  topping mix, prepared
1 (9-inch) graham cracker crust

Heat marshmallows, milk, and chocolate over medium heat, stirring constantly, just until marshmallows and chocolate melt and blend. Chill until thickened.

In chilled bowl, beat cream until stiff. Stir marshmallow mixture to blend; fold into whipped cream. Pour into crust. Chill at least 8 hours or until set. If desired, garnish with toasted, slivered almonds.

A Mormon Cookbook

Pack Creek Campground Shoo Fly Pie

½ teaspoon baking soda
¾ cup boiling water
1 egg yolk
½ cup molasses
½ cup brown sugar
⅛ teaspoon ground ginger
½ teaspoon cinnamon

¾ cup flour
⅛ teaspoon nutmeg
⅛ teaspoon ground cloves
¼ teaspoon salt
2 tablespoons butter or shortening
1 (9-inch) pie pastry

Dissolve baking soda in boiling water, then add egg yolk and molasses. Set aside. Stir sugar, ginger, cinnamon, flour, nutmeg, cloves, and salt together, and mix well. Cut in butter or shortening until mixture looks like coarse crumbs. Pour molasses into pie shell. Sprinkle crumbs evenly over top. Do not stir. Bake at 450° for 15 minutes, then reduce heat to 350° and bake 20 minutes longer. Cool, then serve.

Recipes & Remembrances

Raspberry Pie

1 (10-ounce) package frozen
  raspberries, thawed
Water
1 (3-ounce) package
  raspberry-flavored gelatin
¾ cup boiling water

2 tablespoons lemon juice
½ cup heavy cream, whipped
Dash of salt
2 egg whites
¼ cup sugar
Baked pie shell

Drain raspberries, reserving syrup; add water to syrup from berries to make ⅔ cup. Dissolve gelatin in boiling water; add lemon juice and raspberry syrup mixture. Blend well; chill until partially set. Beat gelatin mixture until soft peaks form. Fold in raspberries and whipped cream (reserve some for topping).

Add salt to egg whites; beat until soft peaks form. Add sugar gradually; beat to stiff peaks. Fold into raspberry mixture. Pile into cooled pie shell. Chill. Top with whipped cream and fresh raspberries.

A Century of Mormon Cookery, Volume 1

Un-Apple Pie

4–5 cups peeled, seeded, and
sliced zucchini
Water
1 cup sugar
¼ cup brown sugar
1 teaspoon cinnamon
¼ teaspoon nutmeg
¼ teaspoon allspice
1½ teaspoons cream of tartar
2 tablespoons flour or
cornstarch
Pinch of salt
2 (9-inch) unbaked pie shells

Cover zucchini slices with water and boil 2 minutes. Drain and set aside to cool. Mix all other ingredients together and stir gently through zucchini. Pour into pie shell and cover with top crust. Bake at 400° for 10 minutes, then lower heat to 350° for 20 minutes or until brown.

How to Enjoy Zucchini

Shamrock Pie

1 cup sugar
¼ cup cornstarch
1½ cups water
3 egg yolks, beaten (reserve
whites)
¼ cup lemon juice
1 tablespoon butter
1½ teaspoons grated lemon
peel
5 drops green food coloring
1 (9-inch) pastry shell, baked

Combine sugar, cornstarch, and water in a saucepan. Stir until smooth. Bring to a boil, stirring constantly. Boil until thick. Stir a small amount into the egg yolks and remove from heat; stir in lemon juice, butter, lemon peel, and food coloring until smooth. Pour into crust.

MERINGUE:
3 reserved egg whites   ⅓ cup sugar

Beat egg whites until foamy; gradually add sugar and beat until stiff peaks form and hold. Spread over filling and bake at 350° for 10–15 minutes or until lightly browned.

Log Cabin Holidays and Traditions

Famous Kelly Pumpkin Pie

3 eggs, slightly beaten
1 (16-ounce) can solid-pack
  pumpkin
¾ cup sugar
½ teaspoon salt
1 teaspoon ground cinnamon

¼ teaspoon ground cloves
½ teaspoon ground ginger
1 (5-ounce) can evaporated milk
1 (9-inch) deep-dish pie shell
Whipped cream or topping

Combine ingredients except whipped cream in the order given, mixing well after each addition. Pour filling into deep-dish pie shell and bake in center of the oven for 70 minutes at 375°. Pie will test done if knife is inserted in the center and comes out clean. Cool. Top with whipped cream or topping.

Log Cabin Holidays and Traditions

Rhubarb Pie

CRUST:

2 cups all-purpose flour
1½ tablespoons sugar
½ teaspoon salt

½ cup plus 2 tablespoons butter
1 large egg
2 tablespoons ice water

Mix together flour, sugar, and salt in a large bowl. Cut the butter in with a pastry cutter. Mix together the egg and water in a small bowl, then add that to the flour/butter mixture. Knead through it with the heal of your hand until it barely holds together. Chill for at least 30 minutes before rolling.

FILLING:

2 cups diced rhubarb
¾ cup sugar

2 tablespoons flour
Nutmeg

Combine above ingredients. Pour into unbaked pie crust. Bake at 375° for 45 minutes.

A Mormon Cookbook

Very Berry Pie

1 (16-ounce) bag frozen
   boysenberries (no sugar added)
1 (8-ounce) bag frozen blueberries
   (no sugar added)
1 (8-ounce) bag frozen raspberries
   (no sugar added)

1¾ cups sugar
½ teaspoon salt
½ cup cornstarch
Pastry for 2 (2-crust) pies

Preheat oven to 375°. Thaw all berries, then pour berries and all of the juice in a mixing bowl. In a separate bowl, mix together sugar, salt, and cornstarch; pour on top of berries. Mix well with rubber spatula. Fill crusts, add top crusts, and bake for 45–60 minutes or until golden brown. Makes 2 pies.

Lion House Desserts

Apple Pie

If you want to make this real easy, get a pie tin that fits down in the bottom of your Dutch oven (10 inch or 12 inch). If you don't have a pie tin, just follow these instructions, but do them directly in the bottom of your Dutch oven.

1 package pre-made pie crusts
5 cups peeled and sliced apples
⅔ cup plus 1 tablespoon sugar,
   divided

2 tablespoons flour
½ teaspoon cinnamon
Sprinkle of salt
2 tablespoons margarine

Dust bottom of Dutch oven with a bit of flour before you put the pie crust in it. Put the first pie crust in the bottom of the pie tin and up the side.

In a separate bowl, mix the apples, ⅔ cup sugar, flour, cinnamon, and salt. Pour this mixture into the first crust. Dot mixture with margarine. Cut second crust into ½-inch strips. Put strips about ½ inch apart over top of pie in one direction first and then the opposite direction, forming a lattice appearance. Push the edges of the top pie crust into the bottom pie crust so that they stick together, then cut away any extra. Sprinkle top with remaining sugar. Cover and bake about 45 minutes to one hour at 375°–400°.

Backyard Dutch Oven

Apple Crumb Pie

TOPPING:
½ cup flour   ¼ cup butter
¼ cup sugar

Combine flour and sugar; cut in butter till crumbly.

⅔ cup sugar   6–8 tart apples, pared, cored, and
2 tablespoons flour   grated
¾ teaspoon cinnamon   1 (9-inch) pastry shell

Combine sugar, flour, and cinnamon; stir into apples. Place pastry
shell in a 9-inch pie pan or place directly in a 10-inch Dutch oven
and turn apple mixture into pastry shell. Sprinkle Topping over
apples. Place pie pan in a 12-inch Dutch oven and bake at 400° for
45–50 minutes until done.

Friends of Old Deseret Dutch Oven Cookbook

Apple Crisp

3 cups peeled and sliced apples   ¾ cup well-packed brown
½ cup granulated sugar   sugar
1 tablespoon plus ¾ cup flour,   ¼ teaspoon baking soda
   divided   ¼ teaspoon baking powder
¼ teaspoon salt   ⅓ cup butter, softened
Cinnamon as desired   Raisins and chopped nuts
¾ cup oatmeal   (optional)

In a greased baking dish, combine sliced apples, granulated sugar,
1 tablespoon flour, and salt. Sprinkle with cinnamon as desired.
Mix oatmeal, remaining ¾ cup flour, brown sugar, baking soda, and
baking powder; cut in butter. Sprinkle mixture over apples. Add
raisins and nuts, if desired. Bake at 400° for 30 minutes until
browned and apples are tender.

Dude Food

Mixed Berry Crisp

Berries in season are always best. When not in season, use frozen.

CRISP TOPPING:

1 cup all-purpose flour
1 cup finely chopped walnuts
1 cup brown sugar

1 cup oatmeal
½ cup (1 stick) butter or
   margarine, melted

In a medium bowl or 1-quart plastic zipper bag, add flour, walnuts, brown sugar, oatmeal, and butter or margarine, and mix. This can be prepared at home and added to the Berry Crisp outdoors. Excellent on cooked fruit or added to coffee cake before baking.

1 (10-ounce) bag frozen
   raspberries, thawed
1 (10-ounce) bag frozen
   blueberries, thawed

1 (10-ounce) bag frozen
   boysenberries or blackberries,
   thawed
¾ cup sugar

In a bowl combine berries and sugar; set aside. Heat a 12-inch Dutch oven over 9 hot coals. Cover with Dutch oven lid and place 15 hot coals on the top. Preheat 10 minutes. Pour the berry mixture into the Dutch oven. Sprinkle Crisp Topping evenly onto berries. Bake, covered, for 30–35 minutes. At home in oven, follow same directions, but cook in a baking dish at 350° for 30–35 minutes, or until golden brown. Serve warm or cold. Serves 6–8.

Recipes for Roughing It Easy

Honey Peach Crisp

6 peaches
¾ cup finely chopped pecans
1 tablespoon lemon juice
⅓ cup honey

½ cup flour
½ cup quick oats
¾ teaspoon cinnamon
⅓ cup butter, softened

Peel and slice peaches and arrange in the bottom of a Dutch oven; cover with pecans. Combine lemon juice and honey and pour over the pecans. Mix flour, oats, cinnamon, and butter, and stir until crumbly. Spread evenly over the peaches and pecans. Cook until peaches are tender and topping is browned, usually about 35 minutes.

Dutch Oven and Outdoor Cooking, Y2K Edition

Blueberry Streusel Cobbler

1 pint frozen blueberries
1 (14-ounce) can sweetened
 condensed milk
2 teaspoons grated lemon peel
¾ cup plus 2 tablespoons cold
 butter, divided

2 cups all-purpose baking mix,
 divided
⅓ cup brown sugar
½ cup chopped nuts

In bowl, combine blueberries, condensed milk, and lemon peel. In a large bowl, cut ¾ cup butter into 1½ cups baking mix until crumbly; add blueberry mixture. Place in a 12-inch warmed and oiled Dutch oven.

In a small bowl, combine remaining ½ cup biscuit mix and sugar; cut in remaining 2 tablespoons butter until crumbly. Add nuts; sprinkle over cobbler. Bake at 350° in your oven in a warmed and oiled 12-inch Dutch oven, or for briquettes, use 10 on bottom and 15 on top for 1 hour and 10 minutes or until golden. If using a Volcano, use 12 coals on the bottom in a circle. Serve warm with whipped cream or ice cream. Refrigerate leftovers.

Log Cabin Presents Lewis and Clark

Kim's Cobbler

1 (21-ounce) can cherry pie
   filling
1 (15-ounce) can crushed
   pineapple
1 (18¼-ounce) white cake mix,
   dry

½–¾ cup butter, melted
Chopped pecans
Coconut

Dump cherry pie filling and pineapple in the bottom of a 12-inch Dutch oven. Cover with dry cake mix and drizzle with butter. Top with pecans and coconut to taste. Bake in hot coals, about 350° for 45 minutes.

Dutch Oven and Outdoor Cooking, Book Two: Homespun Edition

Soda Pop Cobbler

2 cans fruit filling (your choice) or
   lite fruit
1 (18¼-ounce) yellow or white
   cake mix

1 (8-ounce) can diet soda (any
   flavor)

Spray Dutch oven with nonstick cooking spray. Add fruit and smooth. Sprinkle dry cake mix over filling. Pour soda over cake mix. Bake 25–30 minutes at 350° or until done, 10–12 coals under, 18–22 on lid.

Note: Add 2 tablespoons instant tapioca to canned fruit juices to thicken. It's also fun to complement the soda and the fruit (strawberry filling with strawberry-kiwi soda pop on top).

Dutch Oven Delites

Black Forest Cobbler

Loosely defined, a cobbler is a fruit dessert with a cake or biscuit-type topping. There are hundreds of variations. This is usually the first dish a new cook attempts because they are easy and taste so good. Cobblers are very forgiving. It rarely matters if the fruit or the batter is placed in the oven first. Texture of the batter is not compromised whether mixed as directed or using soda pop. Measurements do not need to be exact.

1 (18¼-ounce) devil's food
  cake mix
12–16 ounces cream soda or
  lemon-lime soda

1 (29-ounce) can cherry pie
  filling

Gather all ingredients. Start at least 24 charcoal briquettes. In a large bowl, empty contents of cake mix. Pour soda into cake mix a little at a time, stirring after each addition until it reaches cake batter consistency. Lightly spray a 12-inch Dutch oven with spray oil. Empty contents of pie filling into oven. Distribute evenly with a spatula. Gently pour batter over pie filling. Spread evenly. Bake with 8 charcoal briquettes on the bottom and 16 on the top for 45–60 minutes or until done. Cobblers are done when the top is golden brown, sides are slightly pulled away from the edges, and a toothpick inserted in the cake comes out clean. Serves 12–15.

Note: When baking cobblers, rotate the lid and pot one quarter turn in opposite directions every 15 minutes.

The Dutch Oven Resource

The sego lily was declared to be the Utah floral emblem on March 18, 1911. Kate C. Snow, once president of the Daughters of Utah Pioneers, in a letter dated April 17, 1930, wrote that between 1840 and 1851, food became very scarce in Utah due to a crop-devouring plague of crickets, and that "the families were put on rations, and during this time they learned to dig for and to eat the soft, bulbous root of the sego lily. The memory of this use, quite as much as the natural beauty of the flower, caused it to be selected in after years by the Legislature as the floral emblem of the State."

Apple Phyllo Bundles

Individual packages like these are sometimes called beggar's purses because they resemble a drawstring pouch of coins.

2 pounds (about 4 large) Golden Delicious apples	**¼ cup firmly packed brown sugar**
2 tablespoons (¼ stick) plus 8 tablespoons (1 stick) unsalted butter	**½ teaspoon ground cinnamon**
	⅛ teaspoon ground nutmeg
	8 sheets phyllo
½ cup dried cherries or cranberries	**Confectioners' sugar, to dust**
	1 cup Caramel Sauce, warm

Peel and core the apples. Cut them into ½-inch chunks. Melt 2 tablespoons of the butter in a large skillet. Add the apples and cook and stir over medium heat until they are just tender, 5–8 minutes. Remove from heat and pour off and discard any excess liquid. Stir in the dried cherries, brown sugar, cinnamon, and nutmeg. Let cool.

Preheat the oven to 375°. Line a baking sheet with parchment paper, or brush it lightly with melted butter, or spray with cooking spray. Melt the remaining 8 tablespoons of butter.

Unroll the package of phyllo sheets on a work surface. Cover the sheets with a dampened kitchen towel. Keep them covered while you work so they don't dry out.

Pick up 1 sheet of phyllo, place it on a large cutting board, and brush it lightly with melted butter. Repeat, stacking and buttering 4 layers. Using a sharp knife, cut the buttered stack of phyllo in half, crosswise and lengthwise, making 4 rectangles. Put about ½ cup of the apple mixture in the center of each rectangle. Gather up the corners of the rectangles and gently pinch the dough together just above the apple filling. Butter, stack, and cut another 4 rectangles; fill and pinch into bundles.

Place all the bundles on the prepared pan. Bake 45–50 minutes or until they are a rich golden brown all over. Keep warm in the turned-off oven with the door ajar.

Dust the phyllo bundles with confectioners' sugar. Place each bundle on a plate and drizzle the warm Caramel Sauce generously over the bundles and on the plates. Makes 8 bundles.

(continued)

(Apple Phyllo Bundles continued)

CARAMEL SAUCE:

½ cup sugar   1 cup heavy cream

1 teaspoon fresh-squeezed lemon
    juice or water

Mix the sugar and lemon juice in a heavy saucepan until it resembles wet sand. Cook, stirring constantly with a wooden spoon, over medium-high heat. After a few minutes, the sugar will begin to melt; continue stirring until any lumps dissolve and the mixture turns a deep caramel color, 4–6 minutes. Remove from the heat and immediately stir in a little of the cream. The hot caramel will seize when you add the cold cream but will melt again as it cooks. Return the pan to low heat and gradually stir in the remaining cream. Cook, stirring, until caramel and cream are homogenous. Makes about 1 cup.

Chocolate Snowball

Grandma's Candied Apple Dumplings

PASTRY:

4 cups sifted flour
1½ teaspoons salt
1⅓ cups shortening

1 egg, beaten
1 tablespoon vinegar
8 tablespoons water

Place flour and salt in bowl. Cut shortening into flour and salt with a pastry blender until pieces are the size of peas. Beat egg lightly in a 1½-cup measure; add vinegar and fill cup with ice cold water. Add just barely enough liquid to dry ingredients to hold dough together, about 6–7 tablespoons. Refrigerate the remaining liquid for the next batch of pastry. Handle dough as little as possible. Divide pastry into 8 equal pieces. Roll each piece to approximately ⅛-inch thickness, 8–9 inches in diameter.

SYRUP:

1 cup sugar
¼ pound (1 stick) butter

2 cups water
½ cup red hot candies

Combine sugar, butter, water, and red hots. Heat to boiling and boil for 3 minutes. Pour into a bowl and set aside.

APPLES:

8 medium apples
¾ cup sugar

2 teaspoons ground cinnamon
8 tablespoons butter, divided

Peel apples and slice in thin slices. Mix sugar and cinnamon in a small bowl. Divide apples into 8 equal portions. Place apples on each pastry piece and sprinkle 1 tablespoon sugar-cinnamon mixture on the apples. Place 1 tablespoon butter on top of apples and bring pastry up and fold over top of apples. Place in a 14-inch Dutch oven. Pour hot Syrup around dumplings and cover with lid. Place 8 coals on bottom and 20 coals on top of Dutch oven, and cook for 30–40 minutes or until apples are tender and crust is browned on top. Serve with ice cream, cool whip, or light cream. Makes 8–10 dumplings.

Dutch Oven Secrets

Pumpkin Dessert

4 eggs, slightly beaten	½ teaspoon ground cloves
1 (29-ounce) can pumpkin	3 cups evaporated milk
1½ cups sugar	1 (18¼-ounce) yellow cake mix
1 teaspoon salt	1 cup chopped nuts
2 teaspoons cinnamon	½ cup melted butter
1 teaspoon ground ginger	

Mix together eggs, pumpkin, sugar, salt, cinnamon, ginger, cloves, and milk. Spread into bottom of a seasoned Dutch oven. Spread dry yellow cake mix over the top. Sprinkle chopped nuts over cake mix, then pour melted butter over the top. Bake at 425° for 15 minutes. Reduce heat to 350° for 50 minutes or until knife comes out clean.

To achieve 425°, place 12 coals on bottom and 20 on top. To reduce heat to 350°, place 6 coals underneath and 14 on top.

Championship Dutch Oven Cookbook

Double Chocolate Mint Dessert

CAKE:

1 cup flour	4 eggs
1 cup sugar	1 (16-ounce) can Hershey's syrup
½ cup butter	(1½ cups)

Beat flour, sugar, butter, eggs, and syrup until smooth. Pour into Dutch oven. Bake 25–30 minutes or until it springs back when lightly touched. Cool completely.

MINT LAYER:

2 cups sugar	3 drops green food coloring
½ cup butter, softened	½ teaspoon (6 drops) mint
1 tablespoon water	

Combine ingredients until smooth. Spread Mint layer on cake. To chill, you may pack the Dutch oven in ice. Pour chocolate topping over dessert, if desired. Cover and chill.

Dutch Oven and Outdoor Cooking, Book Two: Homespun Edition

Pete's Prize-Winning Strawberry Shortcake

2 quarts fresh strawberries	½ teaspoon vanilla
Sugar	¼ stick butter, room
1 pint heavy cream	temperature

Just before dinner (not earlier), rinse and hull strawberries. Slice with knives into chunks (crushing makes them too liquid.) Leave a few strawberries whole for garnish. Sugar to taste, little or none, a few spoonfuls should do. Put in icebox. Whip cream, add sugar and vanilla to taste, and whip a few seconds more. Put in icebox.

SHORTCAKE BISCUITS:

2½ cups flour	3 tablespoons sugar
3 teaspoons baking powder	¾ stick butter, softened
½ teaspoon salt	A scant ¾ cup milk

With clean fingers, knead together flour, baking powder, salt, and sugar with butter till it is all smooth, no lumps. Set aside. Grease a cookie sheet. Get all serving dishes and spoons ready. Now you can sit down to eat dinner, or whatever.

About 30 minutes before dessert time, excuse yourself from the table and go to the kitchen and light the oven (you want it hot, about 450°). Now, quickly stir the milk into the flour mixture. Don't waste time trying to make it very smooth. The consistency is much thicker than a cake batter, but not so dry as rolled biscuits, these are drop biscuits. With your finger, push a 2-inch lump of dough off the spoon onto the cookie sheet. You should get at least 8 lumps. Pop them into the oven immediately. Go back to dinner. In about 15 minutes, the table should be cleared, and the serving spoons, dishes and spoons on the table.

Also on the table put the chilled strawberries, whipped cream, and butter that is room temperature. Now comes the time when seconds count. When the shortcakes are tinged with golden brown, take them out of the oven and to the table, pronto. Have someone

(continued)

(Pete's Prize-Winning Strawberry Shortcake continued)

slice each shortcake and put a dab of butter between to melt imme-diately, and place the shortcake in the serving dish. Another per-son should zonk on top a big spoonful of sliced strawberries, then whipped cream, and a few more whole strawberries on top to look pretty. Eat right away! Now you'll know why Pete's is the best short-cake in the world.

Making Magic

Strawberries Divine

1 (8-ounce) package cream
   cheese, softened
3 tablespoons powdered sugar
2 tablespoons orange juice

1 quart fresh strawberries, washed
   and dried (do not remove stem)
Strawberry or mint leaves for
   garnish

Beat cream cheese until fluffy. Add powdered sugar and orange juice. Fill a cake decorator tube with mixture. From the point, slit each berry into quarters (do not cut through the bottom of the berry). Pipe cream cheese mixture into each berry. Arrange on a serving tray and garnish with strawberry or mint leaves.

A Pinch of Salt Lake

Grapenut Pudding

½ cup grapenut cereal
Hot water
4 eggs
⅓ cup sugar

1 teaspoon vanilla
1 (5-ounce) can evaporated milk
½ milk can warm water
Nutmeg

Put grapenuts in casserole dish and add a little hot water. Beat eggs; add sugar, vanilla, and milk and pour into grapenut mixture. Pour ½ can warm water over grapenut mixture. Sprinkle with nutmeg and bake in 350° oven for 40–45 minutes.

Patty's Cakes and Things

Chocolate Custard

2 eggs
¾ cup egg yolks
¾ cup milk
1½ cups cream

7 ounces dark chocolate
   (bitter or semisweet)
¾ cup sugar

In a medium mixing bowl, whip whole eggs, yolks, and sugar together. Set aside. Scald milk and cream in medium saucepan. Add chocolate to milk and cream mixture and stir until melted. Slowly add egg mixture to hot chocolate milk, stirring constantly. Pour into ramekins or custard cups and bake in a water bath for 25–30 minutes at 350°. Serves 6–8 depending on size of cups.

Lion House Desserts

Blueberry Whiskey Sabayon

Sabayon is a mousse-like dessert sauce, the French name for the fluffy Italian zabaglione made with sweet Marsala wine. Sabayon has three primary ingredients; egg yolks, sugar, and alcohol. For a sabayon to accompany chocolate nut torte, omit the blueberries and the first sugar and substitute dark rum for the whiskey. Or prepare sabayon with white wine or champagne, to use as a topping for fresh fruit.

½ cup blueberries, fresh or
frozen
2 tablespoons plus 2 tablespoons
sugar

2 egg yolks
2 tablespoons bourbon whiskey
½ cup heavy cream, whipped

Cook the blueberries with 2 tablespoons of the sugar in a stainless steel (noncorrosive) saucepan over low heat, stirring until sugar dissolves. Continue cooking until the berries are very soft and have released most of their juice, 5–8 minutes.

Place the cooked blueberries and juice, the egg yolks, the remaining 2 tablespoons of sugar, and the whiskey in the top of a double boiler. Place over gently boiling water; the upper pan should not touch the water. Cook, whisking often, until the custard has thickened and reaches 160° on an instant-read thermometer, about 10 minutes.

Prepare an ice bath: Fill a large bowl with ice and nest the bowl of cooked blueberry mixture in it. Whisk the mixture until it is cold. You can refrigerate this sabayon base, covered, for up to 6 days. Before serving, fold in the whipped cream. Makes about 1½ cups.

Chocolate Snowball

Salt Lake City is the site of the nation's first department store. Zion's Cooperative Mercantile Institution (ZCMI) was established in the late 1800s. The store sold a wide variety of goods including clothing, wagons, machinery, sewing machines and carpets. ZCMI was sold to Meier and Frank Company in December 1999.

Mary's Homemade Peanut Butter Ice Cream Sandwiches

Talk about yummy! Wonderful to have in freezer when company comes over.

1 (14-ounce) can sweetened
  condensed milk
½ cup creamy peanut butter
2 tablespoons water
2 egg yolks, beaten

2 cups whipping cream, whipped
1 (15-ounce) roll slice and bake
  refrigerator peanut butter
  cookies

In a large bowl, combine milk, peanut butter, water, and egg yolks. Mix well, then fold in the whipped cream. Pour into a foil-lined 9x5-inch loaf pan and freeze 6 hours or until firm.

Slice and bake cookie dough according to directions. Cut ice cream loaf into 9 slices and then each of those in half. Place between 2 cookies and wrap with plastic wrap, and store in freezer. Makes 18 cookies.

Patty's Cakes and Things

Easy Ice Cream Sandwiches

1 (18¼-ounce) devil's food
  cake mix
⅓ cup oil

2 eggs
½ gallon vanilla ice cream

Preheat oven to 350°. Mix together cake mix, oil, and eggs in a large bowl. The dough will be stiff. Lightly flour a clean surface. Roll out the dough with a rolling pin until it is about ½ inch thick. Use a round cup or cookie cutter to cut out uniform cookies. Spray a cookie sheet with vegetable oil. Place the cut-out dough on the pan. Bake 8–10 minutes. Remove cookies onto a cooling rack.

When cool, place a scoopful of ice cream in between 2 cookies. Wrap the sandwiches in plastic wrap. Store cookies in an airtight container in the freezer.

101 Things To Do With a Cake Mix

Apple-Cinnamon Sorbet

½ cup apple juice
1½ teaspoons lemon juice
⅓ cup sugar, or to taste

¼ teaspoon cinnamon
4 golden delicious apples, sliced
2 cups shaved ice

Pour apple and lemon juice into smoothie container. Add sugar, cinnamon, and peeled apple slices (save a few unpeeled slices for garnish). Add shaved ice. Insert stir stick in top and mix for 30 seconds, rotating stir stick counterclockwise while mixing. Press smooth button and let run for 45 seconds, continuing to rotate stir stick. Press mix while pouring from spout. Garnish with apple slices.

Smoothies & Ice Treats

Christmas Nut Crunch

½ cup butter, melted
2 cups graham cracker crumbs
2 (3.5-ounce) packages vanilla
   instant pudding
2 cups milk

1 quart butter pecan or pralines
   and cream ice cream, softened
1 (8-ounce) container Cool Whip
2 candy bars, crushed (Heath,
   Krackel, or anything crunchy)

In a bowl, combine melted butter and crumbs. Mold in the bottom of a 9x13-inch cake pan or 2 pie tins. In large bowl, beat pudding mixes and milk. Blend well and fold in the ice cream. Fold in Cool Whip, then pour into crust. Sprinkle with crushed candy bars. Freeze for one hour or more and serve when ready. Makes 16–20 servings.

Variation: You may substitute crushed candy bars with chopped nuts, crushed frosted flakes, or use your imagination.

Log Cabin Holidays and Traditions

A Little Bit About Dutch Oven Cooking

OVEN SIZES AND QUANTITIES

8-inch   2 quarts (vegetables, baked beans)
10-inch 4 quarts (baked bread, rolls, small cobblers)
12-inch 6 quarts (most common size used for main dishes)
14-inch 8 quarts (main dishes and cobblers; when cooking for large groups)

COALS NEEDED FOR VARIOUS HEAT-DEGREE

12–15 coals 300°	**16–20 coals 400°**
13–17 coals 325°	**17–22 coals 425°**
14–18 coals 350°	**18–23 coals 450°**
15–19 coals 375°	**19–24 coals 475°**

Coals are ready to use when they are mostly gray in color. If longer cooking time is called for, you will need to start an additional batch of briquettes about the end of the first hour to add as needed. Your oven will function better if you get it as level as possible.

Make sure your lid is set on securely to make a good seal. The heavy lid will act as a pressure cooker when set on correctly. Rotate your oven and lid 90° about every 10–15 minutes while cooking. This will rotate the hot spots and prevent over-cooking the food in one area.

Roasting: Use equal heat on top and underneath.

Stewing or Simmering: Use a 4/1 ratio.

Frying or boiling: All the heat goes underneath.

Baking: Use a 1/3 ratio, one being the number of coals on the bottom and 3 the number on top. When fixing a fire for baking of cobblers, upside down cake, cake, cookies, pies, etc., most of the heat must be on top so you will use a checkerboard pattern on the bottom of only 6–8 briquettes and 18–24 on top in a circle pattern.

Catalog of
Contributing Cookbooks

East Canyon Reservoir is a 680-acre reservoir with excellent camping, boating, and fishing. It is also an attraction for history buffs since trails mark the steps of the Donner Party and the first Mormon settlers. East Canyon is surrounded by low mountains and is located about 35 miles northeast of Salt Lake City.

catalog of contributing cookbooks

All recipes in this book have been selected from the cookbooks shown on the following pages. Individuals who wish to obtain a copy of any particular book may do so by sending a check or money order to the address listed by each cookbook. Please note the postage and handling charges that are required. State residents add tax only when requested. Prices and addresses are subject to change, and the books may sell out and become unavailable. Retailers are invited to call or write to same address for discount information.

ALL THAT JAM: 101 RECIPES TO MAKE WITH A JAR OF JAM

Hollee Eckman and Heather Higgins
Shadow Mountain
P. O. Box 30178
Salt Lake City, UT 84130-0178

Phone 800-453-4532
Fax 801-517-3392
service@deseretbook.com
www.deseretbook.com

What to do with a jar of jam? Add a little of this and a dash of that, mix, cook, serve, and enjoy a surprising variety of tasty treats. From main dishes to desserts, *All That Jam* contains 101 easy-to-make recipes that use jam as one of the main ingredients.

$12.95 Retail Price
$4.00 Postage and handling

ISBN 1-59038-169-6

Make check payable to Deseret Book Company

ALWAYS IN SEASON

Junior League of Salt Lake City, Inc.
526 East 300 South
Salt Lake City, UT 84102

Phone 801-328-1019
Fax 801-328-1048
www.jlslc.org

Through spring, summer, autumn, and winter in Utah, *Always in Season* celebrates the joys of cooking and sharing food with family and friends. Down-home comfort foods, chef's specialties from some of our favorite restaurants, international classics, and local color—it's all here.

$21.95 Retail price
$4.00 Postage and handling

Visa/MC accepted
ISBN 0-9616972-2-9

Make check payable to Junior League of SLC, Inc.

AROMATHERAPY IN THE KITCHEN

by Melissa Dale and Emmanuelle Lipsky
Woodland Publishing
448 East 800 North
Orem, UT 84097

Phone 800-777-2665
Fax 801-334-1913
www.woodlandpublishing.com

With our 85 delicious and aroma-based recipes, *Aromatherapy in the Kitchen* makes the art of cooking even more pleasurable, with great tasting results. Recipes include Shrimp with Ginger Butter, Roasted Salmon with Cinnamon and Cumin, and Lavender Roasted Chicken.

$19.95 Retail price
$1.25 Tax for Utah residents
$2.00 Postage and handling

ISBN 1-58054-348-0

Make check payable to Woodland Publishing

BACK TO THE HOUSE OF HEALTH

by Shelley Redford Young
Woodland Publishing
448 East 800 North
Orem, UT 84097

Phone 800-777-2665
Fax 801-334-1913
www.woodlandpublishing.com

Shelley Young's attractive and comprehensive recipe book, *Back to the House of Health,* features over 100 delicious recipes. From Aspara Zincado Soup to Popeye Mousse Pie, these recipes promote a healthy alkaline environment in the body.

$24.95 Retail price
$1.56 Tax for Utah residents
$3.00 Postage and handling

ISBN 1-58054-071-6

Make check payable to Woodland Publishing

BACKYARD DUTCH OVEN

by Bill LeVere
Backyard Dutch Oven
P. O. Box 12471
Ogden, UT 84412

www.backyarddutchoven.com

Backyard Dutch Oven is written for those just learning how to cook with a Dutch oven. This 28-page cookbook offers over 25 easy-to-cook recipes, including instruction in the basics of Dutch oven cooking: tools, seasoning, cleaning, and cooking temperatures.

$3.49 Retail price
$1.00 Postage and handling

PayPal (online) accepted

Make check payable to *Backyard Dutch Oven*

THE BEGINNER'S GUIDE TO DUTCH OVEN COOKING

by Marla Rawlings
Horizon Publishers and Distributors, Inc.
P. O. Box 490
Bountiful, UT 84011-0490

Phone 801-295-9451
Fax 801-295-0196
www.horizonpublishersbooks.com

Novice chefs will enjoy the useful tips and advice on choosing and using Dutch ovens as well as the great getting-started recipes. However, any cook can enjoy the 130 recipes for easily prepared, delectable dishes as well as the useful recipes and adjustments for cooking for large groups. 144 pages.

$10.98 Retail price
$.71 Tax for Utah residents
$4.50 Postage and handling

Visa/MC accepted
ISBN 0-88290-688-7

Make check payable to Horizon Publishers & Dist., Inc.

A CENTURY OF MORMON COOKERY, VOLUME 1

by Hermine B. Horman
Horizon Publishers and Distributors, Inc.
P. O. Box 490
Bountiful, UT 84011-0490

Phone 801-295-9451
Fax 801-295-0196
www.horizonpublishersbooks.com

The Mormon culture was originally composed of converts who immigrated from many lands to Utah. The delicious ethnic recipes they brought have blended together into wonderful culinary delights. This volume contains a time-proven collection of some of the best recipes in America. 619 recipes in 288 pages.

$18.98 Retail price
$1.23 Tax for Utah residents
$4.50 Postage and handling

Visa/MC accepted
ISBN 0-88290-724-7

Make check payable to Horizon Publishers & Dist., Inc.

A CENTURY OF MORMON COOKERY, VOLUME 2

by Hermine B. Horman
Horizon Publishers and Distributors, Inc.   Phone 801-295-9451
P. O. Box 490   Fax 801-295-0196
Bountiful, UT 84011-0490   www.horizonpublishersbooks.com

This second volume of this collection includes 596 recipes in its 274 pages, each different from the first volume. Like Volume 1, the recipes are divided into eighteen categories such as Appetizers, Breads, Salads, Soups, Vegetables, Pasta & Grains, Meats, Desserts, Cakes, Cookies, Pies, Candy, Sauces, and Preserves.

$18.98 Retail price   Visa/MC accepted
  $1.23 Tax for Utah residents   ISBN 0-88290-725-5
  $4.50 Postage and handling

Make check payable to Horizon Publishers & Dist., Inc.

CHAMPIONSHIP DUTCH OVEN COOKBOOK

by Val and Marie Cowley   Phone 435-753-1778
310 W. 1000 North   Fax 435-753-8033
Logan, UT 84321-2213   www.cookingdutch.com

Over 200 Dutch oven recipes with detailed instructions and helpful hints. Ideal for the beginner or expert. Indoor or out. World Championship winning recipes. Household hints and substitution list included. Many family heirloom recipes.

$9.75 Retail price   PayPal (online) accepted
  $.62 Tax for Utah residents

Make check payable to Val Cowley or Double Dutch

CHERISHED RECIPES

Karen Smith   Phone 801-771-4898
1253 E. 3025 North
Layton, Utah 84040

Collection of recipes from my family and friends over the years. Our military travels include friends from Germany, England, and various states around the U.S. 162 pages with 162 recipes.

$8.00 Retail price
  $.50 Tax for Utah residents
$1.50 Postage and handling

Make check payable to Karen Smith

CHOCOLATE SNOWBALL

by Letty Halloran Flatt
The Globe Pequot Press   Phone 800-243-0495
P. O. Box 480   Fax 800-820-2329
Guilford, CT 06437   www.globepequot.com

From Deer Valley, the Park City Ski Resort renowned for cuisine and service, this book offers 125 recipes for breakfast treats, homemade breads, cookies, and ice creams as well as pies and tarts, elegant cakes, and one-of-a-kind desserts.

$35.00 Retail price   ISBN 1-56044-828-8

Make check payable to Globe Pequot Press

A COMPLETE GUIDE TO DUTCH OVEN COOKING

by Ken and Cheryl Allred
12171 S 2795 West
Riverton, UT 84065

Phone 801-254-1616
Fax 801-886-0522

Complete instruction for beginners to experts. From the basic getting started in Dutch oven cooking, to tips for the novice. All recipes provide excellent family meals and desserts. From the kitchen to the backyard, from the family reunion to the great outdoors.

$9.99 Retail price
 $.65 Tax for Utah residents
$3.00 Postage and handling

Visa/MC/Amex accepted

Make check payable to Kettles and Coals LLC

THE COWBOY CHUCK WAGON COOKBOOK

by Kelsey Dollar
Apricot Press
P. O. Box 1611
American Fork, UI 84003

Phone 801-756-0456
Fax 801-756-9839
www.apricotpress.com

The Cowboy Chuck Wagon Cookbook is full of many of Kelsey's relatives' favorite tried-and-tested recipes. The 100 pages of this book are full of tasty recipes and cowboy information, like "The Code of the West" and other cowboy sayings.

$9.95 Retail price
 $.85 Tax for Utah residents
$2.00 Postage and handling

Visa/MC/Disc/Amex accepted
ISBN 1-885027-18-4

Make check payable to Apricot Press

DOIN' DUTCH OVEN: INSIDE AND OUT

by Robert L. Ririe
Horizon Publishers and Distributors, Inc.
P. O. Box 490
Bountiful, UT 84011-0490

Phone 801-295-9451
Fax 801-295-0196
www.horizonpublishersbooks.com

This book adds a unique contribution with recipes and advice for enjoying the unique tastes of Dutch oven food from your own kitchen as well as outdoor settings. Traditional favorites as well as new taste treats are included in the 87 recipes. Additional insights are given for emergency cooking. 128 pages.

$9.98 Retail price
 $.65 Tax for Utah residents
$4.50 Postage and handling

Visa/MC accepted
ISBN 0-88290-368-3

Make check payable to Horizon Publishers & Dist., Inc.

DUDE FOOD

by Jeannette Wilcox
c/o Jeanie Jensen
P. O. Box 1736
Price, UT 84501

Phone 435-637-1236
Fax 435-637-8030

Tavaputs Ranch is Utah's oldest guest ranch. All the recipes in *Dude Food* are recipes that we use as we cater to our guests that visit Tavaputs Ranch. We hope you all enjoy our ranch recipes!

$11.95 Retail price
 $2.00 Postage and handling

Make check payable to *Dude Food*

DUTCH OVEN AND OUTDOOR COOKING BOOK TWO: HOMESPUN EDITION

by Larry and Jeanie Walker
WH Publishing   Phone 801-756-3951
P. O. Box 824
American Fork, UT 84003

Contains all the delicious recipes you could ever want in a Dutch oven cookbook, with skilled instructions, as well as special sections for low-calorie recipes, recipes for diabetics, time-saver tips and recipes, and "super simple" recipes. Also includes a section on preparing jerky using beef, venison, and other game meats.

$9.00 Retail price   ISBN 0-9676021-1-4
$3.00 Postage and handling

Make check payable to WH Publishing

DUTCH OVEN AND OUTDOOR COOKING Y2K EDITION

by Robyn Heirtzler and Larry and Jeanie Walker
WH Publishing   Phone 801-756-3951
P. O. Box 824
American Fork, UT 84003

Mouth-watering recipes for the Dutch oven method of cooking and for delicious, over the open fire, outdoor cooking experience. Compiled by outdoor enthusiasts, Larry and Jeanie Walker, this outstanding cookbook has sold more than 10,000 copies.

$9.00 Retail price   ISBN 0-9676021-0-6
$3.00 Postage and handling

Make check payable to WH Publishing

DUTCH OVEN DELITES

by Val and Marie Cowley   Phone 435-753-1778
310 W 1000 N   Fax 435-753-8033
Logan, UT 84321-2213   www.cookingdutch.com

Over 160 lower fat recipes that don't taste low fat. Hints, tips, and how-to included. Use indoor or outdoor. Kitchen tips and herb chart.

$9.75 Retail price   PayPal (online) accepted
 $.62 Tax for Utah residents

Make check payable to Val Cowley or Double Dutch

DUTCH OVEN GOLD

by Val and Marie Cowley   Phone 435-753-1778
310 W 1000 N   Fax 435-753-8033
Logan, UT 84321-2213   www.cookingdutch.com

Over 200 recipes for indoor/outdoor cooking. Beginner or expert. How-to and hints. Use and care of cast iron. Home-style recipes including cookies.

$9.75 Retail price   PayPal (online) accepted
 $.62 Tax for Utah residents

Make check payable to Val Cowley or Double Dutch

THE DUTCH OVEN RESOURCE

by Gerry and Chauna Duffin
Camp Chef   Phone 801-254-4265/800-650-2433
10647 South North Forty Way   www.campchef.com
South Jordan, UT 84095

This book is a comprehensive guide to Dutch oven cooking. Drawing from over 15 years of experience in cooking for fun, competition, catering, and teaching, the Duffins make it possible for anyone to become an accomplished Dutch oven cook.

$16.99 Retail price   ISBN 0-9709757-1-6
  $1.12 Tax for Utah residents
  $3.00 Postage and handling

Make check payable to Duffin's Dutch Ovens

DUTCH OVEN SECRETS

by Lynn Hopkins
Horizon Publishers and Distributors, Inc.   Phone 801-295-9451
P. O. Box 490   Fax 801-295-0196
Bountiful, UT 84011-0490   www.horizonpublishersbooks.com

Written by a veteran of World Championship Dutch Oven Cook-Offs, this guide has it all. Suggestions on what accessories to buy, tips for seasoning, cleaning, and storing the oven, 84 delicious and varied recipes, and insights for competition cooking make this a valuable addition to your recipe collection. 112 pages.

$9.98 Retail price   Visa/MC accepted
 $.65 Tax for Utah residents   ISBN 0-88290-372-1
$4.50 Postage and handling

Make check payable to Horizon Publishers & Dist., Inc.

ENJOY! AGAIN AND AGAIN

by Fred Wix (The Gabby Gourmet)
1322 Augustine Drive   Phone 352-750-4481
The Villages   jeancorley@hotmail.com
Lady Lake, FL 32159

Having been involved in the food and media world of Utah for over 20 years, Fred Wix has met the request of his many fans and compiled the best recipes from his television segments in this outstanding 356-page cookbook. Enjoy these fabulous recipes—again and again!

$25.00 Retail Price (shipping included in price)   ISBN 0-9661765-0-2

Make check payable to The Gabby Gourmet

THE ESSENTIAL MORMON COOKBOOK

Julie Badger Jensen   Phone 800-453-4532
Deseret Book   Fax 801-517-3392
P. O. Box 30178   service@deseretbook.com
Salt Lake City, UT 84130-0178   www.deseretbook.com

This time-tested collection of recipes has been gathered from four generations of seasoned Mormon comfort cooks and is the perfect source for the best of Mormon comfort food. All the essentials are here, so dig in—perhaps you'll rediscover one of your favorite childhood recipes.

$16.95 Retail Price   ISBN 1-57008-865-9
  $4.00 Postage and handling

Make check payable to Deseret Book Company

FAMILY FAVORITES FROM THE HEART

by Cheryl C. Huff   Phone 801-489-4383
1122 East 100 South
Springville, UT 84663

This recipe book includes recipes from the Coke and Preston families in memory of Daisy and Eileen Preston. This book has 77 pages including kitchen hints and helps. 177 recipes, indexed.

$10.00 Retail price, postage and handling Included

Make check payable to Cheryl Huff

FAVORITE RECIPES FROM UTAH FARM BUREAU WOMEN

Utah Farm Bureau Women's Committee   Phone 801-233-3010
9865 South State Street   Fax 801-233-3030
Sandy, UT 84070

Utah farm and ranch wives have submitted over 400 taste-tested family recipes for inclusion in this 160-page treasure. These recipes have been created from easy-to-find ingredients and include easy-to-follow directions. Surprise your family tonight with one of these delectable dishes!

$8.00 Retail price   Visa/MC accepted
$3.50 Postage and handling

Make check payable to Utah Farm Bureau

FAVORITE UTAH PIONEER RECIPES

by Marla Rawlings
Horizon Publishers and Distributors, Inc.   Phone 801-295-9451
P. O. Box 490   Fax 801-295-0196
Bountiful, UT 84011-0490   www.horizonpublishersbooks.com

This unique book features 140 recipes, most of which can be traced back to individual first-generation pioneers who emigrated to Utah in the 1850s. Each recipe includes an interesting insight about early pioneer life. A special section of home-made remedies completes the book of 128 pages.

$9.98 Retail price   Visa/MC accepted
 $.65 Tax for Utah residents   ISBN 0-88290-684-4
$4.50 Postage and handling

Make check payable to Horizon Publishers & Dist., Inc.

FIVE-STAR RECIPES FROM WELL-KNOWN LATTER DAY SAINTS

Elaine Cannon   Phone 800-453-4532
Eagle Gate   Fax 801-517-3392
P. O. Box 30178   service@deseretbook.com
Salt Lake City, UT 84130-0178   www.deseretbook.com

Turn your home into a five-star dining experience with proven recipes guaranteed to make mouth-watering dinners, delicious homemade breads, refreshing drinks, and succulent desserts. Some recipes are original, others have been passed down with love for generations. Treat your family to something special tonight!

$15.95 Retail Price   ISBN 1-57008-865-9
 $4.00 Postage and handling

Make check payable to Deseret Book Company

FRIENDS OF OLD DESERET DUTCH OVEN COOKBOOK

Duffin's Dutch Ovens   Phone 801-254-4265
10647 South North Forty Way
South Jordan, UT 84095

This cookbook is a compilation of recipes from nine cook-offs held at This is the Place Heritage Park. Its 232 pages contain a history of Dutch ovens, cast-iron care, and recipe sections for breads, main dishes, and desserts.

$14.00 Retail price   ISBN 0-9716389-0-X
 $.92 Tax for Utah residents
$3.00 Postage and handling

Make check payable to Duffin's Dutch Ovens

HERITAGE COOKBOOK

Junior League of Salt Lake City, Inc.   Phone 801-328-1019
526 East 300 South   Fax 801-328-1048
Salt Lake City, UT 84102   www.jlsic.org

Heritage Cookbook is more than a collection of excellent recipes. It is a tribute to the many people who have contributed to the heritage of Utah, who came from more than twenty-five foreign countries. Over 250 recipes that remind you of your heritage.

$21.95 Retail price   Visa/MC accepted
 $4.00 Postage and handling   ISBN 0-9616972-1-0

Make check payable to Junior League of SLC, Inc.

HOW TO ENJOY ZUCCHINI

by Josie Carlsen
Carlsen Printing   Phone 801-392-0022
1521 W. 2550 South   Fax 801-392-1487
Ogden, UT 84401

How to Enjoy Zucchini has 40 pages with 110 recipes from Josie's kitchen. Recipes include soups, casseroles, cookies, breads, cakes, salads, and even zucchini nutritional information and growing instructions.

$2.00 Retail price   Visa/MC/Disc/Amex accepted
 $.13 Tax for Utah residents
$1.00 Postage and handling

Make check payable to Paul Carlsen

HOW TO WIN A COWBOY'S HEART

by Kathy Lynn Wills
Gibbs Smith, Publisher   Phone 800-748-5439
P. O. Box 667   Fax 800-213-3023
Layton, UT 84041   www.gibbs-smith.com

With more than 150 tasty western recipes, this collection is the perfect way to celebrate America's love affair with the West. Includes cooking tips and advice, and a shopping list for the well-stocked western pantry.

$8.95 Retail price   Visa/MC/Disc/Amex accepted
 $.55 Tax for Utah residents   ISBN 1-58685-192-6
$4.50 Postage and handling

Make check payable to Gibbs Smith, Publisher

JLO ART OF COOKING

Junior League of Ogden
Design Solutions   Phone 801-393-2540
2580 Jefferson Avenue
Ogden, UT 84401

JLO Art of Cooking is a 200-page collection of over 275 recipes combining favorites from our first cookbook, *The Utah Dining Car,* as well as selections from local restaurants and favorites of JLO members. Also features artwork from local artists.

$24.95 Retail price   Visa/MC accepted
  $4.00 Postage and handling   ISBN 0-9740100-0-6

Make check payable to JLO Publications

LADIES' LITERARY CLUB COOKBOOK

Ladies' Literary Club   Fax 801-280-1425
Helen W. Taylor
850 East South Temple
Salt Lake City, UT 84102

Ladies' Literary Club Cookbook is a 3-ring binder with 90 pages containing 218 recipes. It is a collection of recipes that have been prepared by members for their luncheon meetings. These are cherished favorites that are requested again and again.

$13.00 Retail price
  $3.00 Postage and handling

Make check payable to Ladies' Literary Club

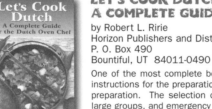

LET'S COOK DUTCH:
A COMPLETE GUIDE FOR THE DUTCH OVEN CHEF

by Robert L. Ririe
Horizon Publishers and Distributors, Inc.   Phone 801-295-9451
P. O. Box 490   Fax 801-295-0196
Bountiful, UT 84011-0490   www.horizonpublishersbooks.com

One of the most complete books for Dutch oven cooking available, with detailed instructions for the preparation, use, and maintenance of the Dutch ovens and fire preparation. The selection of 60 delicious recipes, suggestions for cooking for large groups, and emergency cooking make this "the book" to own. 104 pages.

$9.98 Retail price   Visa/MC accepted
$ .65 Tax for Utah residents   ISBN 0-88290-120-6
$4.50 Postage and handling

Make check payable to Horizon Publishers & Dist., Inc.

LION HOUSE DESSERTS

Hotel Temple Square Corporation   Phone 800-453-4532
Deseret Book Company   Fax 801-517-3392
P. O. Box 30178   service@deseretbook.com
Salt Lake City, UT 84130-0178   www.deseretbook.com

Whether you're preparing for an elegant Sunday dinner, planning for a special event or just preparing an everyday meal, *Lion House Desserts* has just what you're looking for. With the help of easy-to-follow instructions and full-color pictures, you'll enjoy creating these mouth-watering desserts for parties, holidays, and more.

$24.95 Retail Price   ISBN 1-57345-625-X
  $4.00 Postage and handling

Make check payable to Deseret Book Company

LION HOUSE ENTERTAINING

Hotel Temple Square Corporation
Deseret Book Company
P. O. Box 30178
Salt Lake City, UT 84130-0178

Phone 800-453-4532
Fax 801-517-3392
service@deseretbook.com
www.deseretbook.com

This irresistible cookbook offers perfectly planned menus and recipes for every occasion. Whether you're hosting an open house, a formal dinner, or a casual get-together with a few friends, *Lion House Entertaining* will help your event go beautifully. Use the planned menus, mix and match the recipes, or let the book act as a springboard for your own ideas.

$25.95 Retail Price
$4.00 Postage and handling

ISBN 1-57345-972-0

Make check payable to Deseret Book Company

LION HOUSE RECIPES

Hotel Temple Square Corporation
Deseret Book Company
P. O. Box 30178
Salt Lake City, UT 84130-0178

Phone 800-453-4532
Fax 801-517-3392
service@deseretbook.com
www.deseretbook.com

Over the years dozens of good cooks have been employed to turn out the oh-so-good food enjoyed in the cafeteria and party rooms, men and women who love to cook and who have reputations for excellence in their culinary efforts—collected herein are those outstanding recipes. Enjoy!

$19.95 Retail Price
$4.00 Postage and handling

ISBN 0-87747-831-7

Make check payable to Deseret Book Company

LION HOUSE WEDDINGS

Hotel Temple Square Corporation
Deseret Book Company
P. O. Box 30178
Salt Lake City, UT 84130-0178

Phone 800-453-4532
Fax 801-517-3392
service@deseretbook.com
www.deseretbook.com

Whether you need a menu for an elaborate formal dinner, a theme suitable for a backyard reception, or help choosing the perfect flowers for a bridal bouquet, *Lion House Weddings* will guide you through the planning stages necessary to create an unforgettable celebration. Menus and ideas for the perfect reception!

$25.95 Retail Price
$4.00 Postage and handling

ISBN 1-57345-972-0

Make check payable to Deseret Book Company

LOG CABIN CAMPFIRE COOKN'

by Colleen Sloan
900 East Carnation Drive
Sandy, UT 84094

Phone 888-596-1515
Fax 801-523-6240
www.logcabingrub.com

Enjoy 112 pages of mouth-watering outdoor cooking ideas, stories, no-trace camping tips, frying pan and Dutch oven recipes for every age, and campfire activities and fun. Cow Town All Day Breakfast, Cow Camp Enchiladas, and Sour Dough Starter and Bread are just a few of the exciting recipes found within.

$8.99 Retail price
$.66 Tax for Utah residents
$1.70 Postage and handling

Visa/MC accepted
ISBN 0-9630279-7-2

Make check payable to Log Cabin

LOG CABIN DUTCH OVEN

by Colleen Sloan
900 East Carnation Drive
Sandy, UT 84094

Phone 888-596-1515
Fax 801-523-6240
www.logcabingrub.com

Black-pot cooking at its best! Recipes for your oven, outside, or camping. One-pot meals, breads, desserts, and camping sections included. Enjoy 112 pages of good-tasting recipes. Try the Jose's Lasagne or Porky Pineapple Spareribs for a lip-smackin' memory, and partake of the healthiest cooking method ever.

$8.99 Retail price
$.66 Tax for Utah residents
$1.70 Postage and handling

Visa/MC accepted
ISBN 0-9630279-2-1

Make check payable to Log Cabin

LOG CABIN GRUB COOKBOOK

by Colleen Sloan
900 East Carnation Drive
Sandy, UT 84094

Phone 888-596-1515
Fax 801-523-6240
www.logcabingrub.com

With this back-to-basics cookbook including 253 recipes, learn to make crackers, sourdough, noodles, dumplings, and more. Great old recipes like Best Rhubarb Cake Ever and Apple Pie Harvest Cake. Enjoy good soups and stews, sage dressing, helpful household hints, stories, and more.

$8.99 Retail price
$.66 Tax for Utah residents
$1.70 Postage and handling

Visa/MC accepted
ISBN 0-9630279-0-5

Make check payable to Log Cabin

LOG CABIN HOLIDAYS AND TRADITIONS

by Colleen Sloan
900 East Carnation Drive
Sandy, UT 84094

Phone 888-596-1515
Fax 801-523-6240
www.logcabingrub.com

Enjoy 192 pages of holiday information, recipes, crafts, and traditions. Find out how the holidays originated, how they were celebrated, and what they (the pioneers) cooked. Black beans for New Years, cherries on Valentine's Day, and much more. Shamrock Cookies, Corned Beef and Cabbage, and Halloween recipes included.

$10.99 Retail price
$.66 Tax for Utah residents
$1.70 Postage and handling

Visa/MC accepted
ISBN 0-9630279-3-X

Make check payable to Log Cabin

LOG CABIN PRESENTS LEWIS AND CLARK

by Colleen Sloan
900 East Carnation Drive
Sandy, UT 84094

Phone 888-596-1515
Fax 801-523-6240
www.logcabingrub.com

Enjoy 112 pages of over 150 mouth-watering recipes. Learn how Lewis and Clark cooked and survived. Enjoy the history of Sacajawea's contribution and food ideas. Included are the corp's list of firsts, information on what the costs were, where they gathered their food and knowledge, and how we cook it today.

$8.99 Retail price
$.66 Tax for Utah residents
$1.70 Postage and handling

Visa/MC accepted
ISBN 0-9630279-5-6

Make check payable to Log Cabin

MAKING MAGIC

University of Utah
Virginia Tanner Dance Programs and Children's Dance Theatre
1901 E. South Campus Drive, #1215   Phone 801-587-3633
Salt Lake City, UT 84112-9359   Fax 801-581-4091
                                                         www.dance.utah.edu/vtcdt

A beautiful 472-page, 450-recipe cookbook compiled by the Tanner Dance community. Mary Anne Lee sums it up, " . . . you will be overwhelmed by the extraordinary cuisine, good humor, and grace that jumps, skips, and leaps from the pages."

$29.95 Retail price   Visa/MC/Disc/Amex accepted
  $1.98 Tax for Utah residents   ISBN 0-965-1810-1-4
  $5.95 Postage and handling

Make check payable to Children's Dance Theatre

A MORMON COOKBOOK

by Erin A. Delfoe
Apricot Press   Phone 801-756-0456
P. O. Box 1611   Fax 801 756-9839
American Fork, UT 84003   www.apricotpress.com

Our cookbook contains pretty simple recipes with ingredients you have at home. The recipes in this book, along with Mormon trivia, make a great gift. Be sure to check out the green Jell-O recipes on page 8. Includes 93 pages of tasty treats and trivia.

$9.95 Retail price   Visa/MC/Disc/Amex accepted
  $.85 Tax for Utah residents   ISBN 1-885027-16-8
$2.00 Postage and handling

Make check payable to Apricot Press

NO GREEN GELATIN HERE!

Women's Alliance–First Unitarian Church of Salt Lake City
569 South 1300 East
Salt Lake City, UT 84102-3294

This compilation of "culinary treasures" includes anecdotes by contributors and makes for adventuresome cooking and reading. The title of the book humorously hints that the choice of recipes may require wine, coffee, or bourbon to enhance the savory flavors of a recipe and the foreword even suggests that the cook may enjoy a glass of wine while preparing a meal.

$10.00 Retail price
  $2.50 Postage and handling

Make check payable to The Women's Alliance, First Unitarian Church

101 THINGS TO DO WITH A CAKE MIX

by Stephanie Ashcraft
Gibbs Smith, Publisher   Phone 800-748-5439
P. O. Box 667   Fax 800-213-3023
Layton, UT 84041   www.gibbs-smith.com

A New York Times Bestseller! From cookies and breads to unique dessert bars and fancy cake creations, this handy book takes the plain old cake mix a giant leap forward with a wide array of delicious dessert recipes.

$9.95 Retail price   Visa/MC/Disc/Amex accepted
  $.65 Tax for Utah residents   ISBN 1-58685-217-5
$4.50 Postage and handling

Make check payable to Gibbs Smith, Publisher

101 THINGS TO DO WITH A SLOW COOKER

by Stephanie Ashcraft and Janet Eyring
Gibbs Smith, Publisher
P. O. Box 667
Layton, UT 84041

Phone 800-748-5439
Fax 800-213-3023
www.gibbs-smith.com

With 101 easy recipes, now anyone can make hearty, healthy dishes for the whole family the "throw-n-go" way. Includes suggestions for how and what to serve with each dish, time-saving preparation tips, and easy modifications to fit your family's tastes.

$9.95 Retail price   Visa/MC/Disc/Amex accepted
$.65 Tax for Utah residents
$4.50 Postage and handling

Make check payable to Gibbs Smith, Publisher   ISBN 1-58685-317-1

ONLY THE BEST

by Gayle Holdman
10790 N. 6000 W.
Highland, UT 84003

Phone 801-763-9790
onlythebest@holdman.com

Gayle shares 165 "most requested" recipes, including award winners and nationally recognized favorites. A talented cooking instructor and food enthusiast, she thrives on creating and seeking out the most delicious dishes that are also easy to prepare. (Attractive 3-ring binder.)

$12.50 Retail price
$.79 Tax for Utah residents
$2.00 per book Postage and handling

Make check payable to Gayle Holdman

PATTY'S CAKES AND THINGS

by Patty Roberts
1596 South Highway 89
Springville, UT 84663-2430

Phone 801-489-0201
lotsarock@aol.com
www.pattyroberts.com/default.htm

Within these 76-plus pages of 234 recipes you will find most of them easy to prepare with ingredients found in most homes. Helpful hints and suggestions are scattered among them and on the divider pages. Enjoy!

$9.95 Retail price
$.63 Tax for Utah residents
$3.50 Postage and handling

Make check payable to Patty Roberts

A PINCH OF SALT LAKE COOKBOOK

Junior League of Salt Lake City, Inc.
526 East 300 South
Salt Lake City, UT 84102

Phone 801-328-1019
Fax 801-328-1048
www.jlslc.org

A Pinch of Salt Lake Cookbook contains over 400 prize recipes highlighting foods for contemporary lifestyles. We hope this cookbook brings you a glimpse of our colorful Salt Lake lifestyle, success in cooking and entertaining, and a knowledge of our community.

$19.95 Retail price   Visa/MC accepted
$4.00 Postage and handling   ISBN 0-9616972-0-2

Make check payable to Junior League of SLC, Inc.

PLEASURES FROM THE GOOD EARTH

Common Thread, Inc.   Phone 801-943-4970
3601 E. Little Cottonwood Road   Fax 801-733-9711
Sandy, UT 84092   www.commonthreadinc.org

Residents of Transplant House donated many recipes in this book. Some awaiting organ transplants, others recovering from transplants. Recipes also donated by caregivers, organ donors, family, and friends. Cookbook has 134 pages, 300 recipes, contributor's list, helpful hints, and cooking tips.

$10.00 Retail price   Visa/MC/Amex/Disc accepted
 $3.00 Postage and handling

Make check payable to Common Thread, Inc.

THE PRACTICAL CAMP COOK

by Fred Bowman
Horizon Publishers and Distributors, Inc.   Phone 801-295-9451
P. O. Box 490   Fax 801 295-0196
Bountiful, UT 84011-0490   www.horizonpublishersbooks.com

Written by an experienced outdoorsman, this book includes valuable information for the selection of foods, utensils, stoves, and equipment for overnight back-packing to week-long camping. Interesting recipes for using wild game as well as suggestions for more unusual camp foods are given. 43 recipes in 222 pages.

$17.98 Retail price   Visa/MC accepted
 $1.17 Tax for Utah residents   ISBN 0-88290-328-4
 $4.50 Postage and handling

Make check payable to Horizon Publishers & Dist., Inc.

QUICK & EASY COOKING

by Alona S. Perkes
Horizon Publishers and Distributors, Inc.   Phone 801-295-9451
P. O. Box 490   Fax 801-295-0196
Bountiful, UT 84011-0490   www.horizonpublishersbooks.com

This guide for busy people also includes guidelines and sample menus for inexperienced chefs. Speed in preparation and simplicity are the keys of each of the 156 delicious recipes. Ideal for working singles, college students, newlyweds, or anyone squeezing meal preparation into busy schedules and limited budgets. 80 pages

$6.98 Retail price   Visa/MC accepted
 $.45 Tax for Utah residents   ISBN 0-88290-348-9
$4.50 Postage and handling

Make check payable to Horizon Publishers & Dist., Inc.

RECIPES & REMEMBRANCES

Moab Area Chamber of Commerce   Phone 435-259-7814
805 North Main Street   Fax 435-259-8519
Moab, UT 84532   info@moabchamber.com
                                       www.moabchamber.com

This Moab Area Chamber of Commerce cookbook is a delightful collection of area recipes and colorful stories about local citizens. Dedicated to the beloved Home Economics teacher, Rachel McDonald. This book is as diverse as Moab itself.

$7.50 Retail Price
$2.50 Postage

Moab Area Chamber of Commerce

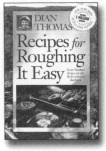

RECIPES FOR ROUGHING IT EASY

by Dian Thomas
P. O. Box 171107
Holladay, UT 84117

Phone 800-846-6355
Fax 801-278-0202
www.campingwithdian.com

Unique recipes for outdoor cooking and backyard grilling, plus many great ideas for creative outdoor fun with step-by-step instructions.

$14.99 Retail price
$1.00 Tax for Utah residents
$3.00 Postage and handling

ISBN 0-9621257-8-4

Make check payable to Dian Thomas Company

RECIPES THRU TIME

Tooele County Daughters of Utah Pioneers
Transcript Bulletin
325 State Route 138
Stansbury Park, UT 84074

Phone 435-882-7678
Fax 435-882-6003
www.bensonmill.org

Daughters of Utah Pioneers have compiled these historic and classic recipes, including everything from Rhubarb Punch to Pony Express Scones, used in kitchens throughout Utah for over 150 years. Included are histories, pictures, quotes, and map of important historic landmarks. Put on your aprons and try a taste of Utah.

$10.00 Retail price
$2.50 Postage and handling

Make check payable to Tooele Daughters of Utah Pioneers

ROUGHING IT EASY AT GIRL'S CAMP

Dian Thomas
Deseret Book
P. O. Box 30178
Salt Lake City, UT 84093

Phone 800-453-4532
Fax 801-517-3392
service@deseretbook.com
www.deseretbook.com

Best-selling author Dian Thomas, dubbed "America's First Lady of Creativity," takes the work out of planning and executing a successful girls camp with *Roughing It Easy at Girls Camp.* Guaranteed to make camp both fun and memorable! Contains awesome recipes, camp themes, organization charts, safety tips, and much more.

$14.95 Retail Price
$4.00 Postage and handling

ISBN1-57345-962-3

Make check payable to Deseret Book Company

SAVOR THE MEMORIES

by Marguerite M. Henderson
1529 Hubbard Avenue
Salt Lake City, UT 84105

Phone 801-582-9204
Fax 801-582-9204
www.margueritehenderson.com

Savor the Memories is designed to inspire the novice cook to feel confident in the kitchen, while adding elegant Mediterranean-influenced recipes to the repertoire of the gourmet chef. Dedicated to her late Italian mother for her influence in the culinary field.

$19.95 Retail price
$1.32 Tax for Utah residents
$2.95 Postage and handling

Visa/MC accepted
ISBN 0-9714942-0-7

Make check payable to Marguerite Henderson

SMOOTHIES & ICE TREATS

by Lindsay Barnes and Amy Shawgo
Back to Basics Products, Inc.   www.backtobasics.com
11660 South State Street
Draper, UT 84020

Lindsay Barnes (nutritionist and smoothie lover) and Amy Shawgo (writer and mother of five) have teamed up to bring you a high-content, low-stress recipe book for smoothie lovers. With delicious recipes for everyone, and categories ranging from meal replacements to special occasions, this smoothie guide offers pure fun!

$9.99 Retail price   Visa/MC/Amex/Disc accepted
$3.00 Postage and handling   ISBN 0-9722418-0-9

Make check payable to Back to Basics Products, Inc.

TASTEFUL TREASURES COOKBOOK

Golden Hours Senior Center   Phone 801-399-5230
650 25th Street   Fax 801-395-2131
Ogden, UT 84401

Tasteful Treasures Cookbook was compiled in memory of Patsy Gimbel, a volunteered in our kitchen and dining room for eleven years. What fun we had compiling this cookbook! Collecting recipes which have been handed down through the generations from seniors willing to share them with everyone is quite rewarding.

$7.00 Retail price
$3.50 Postage and handling

Make check payable to Golden Hours Center

30 DAYS TO A HEALTHIER FAMILY

Peggy Hughes   Phone 800-453-45332
Deseret Book   Fax 801-517-3392
P. O. Box 30178   service@deseretbook.com
Salt Lake City, UT 84130-0178   www.deseretbook.com

Author Peggy Hughes provides an easy-to-follow plan for a healthier lifestyle by simply following this 30-day approach. Develop habits that will stay throughout a lifetime. Included are healthy recipes, physical fitness advice, health goal charts, and more. Finally, there's a practical, fun, and effective way to healthy living.

$12.95 Retail Price   ISBN 1-57008-895-0
$4.00 Postage and handling

Make check payable to Deseret Book Company

ULTIMATE DUTCH OVEN COOKBOOK

Denene Torgenson   Phone 435-529-7633
Camp Chef   Fax 435-529-7633
145 East Main   ddtoutfitters@scinternet.net
Salina, UT 84654   www.ultimatedutchovens.com

Bringing you 112 pages of the "Ultimate" Dutch oven recipes. From Dutch Oven Chicken to Dutch Oven Ice Cream, this cookbook has it all.

$10.00 Retail Price   Visa/MC Accepted
  $.63 Tax for Utah residents   ISBN 0-9709757-3-2
$5.00 Postage and handling

Make check payable to DDT Outfitters

UTAH COOK BOOK

by Bruce and Bobbi Fischer
Golden West Publishers
4113 N. Longview Avenue
Phoenix, AZ 85014

Phone 800-658-5830
Fax 602-279-6901

Utah abounds in breathtaking beauty, colorful history, and a diverse cultural background. Come experience a small part of what makes Utah so diverse . . . the scrumptious cuisine. Sample Cache Valley Cheese Soufflé, Chocolate Lovers' Favorite Mint Brownies . . . and many more! 96 pages of incredible dishes!

$6.95 Retail price
$4.00 Postage and handling

ISBN 1-885590-37-7

Make check payable to Golden West Publishers

VACATION COOKING: GOOD FOOD! GOOD FUN!

by Ruth Atkinson Kendrick and Florence Harris Boss
Horizon Publishers and Distributors, Inc.
P. O. Box 490
Bountiful, UT 84011-0490

Phone 801-295-9451
Fax 801-295-0196
www.horizonpublishersbooks.com

This book shows that careful planning and make-ahead techniques while preparing for vacations give the cook time for fun while providing delicious meals and snacks. Includes 78 easy recipes, and hundreds of tips for camping and family travel, providing fast meals and fun for all. 80 pages.

$6.98 Retail price
$.45 Tax for Utah residents
$4.50 Postage and handling

Visa/MC accepted
ISBN 0-88290-349-7

Make check payable to Horizon Publishers & Dist., Inc.

WORLD CHAMPIONSHIP DUTCH OVEN COOKBOOK

Dick Michaud, co-author
1104 Thrushwood Drive
Logan, UT 84321

Phone 435-752-2631

This Dutch oven cookbook is authored by the founder of the International Dutch Oven Society and the original committee of the World Championship Dutch Oven Cook-off. It's chocked full of good recipes, black pot info, and fun.

$9.95 Retail price
$.65 Tax for Utah residents
$4.00 Postage and handling

ISBN 0-9623918-0-8

Make check payable to Michaud Enterprises

Index

PHOTO © FRANK JENSEN, STATE OF UTAH DIVISION OF TRAVEL DEVELOPMENT.

Mt. Timpanogos rises 11,750 feet, making it the second highest in the Wasatch Mountains. It is considered the most popular mountain climbing destination in Utah.

Index

Index

Index

Index

Index

Index

Index

Index

Index

Special Discount Offers!

The Best of the Month Club

Experience the taste of our nation, one state at a time!

Individuals may purchase BEST OF THE BEST STATE COOKBOOKS on a monthly (or bi-monthly) basis by joining the **Best of the Month Club**. Best of the Month Club members enjoy a 20% discount off the list price of each book. Individuals who already own certain state cookbooks may specify which new states they wish to receive. No minimum purchase is required; individuals may cancel at any time. For more information on this purchasing option, call 1-800-343-1583.

Special Discount

The entire 41-volume BEST OF THE BEST STATE COOKBOOK SERIES can be purchased for $521.21, a 25% discount off the total individual price of $694.95.

Individual BEST cookbooks can be purchased for $16.95 per copy plus $4.00 shipping for any number of cookbooks ordered. See order form on next page.

Join today! 1-800-343-1583

Speak directly to one of our friendly customer service representatives, or visit our website at **www.quailridge.com** to order online.

Recipe Hall of Fame Collection

The extensive recipe database of Quail Ridge Press' acclaimed BEST OF THE BEST STATE COOKBOOK SERIES is the inspiration behind the RECIPE HALL OF FAME COLLECTION. These HALL OF FAME recipes have achieved extra distinction for consistently producing superb dishes. *The Recipe Hall of Fame Cookbook* features over 400 choice dishes for a variety of meals. The *Recipe Hall of Fame Dessert Cookbook* consists entirely of extraordinary desserts. The *Recipe Hall of Fame Quick & Easy Cookbook* contains over 500 recipes that require minimum effort but produce maximum enjoyment. *The Recipe Hall of Fame Cookbook II* brings you more of the family favorites you've come to expect with over 400 all-new, easy-to-follow recipes. Appetizers to desserts, quick dishes to masterpiece presentations, the RECIPE HALL OF FAME COLLECTION has it all.

All books: Paperbound • 7x10 • Illustrations • Index
The Recipe Hall of Fame Cookbook • 304 pages • $19.95
Recipe Hall of Fame Dessert Cookbook • 240 pages • $16.95
Recipe Hall of Fame Quick & Easy Cookbook • 304 pages • $19.95
The Recipe Hall of Fame Cookbook II • 304 pages • $19.95

NOTE: The four HALL OF FAME cookbooks can be ordered individually at the price noted above or can be purchased as a four-cookbook set for $40.00, almost a 50% discount off the total list price of $76.80. Over 1,600 incredible HALL OF FAME recipes for about three cents each—an amazing value!